Touched by the Spirit

Testimonies That Will Fill Your Heart

ISBN: 0-88290-771-9
e.2

Published by Cedar Fort Inc.
www.cedarfort.com

Distributed by:

Edited by Janet Bernice
Cover design by Nicole Shaffer
Cover design © 2003 by Lyle Mortimer

Printed in the United States of America
10 9 8 7 6 5 4 3 2 1

Printed on acid-free paper

Library of Congress Control Number: 2004111335

Touched by the Spirit

Testimonies That Will Fill Your Heart

Compiled By

Joy Robinson

CFI
Springville, UT

Dedication

To good and true friends whose hearts rejoice with me during good times and whose arms enfold me during the trials:

Patricia K. Hill

Mary T. Oniki

Minnie Jo Seely

Lanece W. Ballif

Afton N. England

Acknowledgments

This book began with one story from one journal, and grew story by story. The testimonies are from valued friends, from members of our Ward and Stake family, (Canyon Road Ward, the Ensign Stake), and members of my own family. Many testimonies came from personal and family journals; some were experiences written down for the first time.

I testify that all the stories are true. For three months, while editing these contributions, I have been blessed with visits from spiritual beings, who came to check my progress with the stories of their 'doings' with mortals, to see if I was getting it right. At times I felt another presence so strongly I would turn in my chair, thinking someone had come into the room, but I was alone, except for the 'feeling' that I was not alone.

I am grateful to those who placed their trust in me and were willing to share meaningful, and sacred parts of their spiritual life.

Special thanks to a good friend, Joan Oviatt, for gathering stories from her Pahoa Ward on the Keaau Island. She also gave advice (via e-mail), and encouragement. She was generous in sharing her own 'touched by the Spirit' experiences, in an altruistic effort to help a friend.

Judith Locke reached down and rescued me from despair with her computer expertise when I did not know how to do the publisher's final bidding. Without her hours of work there could not have been a finished product.

My deep appreciation also to Duane S. Crowther, President of Horizon Publishers, who saw the potential in my manuscript to touch many lives for good. I appreciate his patience and kindness in shepherding me through the manuscript preparation process and in editing the book for publication.

Finally, there are not adequate words to express thanks to my husband, George, who quietly holds everything together, leaving me free to follow the Muse, without feelings of guilt for things left undone.

TABLE OF CONTENTS

Music

For my soul delighteth in the song of the heart; yea, the song of the righteous is a prayer unto me, and it shall be answered with a blessing upon their heads.

D&C 25:12

Outside the Walls of Temple Square

To be a missionary on Temple Square during General Conference is absolute heaven. Some members of the Church travel hundreds of miles for the opportunity of listening in person to the Prophet, the Apostles, and other General Authorities. The feelings within the walls of Temple Square are of peace, sacrifice, love, and testimony. Some members of the Church who do not have tickets for a session of Conference wait in lines inside the Square for hours in hopes of crossing the street to go inside the beautiful Conference Center. No one is impatient or grumpy as they wait. Even when it hails, rains, or snows, smiles are seen, and laughs are heard as members try to squeeze under umbrellas of those in line with them. As a missionary I found it was a joyous, happy thrill to share this experience with the good Saints.

Outside the walls of Temple Square, however, the scene is quite different. A large group of highly vocal men, calling themselves street preachers, have been attending Conference for a number of years. They have begun to multiply, and their attacks have become more vicious. Some are local men. Many have traveled hundreds of miles to be there. Their aim is to do all they can to disrupt the peace and sanctity of Latter-day Saints at each Conference session.

These men yell and scream profanities; they say beastly things to LDS women in front of their husbands and children; they verbally attack the leaders and doctrine of the Church. At the top of their voices they say *they* are Christian, and claim that we are not. Each year their posters and billboards are larger, their voices get louder, (they use megaphones for voice enhancement) but the result is the same: families scramble to get past them, covering the ears of their little ones, as they hurry across the street between the Conference Center and Temple Square where, within the walls, they can feel peace again.

In September 2003, leaders in the Church came up with a plan they hoped would circumvent some of the ugliness that detracts from the Spirit of the Lord. Anti-Mormons can buy a permit from the city to stand in a specific spot and conduct their protest. The Church decided to purchase their own permits, as well. They purchased one permit on the Conference Center side of the street, and one on the Temple Square side, just outside the gates. People in the Church called a special meeting with sisters who served in leadership positions on Temple Square. They asked us to be brave and set ourselves smack dab in the middle of all the street drama.

Can you visualize two groups of young sisters standing at their designated posts, in the midst of mobs of angry men holding vitriolic posters, yelling, and blowing their noses on sacred garments, then waving them in the air? We were a small force against their profane anger. We had two-hour shifts. This gave us a chance to go inside the walls and recharge our spiritual batteries before going back to face the lions.

An interesting thing about these men is that they receive pay from organized groups to do this. It is a job. When Conference sessions begin, there is no one to yell at. The men then put down their posters and megaphones and relax.

The sisters and I used this time to chat. We called one of the Anti's over and asked why he was there. His answer was that he "didn't really know." He said he was cold, and that he "kind of wanted to make enough money to get back home." He had come from the east coast to do this. We noticed another young man who seemed a bit slower than the others. As people entered the Conference Center, he was holding a sign with a large arrow that said "False Prophet," but it was pointed at the Anti-Mormon standing next to him. His partner noticed this, and redirected the arrow so it pointed at the Conference Center. We chuckled. We made eye contact with this man and smiled. He smiled back, and waved as if he wasn't aware of what he was being paid to do.

When each group of sisters went inside the walls of Temple Square, we prayed very hard for our presence out there to have an impact. Conference let out. Twenty-one thousand people came streaming out of the Conference Center. They had been spiritually fed and strengthened. I said one more prayer as the men picked up their posters and megaphones. We watched as peace was wiped from the faces of members and replaced by fear of the loud, ferocious, angry men.

My companion, who has an incredibly strong voice, turned to me and said, "Lets sing hymns and see if we can drown out these guys." We began singing hymns as loudly as we could. A few missionary sisters joined in. As members crossed the street, they heard the music, and looked around to see where it was coming from. Some joined in.

Our small sisterhood became powerful. This angered the men and caused them to yell louder. It didn't matter. The faces of the members turned from fear to happiness as they saw a small army of Saints standing bravely for truth.

More Saints began joining us in our songs. As the street protesters chanted "false prophet, false prophet," we sang with power, *We Thank Thee Oh God For a Prophet*. As they chanted, "the Book of Mormon is false," we sang with fervor, *We Are as The Armies of Helaman*. They yelled into their megaphones that we were going to "burn in hell." We sang with full hearts, *The Spirit Of God Like A Fire Is Burning*.

The feeling was unmistakable. The presence of the Spirit was powerful. The sister missionaries, and those who sang with us, were brought to tears. Never had the contrast between good and evil been so clear to those standing there that day.

In the midst of it all, my eyes were drawn to one man among the Anti's who had stopped yelling. I watched as the spirit of the music utterly stopped his mouth. He lowered his sign and looked at us as we lifted our voices in song. The expression on his face seemed to say, "What am I doing here?"

He stood quietly with his head bowed. My eyes welled up and spilled over with tears. The Spirit bore witness to me at that moment that the gospel of Jesus Christ will go forth boldly and nobly. No unhallowed hand will stop it. An army of yelling men cannot change what is true, nor cause me to doubt the confirmation I received that day.

Submitted by Tiffany Wilde

The Spirit Speaks in Kansas

My husband, George, and I were called to serve a mission in Zimbabwe, Africa. We needed visas, which normally took about six months to obtain. We were ready to go, and asked if we could serve somewhere else while we waited for the visas.

Yes. We could. CES needed a couple at the Haskell Indian College in Lawrence, Kansas. Our assignment was to clean up the house and grounds of a building across the street from the College owned by the Church.

We were to paint walls, cupboards, clean carpets, and purchase furniture for the house. It was to be used as a permanent home for senior couples who would be called to serve missions there. We were also to reorganize and refurbish the Institute building which was close by. As we were going about our duties, the Holy Spirit decided to take a hand in my life.

There were two pianos in the Institute building and not enough room for both of them, so we moved one into the living room of the house. As the piano was being moved, the Spirit spoke forcefully to me, *You must learn to play this piano.*

Not I, Lord.

Yes, you!

I was nearly sixty years old. I'd had a piano in my home for thirty years. Five children had learned to play it. Five children learned to read music. I had sat beside them as they practiced, giving encouragement. I knew when they hit a wrong note, knew when their timing was off, but I could not read a note of music. I did not know do-re-mi from fa-so-la-tee-do. I didn't have a clue about F A C E.

There was no time for music lessons and I did not consider it. The Spirit had had years of opportunity to speak to me about learning to play the piano and had never witnessed to me before.

Now I was being directed to play the piano?

Why now, Lord? Why now? No answer came to my questions. Only one simple declarative statement—*Learn to play this piano.*

It happened that a young woman who had a degree in music from BYU lived in our ward. I reluctantly approached her about piano lessons. She smiled pleasantly, and said, "I give lessons four days a week. When would you like to come?"

So, in our first month at Haskell, I began lessons two days a week, and promised to practice two hours a day. At the end of our six-month mission, I could read music, and play simple hymns using both hands.

I did not hear another word from the Spirit until we arrived in Salt Lake City, Utah, preparing to fly to Africa. Two days before our mission training sessions I heard, *You must buy a keyboard. You will need a keyboard.*

I bought a keyboard, and more music for simple hymns.

In Zimbabwe, I discovered why the Spirit had been so insistent. George was director of seminaries in Bulawayo, Zimbabwe. We began going to seven different branches in the areas where our seminary students went to Sunday services.

There was one song leader in one branch, and only a few ragged hymn books in any branch (which the women kept at home and carried to church on their heads). There were no musical instruments.

I was always asked to conduct. Africans suppose that all white women are born knowing how to sing and conduct music, but I was one white woman who did not. And, if my life depended on it, I cannot sing an on-key note. When I was rocking my youngest baby, singing him a lullaby, he put his hand over my mouth and said, "Please, mommy, don't sing."

I was alone in alien territory. The Holy Spirit made no effort to communicate. He had done his part. The rest was up to me.

I sent home for six keyboards. In the building where white people went to Church there were three pianos. I asked two people from each branch to come to that chapel at a certain hour on Saturdays. They were going to learn to read music, learn to conduct music, and learn to play the piano.

Everyone who attended regularly and learned would be given a keyboard which they could keep in their homes, but must take to church on Sunday and play for the services. Sixteen people came that first Saturday.

I asked a missionary sister, who was there with her husband on a proselytizing mission, to teach the classes on reading music and conducting. Then, running from the chapel to the recreation hall to the Relief Society room, I began teaching the basics of piano playing to sixteen people.

When the students progressed past my limited expertise, we hired an African woman to teach them. One young man showed exceptional talent. He was also a Branch resident. He was overjoyed at the opportunity to learn to play a piano, and soon became the star pupil. He worked for the postal service, and was the only one with transportation—a bicycle. Everyone else walked long distances to be there.

Finally, the keyboards arrived. I had counted on some of the students dropping out. Only three did. I had seven keyboards, counting my own, and thirteen people who wanted one. But of the thirteen, only eight had learned well enough to play the hymns, and stay on the correct beat.

Two of the eight who had learned were sisters. That made the job of deciding who got one keyboard easier. Anticipating this predicament, I had sent home for six recorders, and the music. The piano teacher also played a recorder. She taught the six who did not receive a keyboard to play the recorder.

Eighteen months later we had managed to get more hymn books for the branches. Each branch had music every Sunday, with someone to conduct who could also sing.

The Holy Spirit wins every time, if we listen and follow through.

Submitted by Joy Robinson

Our Introduction to *I Am a Child of God*

This is an account of our family's experience with what has become a beloved Latter-day Saint hymn.

Although we are both natives of Utah, we were married in St. Louis County, Missouri, on New Years Eve, 1941. In 1957 we had been living in the South St. Louis Branch for about eight years, We had five living children, Denise (14), Christine (13), Louise (9), Matt (7), and Sam (3 1/2). We lost a little girl, Virginia, to leukemia in 1955, when she was four years old.

In the fifties, the meeting schedule in wards and branches was somewhat different from the current block schedule. Typically, Priesthood Meeting and Sunday School were held on Sunday morning. Sacrament Service was in the evening. Relief Society met on a week-day afternoon. The MIA met on an evening during the week. The Fast and Testimony meeting was held immediately following Sunday School. On the first Sunday evening of each month, special presentations were scheduled by the Priesthood, or one of the auxiliaries.

In the spring of 1957, the Primary Association held a special program for the ward and branch Primaries. The presentation was on the first Sunday in May. The program called for a family tableau, climaxed by a child singing a new composition: *I Am A Child Of God*.

Our family was selected by the branch Primary presidency to make the presentation. A special platform was built to seat us, since the chapel was not designed for presenting acts of drama. The program focused on the family; the need of children to be taught the gospel. We only recall one detail; our daughter Louise, singing the new composition, *I Am A Child Of God*. She had then, and still has a beautiful singing voice.

That musical number, which was first introduced at the Primary General Conference in April, 1957, was later published in the *The Friend*, the *Children's Songbook*, and in the current edition of the Church hymnal. Louise has sung the hymn a number of times in our presence since that original performance, and it never fails to bring tears to our eyes.

I Am A Child Of God has a special place in our hearts, and within the family circle.

Louise sang Naomi W. Randall's original lyrics, which included the phrase "Teach me all that I must know to live with him someday."

It is a matter of history that, after listening to the hymn sung for him in private, Elder Spencer W. Kimball (then a member of the Quorum of the Twelve Apostles) asked Sister Randall if she would consider changing "know" to "do."

A post script to this story: In the mid-fifties a young resident in Ophthalmology, Dr. William A. Pettit, Jr., served as Dell's counselor in the presidency of the Fourth Quorum of Elders of the Central States Mission. It was not until he had returned to California to establish his eye-care practice that we became aware of the fact that he was a son of Mildred T. Pettit, composer of the music for *I Am A Child Of God*.

Submitted by Dell and Marie Madsen

And a Little Girl Shall Lead Him

In the years of World War II, my father, Karl Herbert Klopfer, served as President of the East German Mission. During this time he also served a mandatory tour of duty in the German Army. He directed the affairs of the mission from the battlefield, through his capable counselors. Our family saw him for the last time in November 1943, while he was on a furlough.

The Mission Home in Berlin had been completely destroyed at that time. Our family was evacuated to central Germany. My father was sent to Denmark. What happened to him there, and subsequently in other locations, is a matter of record in personal journals of others since we did not see him again. We know that he died of starvation in

March 1945, in a hospital in Puschka near Kiev, Ukraine.

At age thirty-two, my father was stationed in or near Esbjerg, Denmark, in December 1943. He was very lonely and wanted to attend sacrament meeting on one of the two Sundays preceding Christmas. He did not know whether or not there was a branch of the Church in Esbjerg, but he assumed that there would be one some-where in the city. He was in an enemy country dressed in full military uniform and did not speak the language.

Knowing that music is the same in any language, he hummed the tune of a favorite hymn as he walked on the city streets, hoping to attract the attention of someone who would recognize the tune and lead him to the place of worship.

A little girl was skipping along the sidewalk on her way to Church. As she passed my father, she recognized the tune and asked him in Danish: "Mormon?" He nodded his head. She took him by the hand and led him to the branch meeting house.

His arrival at the door of the chapel created a few tense moments for the Saints who were gathered there. They knew the little girl who entered holding the hand of my father—but who was this man dressed in enemy uniform? Was he there to do them harm?

The 30-year-old branch President, Erik R. S. Thomsen, had already started the sacrament service. He was afraid and very concerned. He stopped the meeting and left the pulpit. He walked to the doorway where my father stood and asked who he was.

My father identified himself and asked for permission to worship the Lord with the Saints, and partake of the sacrament. President Thomsen invited him to come and be seated at the podium. He also asked my father to deliver the gospel message for that day. He did so in beautiful English, since German was not appreciated by the Danes. Brother William Orum Pedersen, a visiting salesman from Copenhagen, who was also afraid, translated my father's message.

Sister Thomsen recalled for me, "Your father was the most mild-mannered German we had ever met." She also said that during the time he was there, the branch members treated him as they would a friend and a brother.

My father risked his life going to sacrament meeting in an enemy country. He fully realized that his discovery by Nazi officials among enemy people in their worship services would bring a charge of trea-son, which was punishable by death. The chance of this was further amplified by his surrendering his weapon belt to the branch President, and taking an active part in the meeting. But his desire to worship the Lord was stronger than the fear of death. He had been led to the place of worship by the power of the Lord.

A little girl provided my father with the opportunity to fellowship with the Saints because of the simple power of music. The sound of a man humming a familiar hymn touched her heart. She put her hand in his and led him to the place where he wanted to go. She was not concerned that he wore the dreaded Nazi uniform. "Mormon" was all she needed to know.

Submitted by W. Herbert Klopfer

The Spirit Is Willing But Something Interferes

I received a telephone call from the *Ensign* office. They had received a letter from a woman in England. She had also sent a picture of two missionaries that the *Ensign* people hoped I could identify.

I went to their offices to read the letter and see the picture. Lo and behold, imagine my surprise to see a picture of myself and my companion taken twenty-seven years earlier in London! I even recalled the father of the woman who had written the letter. Through the years I had been retelling a story about him whenever anyone asked me to sing in a choir. "Let me tell you a story," I would say.

Then I would tell of meeting the Reynolds family while tracting in Leeds, England. We left a copy of the Book of Mormon and went back a few days later for a cottage meeting. After the meeting, we asked them to set a time for another discussion.

"No thanks," Mr. Reynolds said, "and here is your book back."

We left feeling very discouraged. A few days later there was a knock on our door. It was Mr. Reynolds's son. He said his father wanted to see us right away.

We put on our jackets and lost no time in returning to the Reynolds family home. We were shown into the bedroom where Mr. Reynolds was lying in bed. He had been taken ill immediately after we left his house. The doctor had said he would be bedridden for some time.

We had a captive audience. We were back almost every day, giving all the missionary discussions. One day, as we were leaving, he handed us a letter. He stated in the letter that he had read the Book of Mormon. He believed it to be true and requested baptism.

My companion and I were thrilled. We wanted to do something special for him. We chose a hymn and sang it through. He never was baptized. From then on I told that story if I was ever asked to join a choir.

The letter sent to the *Ensign* had a name, and a return address. When I got home I began trying to find a telephone number for this person. I got right through to a woman named Mary Reynolds Breeze. She was surprised to hear from me. She had just come in the door from Primary where she served as a teacher.

She said that ten years after our visits with her father, he announced one day that he wanted to go to the "Mormon" church, and asked if she would go with him. She went along, and was later baptized. Now she had a son ready to be baptized.

I asked when this was going to happen. She told me. I said I would try to be there. This really shocked her, to think I would be interested enough in her family to come such a long distance for her son's baptism.

After much searching, I located my former missionary companion, Russell Robertson. I told him about the letter and the picture, and asked if he would be interested in going to the baptism. He agreed, and we made travel plans. .

Meanwhile, we corresponded with Mary Breeze and her parents. The parents had set several dates for baptism through the years, but something would always happen to prevent it.

Knowing we were coming for their grandson's baptism must have given them added impetus. By the time we arrived in England, Mary Breeze's parents had been baptized. We met them as members of the Church.

My singing had not kept them out of the church. It only set them back 27 years.

The Rest of the Story

Mary Breeze wrote in her letter to the *Ensign*:

"Twenty-seven years ago two missionaries visited the home of my parents. They did not join, but seeds were planted. My father never forgot the missionaries and their message. Several years later, after I had married, my father said, 'I think I'll start going to the "Mormon" church. Would you go with me?'

"As a result of attending Church with my father, I began absorbing the teachings and was baptized. The years that followed have not been without trial and sorrow, but through everything, I have been given joy in the sure knowledge that God lives, that Jesus Christ is his Son, and my Savior.

"I have three lovely children who are growing up in the Church. My eldest son will soon be baptized. It is my prayer that I have prepared him well, and implanted in him the desire to serve the Lord as a missionary.

"Do not be downhearted, you returned missionaries, maybe you have not been blessed to see the fruits of your labors, but in time your work will be rewarded. Thank you, Elder Glen Seely, and Elder Russell Robertson. You have brought eternal joy to my family lines."

Submitted by Glen Seely

African Experience

My husband, George, and I were called to serve a mission in Zimbabwe, Africa, for the Church Educational System. We were just home from the Haskell Indian College at Lawrence, Kansas, where we had been asked to clean and refurbish the Institute, and do the same for the house next door. CES wanted to make a home for permanent senior missionaries.

While in Lawrence, the Spirit had worked overtime with me. We went one evening to see a play put on by the Stake youth; *My Turn On Earth*. I had not seen the play before, and thought it was delightful. During the last act of the play the Spirit spoke to me; *You are going to put on this play in Africa*. I smiled incredulously.

"Ha ha," I said. "You should know better than that. I cannot sing or dance. My only directing experience is with my husband, a few roadshows, and a one-act play."

When you get to Salt Lake City, buy the play rights, and all else you will need.

I kept smiling, and the Spirit kept saying, *You will do it.*

There was no let up. At odd and unexpected moments the Spirit would whisper two words: *the play.*

When we arrived in Salt Lake City I called the office where material for the play could be had. When I heard the price, I gasped, said "Thank-you," and hung up the phone.

"No way," I said to my husband, and went off to Zimbabwe without the play. The Spirit was silent—an ominous sign.

We arrived in Zimbabwe—an alien place where the figure on the moon was a long-eared rabbit; water ran clockwise down the drain; goats, monkeys, deer, and wart hogs became road kill if you were not constantly on the alert.

In an area roughly the size of Utah, there were more than ten million black Africans, and approximately a quarter million Caucasians. Wherever we went we were a minority of two, which was intimidating at first, but after a few weeks we never thought of it. In fact, before we finished our mission, the time came when I was surprised to look in the mirror and see a white face looking back.

The Play. After a few weeks, I began to understand why I was supposed to buy the rights and do the play. George was director of seminaries in the area of Bulawayo. The young Africans were segregated, and disenfranchised whenever possible, by white young people. In the Church? Yes. In the Church.

The play would have been a means for bringing black and white young people together in an activity that was fun, creative, and spiritual.

I had a long talk with the Lord. We have had these talks for years; I get on my knees, admit I was wrong, promise to do better, and ask for further direction.

Get the play, and get to work, were my instructions. The Spirit did not say, "I tried to tell you. You would not listen," but the implication was certainly there.

My daughter was handling my bank account in Utah. I called her. She agreed to get everything I needed, and send it as quickly as possible. In the end, this way of getting it all together added greatly to the cost. I don't learn easily.

Meanwhile, I had been observant about the young people who were taking seminary classes. I began quietly choosing the young people who sang well, who were outgoing, fun-loving, and bright.

The material arrived. I invited the young people I had chosen to our house. George and I were going to tell them about my plans, and then show the play on video. Only black Africans came. They were excited beyond expression at the thought of being in a real American play. When they saw it they were a little less exuberant. They loved the play, but the cast on the video was beautifully white—obviously talented singers, dancers, and actors.

"Sister Robinson," they said, "do you really think we can do this? We can't dance. We can't act. We can't sing except in church. Who will teach us?"

"I can't teach you to dance or sing, but I can teach you to act. We will find people who can teach you everything else."

They looked dubious, but they totally believed anything I told them. If I said they could do it, then they could. I was not so certain about anything as I pretended to be. Doubts were beginning to creep into my mind. But I believed without question that this was a play the Lord wanted His African children to perform.

I began the search—first for a pianist, then for a dance instructor.

Every member of the white branch who played the piano turned me down. Each one had a valid reason. I found a young woman who was a dancer. She had come back from South Africa where she had performed for several years. She wanted to live closer to her family who were active Church members.

I approached her about teaching the young people to dance. When she learned that the entire cast was black, she was incredulous.

"Black people can't learn," she flatly stated.

"These black people can," I said. "In America, many of our best entertainers are black."

"Oh, well," she said, "black Americans and black Africans are not the same."

I talked with her for some time, trying to change her attitude.

Finally she said, "I will think about what you asked, and call you tonight."

She did call. She would try it and see how things went. We set a time for practice in the recreation hall of the large chapel where all the white people attended meetings. I told the young people to be there. They were there ahead of time; excited that this young woman, whom they knew of and admired, had agreed to teach them to dance.

We began with those who would be in the entry act. They were intimidated by her whiteness, her beauty, and who she was. They followed her directions exactly, and tried very hard to please.

At the next practice, the entry act was gone through again, and

14

the beginning dance number for the play. The instructor became quite cross with some of the young people.

She walked away, came to where I was standing, and said, "You see, they can't learn. They have forgotten everything I taught yesterday."

"Be patient. Give then a little time. They will practice. They will get better."

"They can't remember from one minute to the next," she said.

"When you were first learning to dance, did you know right off all the steps?"

The young people were watching us from the stage. They huddled together. I could tell they were becoming concerned. They definitely felt the bad vibes.

"Give us a little more time, please," I said. "I promise they will learn the dances."

"All right," she said, and left the hall.

She didn't give us more time. She came to see me the next morning.

"I'm sorry," she said. "I feel bad about it. I know I'm letting you down, but I can't do it."

I sensed that to argue and plead would be useless. It was a terrible blow, but I felt calm.

"All right," I said, and gave her a hug.

"What will you do?" she asked.

"I don't know. I only know one thing—we have a saying in America, 'whatever happens, the show must go on.' This one is meant to go on, and it will."

I got in touch with our three most versatile young people: Kelvin, Jackie, and Mildred. They each had a lead in the play. They came to our house. I told them the whole story: of how the Spirit had touched me in Kansas, and again in Salt Lake City. I said that for the Lord's own reasons, He wanted this play to go on.

Then I broke the news that the dance instructor had quit. I said she did not have enough time to do it. We must carry on without her.

The young people looked at each other. It didn't take a clairvoyant to read their thoughts. "Sister Robinson is crazy. We can't do this without help."

"What we will do," I said, "is choreograph the dances ourselves from the video, step by step. I have watched you. You can do it. You have an inborn sense of rhythm."

There are twelve dances in the play. The three young people came after school for five days, and all day Saturday. We gave them supper, and they worked until late. On week nights, we drove them home in time to do their homework. They were top students. Kelvin was Head Prefect over 300+ boys at his school.

We had hardwood floors, we pushed the furniture back, clearing a stage-sized area in the living room. At the end of six days, they had the choreography down pat. It was a joy to watch them.

The dances are done while singing. I had given each of the five leads a tape of My Turn On Earth. They loved the music, and learned each song perfectly.

An African member of the Church was the director of a center (Jairos Jiri) where disabled young people came from all over Africa to learn a trade. He offered to have his carpentry students make the props, which were seven large boxes painted in primary colors. The dancers stood on them, danced on them, made a train, built stair steps; singing and dancing their way through the play.

We were using a tape played on my boom box for practice. We desperately needed a piano player. Every day George and I were out following leads. We found a middle-aged East Indian woman who agreed to play for us. She charged by the hour—a large fee even in America.

But we were desperate. We agreed to what she asked. George picked her up on practice days. She did not own a car. She had him drive her all over town while she ran errands. She was arrogant during practices. She did not like black Africans. She did not like the play. She wanted to change it. She was an expensive 'carper.' My heart felt good when I fired her. The cast was happy to see her go, but they worried.

"What will we do, Sister Robinson? Only two weeks until opening night."

I was always honest with them. "I don't know. But I have a peaceful feeling. It is going to be all right."

I found a man who had toured throughout Europe with Jimmy Dorsey. He heard my story, read the music, and agreed to do it. Two days later, he fell and fractured his knee cap. He had to go to South Africa for treatment.

Nine days before opening night. No musician. I wept from frustration. But I did not despair. The Lord wanted us to do the play. Something would happen. George and I sat on the living room couch holding hands, and praying for a miracle.

The Relief Society President, Sister Watson, and Sandra Bentley, her first counselor, drove up. Johannes, our houseman, brought them inside.

"People come," he said.

"We've been worried about you," Sister Watson said.

"That makes four of us," George said, and updated them on what was happening.

Sandra said she knew a woman who had studied to be a concert pianist, but she had given it up to have a family. She now taught French at the school her son attended. She was a born-again Christian.

"Would you let me take the music to her? I will tell her the story and show her the music. Maybe she will do it."

"With our blessing," we said.

We watched them drive away. I prayed so hard that this woman, whoever she was, would be touched by the music, and the Spirit, and want to help us.

In about an hour we got a phone call from Sandra.

"She won't do it. When she found out you were Mormons, she said, 'I wouldn't lift a finger to help a Mormon.'" She told us that her Church had shown the members a movie called 'The God Makers.' "Mormons are evil," she said.

Then Sandra said, "I left the music with her. I asked her to please play the music. I said I would come by tomorrow and pick it up. I hope that's okay."

"Yes, that's fine. Thank you for trying. Pray," I said. "Pray hard."

I hung up the phone and told George. It was time for rehearsal at the chapel. We got in the car and left.

When we walked into the hall, with almost one voice, our kids wanted to know if we had a pianist yet.

"No," I said. "But do not despair. Something good is going to happen. I just know it."

They gave each other 'the look' that I had become familiar with, but said not a word.

We got on with the rehearsal. In about an hour a very tall, very large lady came into the recreation hall. She had the majestic look of the carved prow on a ship. She sailed into the room, skirts flying around her, long blond hair flying behind her, and wearing a smile.

The kids stopped singing.

The woman came up to me and said, "Sister, I'm Pamela

Delahaney-Smythe. I hear you have a problem." She pulled the book of music from her large bag. "This music is so beautiful. The lullaby made me cry. How can I help?"

My goodness! We sat down together. I related all the problems we had had. I told her that three of the kids had choreographed all the dances, and then taught them to the others. "But through it all, I knew that the Savior intended for this play to be heard. And I knew something else; He wanted it to be dome by his African children. No matter what went wrong we kept that belief."

"Well," Mrs. Pamela Delahaney-Smythe said, "lets see what we can do." She opened the music, and sailed to the piano. For the first time she looked at the dancers.

"Kelvin," she said, "I know you."

Kelvin was our 'Satan.' No one ever played the part better. He smiled at her. "Yes," he said, "you taught me French at Price Academy. I was sorry when you left." .

"So, you sing and dance, and act? You have many talents "

Quietly, she said, "Kelvin is one of the brightest students I ever had."

Mrs. Delahaney-Smythe stayed for two hours, going through every song with the cast. She then set up a practice for the next afternoon, which was Saturday. "After that we will practice as often as necessary to get this put together."

"Amazing," she said to me, as she was getting ready to leave. "This has been an amazing experience. What a beautiful message this play has. I've never heard anything like it."

We walked toward the door together. I was still in shock. I felt like Dorothy in *The Wizard of Oz*, caught up in the eye of a storm, whirling through space with no control over what was happening. Since it had all begun in Kansas, that was fitting and proper.

"Are you really going to do it?" I asked. "I can count on you?"

She smiled, "Try and stop me." she said. And then seriously, "Yes, Sister, I am really going to do it. I've heard some wrong things about Mormons. I am going to my Pastor and inform him that he has been misled about the Mormons."

We needed to get down to business. In Zimbabwe no one does anything without money. "How much do you charge?" I asked

She stopped dead in her tracks. "Who are you doing this for?" she asked.

"The Savior."

"I should charge you money to teach the word of the Lord? No, my dear. We will do this together for the love of the Lord." She enveloped me with a hug.

"See you tomorrow," she said, and sailed away.

The Rest of the Story

The play went on as scheduled. My daughter had sent bright colored T-shirts from Utah. A member of the Church had one of her domestic workers fit and make matching skirts for the girls, and shorts for the boys who were in the entry act. They looked beautiful. They were proud of themselves. They had never been to a movie; never seen anything but State-run television shows which were political—not entertaining; they had never seen a play—and now they were the stars of one.

A few days before we did the play, a member of the Church introduced me to the manager of the television station in Bulawayo. He agreed to let our young people do a spot on his evening show. They did their favorite song and dance, 'Look For The Light.' The show was seen across the Nation. Young missionaries arranged for their investigators to watch it.

Mrs. Pamela Delahaney-Smythe was in love with the play. She wanted us to rent the downtown theater and show it for a week. She offered to put her piano (which she prized) on a truck, and go from town to town showing the play.

"This is the Word," she said. "People need to see this. People need to hear this message." We were unable to do any of those things. Our main focus had to be on the Seminary program. George had carried on with that while I was involved with the play.

Pamela came and played the music for our Youth Saturday, which was held a few weeks later. She was astounded at the number of African young people who belonged to the Church. George taught her the gospel but she would not be baptized.

Among those who traveled 250 miles from Harare that night to see the play were our Mission President, Vern Marble, and his wife Mary; the office missionary couple; Alan and Carma Tuttle. The senior missionary couples from all over Zimbabwe came. They knew what the young people had done in order to put the play on.

Afterwards, they couldn't stop talking about the play, and how proud they were of all the kids involved. To this day, when we get together with the senior missionaries, they never fail to mention the play and what a wondrous thing it was. I keep in touch with the young people. I recently sent new music tapes to replace the worn ones they had.

The Spirit didn't stop talking about the play either; not until it was over. And then He went on to whispering about other things.

The young woman who had thought 'black Africans can't learn,' was there.

She came to me afterwards and said she was wrong. "I really can't believe they did this alone," she said. "If I hadn't seen it, I would not believe it."

"They were not alone," I told her. "God had a hand in it."

Submitted by Joy Robinson

The Spirit of God Like a Fire is Burning

In my last area as a missionary, we worked in a place called La Providensia (Providence), Mexico. This was a special place, an amazing place. Elder Porter was my companion. By the end of our time there almost forty people in that little village got baptized. We were blessed to open a new branch of the Church there. We started out by renting a little place where we could hold Church services. It cost fifty dollars a month. We could fit about 150 people in there for sacrament services. We cleaned the house, set up chairs, and arranged everything for services.

On Saturday, we put flyers all over town, announcing the meeting we were going to have that night. We said there would be a free video to watch. It was the movie where the Apostles bear their testimonies all over the world about Jesus Christ.

Fifty investigators came. That was very exciting for us. The next day at Church, about sixty-seven investigators showed up. We had three talks in the sacrament meeting.

President Alexander, our new Mission President came. He gave a talk on faith. Elder Pratt (who is a descendant of Parley P. Pratt) spoke on repentance. I spoke on baptism. As I finished my talk, I invited everyone in the room to get baptized. Seven people stood up and requested baptism.

We had a portable baptismal font in the other room with a hose in it. We filled up the font. All seven of those people got baptized after sacrament meeting.

After that we started taking down the names and addresses of people who were there. In a small village like that it was easy to find people. We were outside. They would point and say, "I live over there."

We got everybody's address. One lady in particular wanted us to come to her house. We went there in the next day or two, as soon as we could. When we went into the house we visited a little bit, and then she began to tell us about her family. She had four children. Her husband had committed suicide the year before. This had pretty much destroyed the faith of her oldest daughter. The woman became very emotional as she talked about the devastation this event had brought to her family.

We testified about Jesus Christ and the Atonement for a few minutes. Then we told the family that we were going to sing them a song. We asked them to close their eyes and listen to the words. They all put their heads down and closed their eyes. We began to sing a hymn. Before we got to the end of the first line we could see tears falling on the floor from the eyes of the mother. This happened with the children also. They all had their faces in their hands; they were kind of hunched over, and tears were falling on the floor.

Elder Porter and I looked at each other when we got to the end of the hymn. The family still sat with their heads bowed, their faces in their hands. We began singing another hymn. As we sang, the Spirit of the Lord came into the room. It was amazingly strong, and kept getting stronger. By the time we sang the fourth hymn the room was just thick with the Spirit. It filled the room.

We stopped singing. The family members sat up then and looked at us. Elder Porter and I bore testimony that what they were feeling was the Spirit of the Holy Ghost bearing witness to them that our message was true. We said that we represented the true Church of God, and that Jesus Christ was the head of this Church. That he had sent us to their home so they could be baptized and become members of His Church.

The Spirit was so powerful in the room that it was impossible for them to deny the things we had testified of. We told them that they needed to be baptized. They all nodded their heads in agreement.

They were baptized that week. The mother was soon called to be the Young Women's President.

I know that this is the true Church of Jesus Christ. I know that Jesus Christ lives and he is the son of God. I know that the Spirit testifies of this Church, and of the sacred mission of Jesus if we will take the time to listen.

Submitted by Kyle Bills

(Editor's note: Elder Bills is enrolled at BYU. He married a young woman in July 2003, in the Monterey, Mexico Temple: his Mission President's daughter, whom he did not know until after his mission. He teaches Spanish at the MTC, bearing testimony daily of his love for the Lord. His wife told me that he receives many letters from the Elders he teaches, expressing their thanks for all they have learned from him).

Resilience of the Human Spirit

Finally, the year 1944 came to an end. I was fifteen years old, living in a little town called Landsberg, in East Germany. My mother and twelve-year-old sister were all that was left of my family. My father was a soldier fighting somewhere in the war. A few months earlier my brother, Seigfried, who was only seventeen years old, had been drafted. In the same year, when we were having a small celebration of Christmas Eve, an official of the city came and informed us that our brother, Horst, had been killed in action on the Russian front. The only reason I was able to stay at home was that I had volunteered several months before to serve as an orderly for the Red Cross.

I was trained and had to pass a test before receiving my certificate. I then had to work at any time when needed to assist to bring wounded German soldiers, who arrived by train from the Russian front, and to transport them to our army hospitals. Many of them were in terrible condition; they had not been cared for since receiving their injuries. The air was filled with the odor of dead flesh, gangrene, and other infections.

I prayed constantly to my Heavenly Father to give me emotional and physical strength to do my job. I would become very tired and was afraid I might drop a wounded soldier. At other times I had to take care of civilians who had been wounded in air raids.

It was clear at this time that nothing could save us from the advancing Russian army. But our government wanted us to believe that we could still win the war. The closer the end came, the more desperate measures were taken to turn the tide. Boys younger than fifteen and old men who could barely walk were forced to take up arms, which were too heavy for them to carry. They must stand up against the Russian tanks and an army of well-trained communist soldiers who were fighting for the glory of their beloved Mother Russia.

Christmas came again. It was our last Christmas as a free people in a free country; it was also our darkest as a family torn apart by war. Our condition worsened as the enemy came steadily nearer. Every evening, just before bed time, I would go outside and listen to the sounds of war coming closer. The heavy guns of the enemy sounded like rolling thunder. As I stood there each night, I thought of the boys and men who had to face the Red Army, be slaughtered and die in vain for a lost cause. These soldiers were not Nazis who had volunteered to fight in the war. They were grocers, farmers, mercantile men, house painters, who had not been trained for the military. Had they refused to fight, they would have been shot. In those lonely hours while I stood outside and listened, my heart cried out for my people, for my country, for everything that was dear to me--my religion, and my freedom.

At this time we had no electricity, no running water, no heat and no food. Our local government had left us alone without instructions or advice on where to go or what to do. Before they left they blew up the bridges that crossed the Warthe River. We were isolated. From then on our town was without visible life. It was a ghost town. The whole city was covered in a dark, deadly silence.

One early morning I went outside the house to view the situation. I saw in the not so far distance long columns of army troops. The thought struck me like lightning: "The Red Army. The Russians are here. All is lost." Fear gripped the hearts of the people left alive. Everybody had to care for themselves. One word only can describe what happened next: chaos. There was no order, no government, no rules, and no laws.

The Russians presented a horrible sight. Their faces were rough and hardened. These first soldiers came from Mongolia. They had Asian features with bronze-colored skin, black hair, small eyes and sharp, outstanding cheek bones. They wore gray fur coats and big fur hats. They came down the street in little wagons pulled by small horses that had heavy hair, long manes, and bushy tails. A reign of terror followed them. Any houses left standing after the bombings were burned to the ground. They looked for any kind of woman, old or young, it did not matter.

Our Fuehrer had no regard for the life of his people. He ordered us to fight until every last drop of blood was shed. Lives were senselessly sacrificed while Hitler was in his fortified bunker. He married Eva Braun as the Russians closed in. Then he planned and carried out the suicide of his new wife, Blondie, his beloved German shepherd dog, and himself. A few days later, Joseph Goebbels killed his children, his wife, and then himself.

Then came a night I will never forget. In the dark silence I heard the voice of a young girl begin to sing, "Nearer My God To Thee." Other girls began to join in like a choir of angels. This hymn was sacred and dear to my heart because I was brought up in a religious environment. The young girls sang, "Nearer my God to thee, nearer to thee, even if I am depressed because of sorrow and pain, and being threatened, and if this should be my fate, in spite of pain and worries, nearer my God to thee."

No other hymn could better express the feelings of these frightened, crying young souls being dragged away from their loved ones, lying on the cold, hard floor of a dark prison cell, not knowing what would happen to them. They sang as though they were praying to the Lord, and maybe found some solace and comfort in these words of the last verse of the hymn: "And when night is over, and the sun is shining again, I will submit myself to thee before thy throne. I will build my Bethlehem for thee, and shout for joy, nearer my God to thee, nearer to thee."

Even today, fifty years later, when I hear this hymn, I cry out inside for these pure innocent young ones who had to suffer terrible afflictions. My only comfort is that they were soon taken back to their Heavenly Home, to their Heavenly Father, before they had to suffer more.

Submitted by Werner Klein
From the pages of his journal

Missionary Service

Called to know the richness of his blessing
Sons and daughters, children of a King
Glad of heart His holy name confessing,
Praises unto him we bring.

"A Lamb To The Slaughter"

I arrived in Valparaiso, Chile during the first days of August, before a military coup overthrew President Salvadore Allende, on 11 September 1973.

As a new missionary, in a country torn between Communism and democracy, life was unpredictable. Occasionally, someone would accuse us of being spies for the CIA. Always, whatever we did, we battled long lines of people. American dollars were stable, and highly valued compared to the devaluing Chilean "escudo." Old bills were so worthless they were lying in the streets like pennies in America.

Transportation was in short supply causing commutes to be a time consuming challenge. Buses were usually so packed that all the seats were full, the aisles jammed, and people would be hanging out the doors. I really enjoyed hanging out of a speeding bus. It was exhilarating to ride on the edge, and feel the wind blowing through my suit. It sure beat standing in a crowded aisle with warm bodies pressed against you.

I was several inches taller than most everyone. I had brown hair amongst a sea of black. My looks screamed "American." If that didn't draw enough attention, my pathetically poor Spanish with an American accent attracted eyes like a magnet. When I spoke, I felt incredibly self-conscious.

When it was time to exit the bus, if I had got stuck inside, I had to plow through tightly packed bodies, and they did not help by sucking in, bending, or moving over. Only the really bright, forward thinking person could get off the bus at the right stop. That is why I liked hanging out the door, feeling the wind, and dodging an occasional lamp post as we rounded a corner.

My companions and I were held up several times at gun-point by Chilean soldiers. We were shot at once. But one experience stands out vividly, above all the rest. It was the end of September. President Salvador Allende had definitely acknowledged his defeat by committing suicide with the machine gun given him by Fidel Castro.

Skeptical about the accuracy of the news; I pondered how many times a person could shoot himself with a machine gun. His presidential palace, the Moneda, in Santiago, had been riddled with bullets. Gun battles in the neighborhood where we lived quieted down considerably. Military enforced curfews had been relaxed incrementally from "all day lock in" to 9:00 P.M. Curfew was passionately enforced by the military.

I had just received a new missionary companion, Elder Taggart. He was to be my senior companion, and the District leader. He was energetic, ready to work, and so was I. The past month had not been productive for any of us, with all the political problems, and the curfews.

Our first time out together, Elder Taggart and I headed up the hill to present a discussion. In Valparaiso you were always going up or down. There was very little flat ground.

I told my companion we needed to finish the discussion and be back on the main road by 8:30 P.M. I sensed that he thought I was being lazy. But I had heard too many scary stories about people caught out after curfew. I did not want to verify the rumors for myself.

We were late finishing our presentation. It was 8:40 when we arrived back at the main road. We began trying to flag down taxis and buses without success. We tried hitch-hiking. No one would stop. I started running. My companion refused to run. I explained that the road was downhill all the way. If we ran we could make it in good time.

Elder Taggart said, "If the police see a couple of gringos running, they'll shoot us for sure." I disagreed. I pointed out that even old ladies and dogs were running. Running was the smart thing to do. It was expected. My companion was unmoved. He refused to run. Finally, so we could stay together as Mission rules demanded, I agreed to walk with him.

However, I emphatically stated, "Close calls I can deal with, but you better not get us hurt."

At 9:00 P.M. the streets were totally deserted. It was an eerie feeling to see busy roads become suddenly desolate. We could not see a sign of life in any direction. We were on the street alone. Then, in the distance, we noticed the lights of a vehicle coming down the hill behind us. It was traveling very slowly. I wondered why the people in it were not in a hurry. We continued walking until they were even with us. The vehicle was a flatbed truck driven by a man, with a woman passenger. They seemed like lovers out enjoying the evening. We asked for a ride. The man allowed us to sit on the back of the flatbed truck. Still, they were in no hurry. The truck moseyed on down the road.

We noticed the headlights of another vehicle in the distance. It was coming fast. Soon, it was on our bumper with the lights turned on blinding bright. The flatbed truck began to maneuver around a sharp curve. The vehicle behind us pulled in and cut us off. The instant we stopped, four men jumped from a pick-up truck, pulled guns on us and demanded that we get down from the truck. I assumed they were Communists because they were not wearing military uniforms. This was bad for us. The Communists in Valparaiso were extremely anti-American.

The four men had a discussion about what they were going to do with us. They came to a decision. Two of our captors escorted us at gun point over to a ditch at the side of this very dark road. Two men waited in the truck.

I was convinced they intended to shoot us, and there was nothing I could do about it. I had this incredibly calm feeling come over me. It was the feeling you get on a beautiful warm spring day when everything is just perfect. I was totally at peace. I never imagined I could feel so calm and submissive while being escorted to my death.

It came to me then that this is exactly how Joseph Smith felt when he said, "I am going like a lamb to the slaughter; but I am calm as a summer's morning."

The gunmen dumped our scriptures, pamphlets, and a sweater on the ground. We were frisked from head to foot. Suddenly one of the men in the pick-up yelled. Our assailants immediately turned, jumped into the truck and sped away. My companion and I were left standing in the dark; very much alone. Both vehicles, the four gunmen, and the couple, all disappeared into the darkness.

After gathering our stuff, my companion and I continued the long walk home. We were spotted by a soldier with a machine gun. He escorted us at gun point to the city plaza. Once there, he demanded that we should sit on the sidewalk with our hands on our heads, and our elbows on our knees. He stood above us, pointing the gun at our heads. Elder Taggart tried to talk with him but the soldier refused to answer.

A group of soldiers approached and began questioning us. When they were satisfied with our answers, they ordered us to start walking, and to stay in the middle of the street. After walking a few feet, I turned to see what the soldiers were doing. To my surprise, they were trailing us on the sidewalks, but they were staying in the shadows, and hiding in doorways for protection. We were being used as bait for rebel snipers. This was not a comforting thought.

We began approaching a huge line of "curfew violators" who were also in the middle of the street. There must have been close to a hundred people waiting to be processed. There were sounds of fear coming from the group; crying and whimpering.

"Oh, great," I thought. "We are all going to be hauled off to some stadium for the night." Soldiers came and began herding the group away. To my complete surprise, and that of my companion, we were not required to go with them. We were allowed to continue our walk home.

About 10:30 that night, we entered our apartment where we were happily greeted by the two other missionaries who lived in the building: Elders Black and Andersen. Because we were so late, they had envisioned all the worst possibilities happening to us. They listened in amazement as we recounted our adventures.

Through this experience, I came to identify with Joseph Smith in a way I could never have imagined. It's hard to know what we ourselves might feel while reading of another's experience. It's easy to gloss over feelings other people describe. I learned that emotional feelings build powerful testimonies. I came away from Valparaiso knowing that Joseph Smith was completely honest in describing how he felt. My own experience facing death helped me to trust Joseph Smith more than ever.

We felt divine protection during that scary and adventurous night. And, as a final lesson, Elder Taggart and I never again had problems getting home before curfew.

Submitted by Rod Olsen

Called To Serve

These stories have to do with the Holy Spirit working in our lives as we went out to teach and proclaim the gospel in Torreon, Mexico, from March 2001 to March 2003.

The first story takes place in a town called Matomoros. I was working with two companions. We went to see an investigator named Montecruz. She had been to church a few times, but she was one of those investigators who was right on the edge. She had not taken the step she needed to for baptism. She was right there, she just needed a final push.

We went to her house on Saturday evening. We began to teach her, and she brought up the same doubts that she had been mentioning for a long time. She just wasn't sure the Church was true, and when she prayed, the Spirit did not speak to her.

We taught her again about the apostasy and the Restoration. We taught her about Jesus Christ and testified of the Atonement. But it was not quite enough. Then we suggested that we all kneel and pray, and have her ask the Lord, to put an end to the doubt.

We went in the other room. There were four or five of us in the room. We knelt down. The first missionary prayed. Then Elder Brown prayed. And then I prayed. During the prayer we used an ordinance and called the Spirit down from Heaven.

Then Montecruz began to pray. She said, "Father, I need to know if the Church is true so I can make correct decisions in my life."

Right when she said those words, the Spirit in the room became absolutely, amazingly strong, and overwhelming. There are not proper words to describe it. It over came her. She fell lifeless and motionless on the bed. We looked at each other and did not know how to react. This had not happened to any of us before. We stayed on our knees and continued to pray. We were very excited. We knew this was from the Spirit and it was a good thing that was happening.

After about five minute of lying there seeming to be dead, she stood up and pronounced that she had seen a vision. She said that she had seen a long dark tunnel and at the end of the tunnel was a bright light. (People in Mexico do not know about the life after life experiences that have happened to North American people and been written about).

She was told that the dark tunnel represented her life, and the bright light represented the gospel.

She testified that she now knew that what we had been teaching her was true. She committed to baptism the next day. So far as I know she has remained true and faithful.

This next story took place in a town called Modrero. My companion was Elder Henderson. We had been teaching a family of seven people. A mother and her six sons, all of priesthood bearing age. We were very excited about that. The father was not interested in hearing the gospel.

As we taught them they were getting closer and closer to being baptized. They had been reading and praying, and attending church regularly. In Mexico things can change pretty quick day to day. A family can commit to baptism and someone close to the family may come by and say, "Why are you doing that? You don't want to do that. You are going against all our traditions. Mormons are evil. They have horns just like the devil."

That night as we prayed, we pled with the Lord about this family that had agreed to baptism. My companion and I prayed together. Later I knelt in my bed and prayed to the Lord about this family. I tried my best to convince Him that our desires were just, and that this was a good family. They wanted to serve the Lord; they were trying, and they had done all we had asked them to do.

The Lord came to me then. He told me through the Spirit, as clearly as possible, that we had done as much as was required of us. He promised that this family would be baptized the next day. And He covenanted with us. I knew from that point on that all He said would transpire. His Spirit came down from Heaven and just landed on me. It was the most comfortable feeling I have ever experienced. I lay on my bed musing about what had happened, and enjoying the Spirit that I had felt.

The next day we went to the home of our investigators. All seven of them were there, and two extra people. They had been present for some of the discussions, but not all of them. They said, "Listen, you need to teach us the rest of the discussions right now, because we want to get baptized with our family."

We were pretty willing to do that. We said, "Okay."

We took them all to church. We taught the discussions the two had missed, and all of them were baptized. I'll never forget how good it felt to baptize all those people of one family. .

There was one problem. We did not have enough baptismal clothes. We went to the hospital that was next door. We got some of those white patient gowns that tie in the back. We gave them to some of the smaller kids. They didn't realize how they tied. They stripped down completely naked, and put on those gowns. They came out for the baptism, and there they were with their little bums hanging out the backs. It was pretty funny. But no one paid any mind. Little kids running around with naked bums is not unusual in Mexico. It was a happy day for all of us.

This story is about a really neat man. I was walking with some Elders in a zone called Torreon, Mexico. This was close to the Mission office. We got up that morning and we prayed, and we studied and then we went out to do the Lord's work.

We had made some plans, but then we both felt that we needed to do some more praying because we were not feeling where the Spirit wanted us to go. As we were praying we were told there was a man we needed to visit; a home we needed to go to.

My companion pointed across the street. "That house, right there," he said.

We went over and knocked on the door. A man's voice said, "Come in."

We opened the door and went in. A man was there sitting in a chair. He had a bag beside him. His baptismal clothes were inside the bag. He looked us in the eyes and said, "I knew you were coming. I've been waiting. I need to get baptized."

To say we were taken aback would be an understatement. My companion and I looked at each other. We were thinking the same thing, "Hey, whoa. What's going on here? Who is this guy?"

As missionaries, we knew he couldn't get baptized until he had gone to Church. We sat down with him and asked him a few questions. Our first question was, "Have you been to church?"

He said, "Yes." So we said, "Well tell us a little bit about church."

He described the teachers blessing the sacrament and the deacons passing it. So we thought, "Well, I guess that covers that. He's been to Church."

Then we asked him if he had been taught the gospel. He told us "Yes, I know what I need to know. I am ready to get baptized." We began then to try and find out what he really knew about the Church. We asked if he had heard of the Word of Wisdom. He said he knew all about it. "You can't drink alcohol, tea, or coffee. You can't smoke." He knew about Joseph Smith. All the questions we asked he had an answer for.

The Spirit spoke clearly to each of us, my companion and I, that this man was supposed to be baptized. So we went over to the Mission office, got everything cleared, and he was baptized that same day.

This was a wonderful example of how the Spirit works if we are connected.

Another story has to do with Elder Conover and myself. We were companions. We were in a small village on the outskirts of Torreon. There were dirt streets; it was a hot day. We had worked hard. We'd knocked on a lot of doors, talked to people on the streets, but we had not had much success. We were hot and tired. It was noon and we were hungry. But we did not want to stop and eat until we felt better about our morning's work.

"One more try," we said. We decided to find a secluded place in this little village where we could have a prayer. We carried with us a map of the streets of this little village. We opened up the map and asked the Lord where he would have us go to find someone who was seeking; someone we could teach, someone who would be baptized. As we were praying, I had an impression, and Elder Conover had the same impression. When our prayer was finished we both pointed to the same street on this little map. We walked down a few blocks and found the street.

There was this man. He was standing outside his home, waiting for us. We said hello. He said hello back. We asked if we could come in. He said yes. So we walked back to his little house and went in. He lived in a tiny place, a little hut really, that was made of some tin, tarpaper, pieces of wood, bicycle parts, whatever he could find to make walls and a roof.

We sat down in his home with him, and began to teach him the gospel. We found out a little bit about him. He had two young kids. About five minutes into the discussion, he interrupted.

"Could I tell you guys about a couple of dreams I've had? Maybe you can tell me what they mean."

We said, "Yeah, go ahead."

He said that in one dream he saw two white personages. They were standing in the air. They had silver white hair and beards. They were exceedingly bright like a light was shining around them. They also looked like each other. They were wearing long white tunics.

We pulled out the flip charts and showed him the picture of Joseph Smith in the Sacred Grove looking at God the Father, and His Son Jesus Christ.

The man got all excited. He said, "That's exactly what I saw. That's it right there."

We were pretty excited ourselves, but we held it down, and waited to see what was going to transpire.

"Let me tell you about the other dream," he said. "I saw a white castle in the mountains. It was the most beautiful thing I have ever seen. It had a whole lot of towers. I also saw inside the building. I saw people walking around in there. They were dressed in white clothing."

My companion and I were both thinking, "Wow, that's pretty interesting."

He then said that there were three levels inside this castle. The bottom level had a deep hole. In his dream he wondered what was inside the hole and where it went. He said the second level was pretty, and an okay place to be, but the third level was more beautiful than a person could imagine. That was where he wanted to be.

In the middle of this third level was a fountain, a large white fountain, and pure clear water was coming from it. He said it was the most amazing place. He longed to be there, and he wanted to be there forever.

We pulled out a picture of the Salt Lake Temple on the flip charts, and showed it to him. Again he pointed, very excited: "That's it. That's the building. That's the castle."

This time, we couldn't hold it any longer. We began to teach him, and to preach to him about the Savior, and about the Apostasy, and the Restored Church. We told him about Joseph Smith. We taught him for a good hour that day. We were not hungry. We were not tired. We looked him in the eyes and said, "Heavenly Father has been preparing you. You need to be baptized, and become a member of His Church."

He looked back at us and said, "You are right."

That was on a Wednesday or Thursday. He was baptized that next Sunday. About a week later he was called to be a counselor in the bishopric. That was a pretty exciting day for Elder Conover and myself.

A footnote to the story: the Saturday night before he was going to be baptized, he was on his knees praying. He was telling Heavenly Father everything that had happened, and that he was going to be baptized. (This was a pure man. He had a Catholic background, though he had not attended church for some time). He told the Lord, "And this is what I am going to do now. I'm going to pour gasoline on my feet and light a match to it. If I don't get burned I will know for sure that this is Your Holy Church."

He poured gasoline on his feet, struck the match and dropped it. Fire consumed the gasoline, but his feet were not burned. He went happily to bed.

The next morning when we came to get him for Church, I could smell the gasoline. I asked him about it. When he told us what he had done we were pretty amazed.

"Please," we said. "Don't tell anyone else that you did that."

He said okay, as if it was nothing, and we all left to get him baptized.

In the Stake at Durango, Mexico, for a few days we had three companions working together. Elder Hill, Elder McConkie, and myself. Our Mission President was Mauro Gil. President Gil had the Elders call on Wednesday and Sunday night. On Sunday night We reported how many baptisms there had been. On Wednesday night we reported how many baptisms we expected to have on Sunday.

Things in that area had been going very well. The Lord had really blessed us. We had eight people ready for baptism on the following Sunday. We reported this to President Gil. He was pleased.

On Monday, we began following up on our people who had committed to baptism. We had a really disappointing day. One after another, for one reason or another, each of the people told us that they could not be baptized. My companions and I talked together about what we would do. We couldn't think about calling President Gil on Wednesday and telling him all our baptisms had fallen through. We had each had the experience, and none of us wanted to repeat it. Somehow, it fell on me to phone him.

There was dead silence on the other end of the phone when I made the report that no one was getting baptized. Then the prophesying began.

"Elder Bills, the Lord wants seven people from that area baptized this week. You and your companion go out and find those seven people. If you have any faith in the Lord you will find those seven people and baptize them." Then he hung up the phone.

My companion was chewing his nails waiting for me to finish the call. As soon as I hung up he said; "Well, what did he say?"

"Umm. Well, he said that if we have any faith in the Lord, we will baptize seven people this week."

"Oh, man," he said. "Where will we find seven people?"

We had one man that we had just begun to teach, and no one else. We looked at each other kind of desperately.

I said, "If we don't baptize seven people this week then it means that we don't have any faith. This isn't good."

There was only one way open to us. We dropped to our knees and started pleading with the Lord. We told him how silly we were, and how much we didn't know, and how much we needed his help.

We said a lot more as a companionship, then we separated and began praying individually.

As I was praying alone, I poured out my soul to the Lord. I told him that I knew I was weak in many things, but that I loved him. I wanted to find these seven people, and I did have faith in Him.

As I was praying, He opened up my mind. I saw the place where these people were. He told me the name of the place, and the number of people who would be baptized. The name he told me was Ampliacion PLI. This was a small colony not far from us.

I stood up after my prayer. I told my companion that the Lord had shown me where we needed to go. The next morning we got up, had our prayers, studied and went out to work. We knocked on the door at the house the Lord had shown me. There were seven people living in that house. And they were waiting for us. We baptized every one of them on Sunday. We got down on our knees and thanked the Lord for blessing us and showing us where those people were. It was really great to call the Mission President and tell him what had happened.

Baptizing those seven people was just the beginning. An entire city block, about thirty people, were taught and baptized. The Lord had sent us to a golden area where He had prepared a group of people to be taught His Gospel. My companion and I felt truly blessed to be a part of that.

Submitted by Kyle Bills

Experience in Zacatlan

On the 28th of March, 2000, I was in an area in the northern mountains of Puebla, Mexico. It was called Zacatlan by the people. The landscape was green, with towering mountains, 200-foot-high waterfalls, and a people that were starving for the gospel. The church had only been in Zacatlan for six months and was beginning to grow considerably.

I had been the branch president for a few months. I had seen many miracles, and much spiritual growth in this beautiful land. In February we started teaching the family Luna Leon. It was an entire family with four future priesthood holders, and one very sweet mother. Normally, in Mexico, the women are receptive to the missionaries, and to hearing us teach the gospel plan. But the men are more stubborn. They don't want to change their way of living.

After teaching all the discussions to the Luna Leon family, and spending many hours teaching, and learning from them, the time had come for their baptism. It was now the 28th of March. We rented Volkswagen minivans to transport the entire branch to the river Quesalapa where we performed the baptismal ordinance. Some other missionaries came in to help us with the baptismal interviews for the eight people that had accepted the invitation to follow the Savior and enter the waters of baptism.

I was interviewing Rosa Maria Luna Leon. Her husband Rene and three sons, Rene, Uriel, and Erick were already dressed in beautiful white clothes. We started the interview and ran into a rather large speed bump in the road. Rosa Maria believed the Church was true and everything about it, but did not have a testimony of the Prophet Joseph Smith.

It is impossible to believe it is all true and not believe in the one man that restored these wondrous eternal truths. After two hours of talking and crying, I felt that we should kneel in prayer and find out right now. She admitted to never praying about Joseph Smith. We both got on our knees. She offered a very simple prayer. I was pleading with the Lord to confirm her decision, and please do it now. We agreed to not leave our knees until the answer came.

After three or four minutes she sat up and said that she still questioned it. I slowly got up, and sat down on my chair. Suddenly, Rosa Maria was overcome with happiness and started to cry. She blurted out three times "Joseph Smith is a Prophet and I know if for myself." Her face was all smiles, and she was clapping her hands.

We knelt in prayer again to thank the Lord for the Spirit that had touched our hearts. Within the hour she, and her family, had all made sacred covenants with the Lord by being baptized and confirmed members of the Church of Jesus Christ of Latter-day Saints.

The second story was when I was serving in La Libertad, Puebla. My first day there I met with the Mission President and the Stake President. In that zone there had only been six baptisms in six months. It was late June and we set a goal with both presidents to baptize twenty-eight people on the 25th of July.

They were just finishing up a new stake center and wanted to have a baptism on the first day of church in the new building. That night I prayed and pleaded with the Lord to help us know the way to find people that were ready to accept the gospel; and I asked Him to help us, as missionaries, receive an awareness of how we could help them come unto the Savior. I felt that we needed to understand how to call upon the powers of Heaven and be a part of a miraculous work and a wonder.

The next day we met as a zone and each shared stories of miracles we had seen in our lives. We then decided to pray for each investigator in the zone, for their families, doubts, concerns, problems; and for the spirit to touch their hearts and minds. We each decided that we would pray for them every night and every morning. It would take about thirty minutes to finish each time. As the month progressed, we found the families, taught them, prayed for them, and on the 25th of July, we had twenty-eight people dressed in the white beautiful clothing. The baptisms lasted three hours. It was truly a miracle. We prayed with our whole faith as a team. Under the Lord's direction, the missionaries in our zone were guided to the homes with wanting souls. We were given the power to bless those people with the knowledge and truth needed to enter into the waters of baptism, and take upon themselves this holy covenant.

Submitted by Jeffrey Hall

A Nephite Missionary Companion

In 1866 the first John Morgan came to Salt Lake City, but not because of the Church; he was not a member at the time. He came to fulfill a contract which he and his friend had made with William Jennings: to drive a herd of Texas Longhorns from St. Louis to the Great Salt Lake Valley.

When they finally arrived in the valley with their herd of Longhorn cattle, they found Mr. Jennings out of town on business. He was not expected back for several weeks. They decided to wait for his return, in order to be paid for their services.

While waiting, John stayed at the home of Joseph L. Heywood, Bishop of the Seventeenth Ward.

One morning after sitting down to breakfast, he related to Mrs. Heywood an impressive dream he had had during the night. He dreamed that he was back in Georgia near the battlefield of

Chickamauga, where he had fought during the Civil War. He was traveling southward on a road running from Chattanooga, Tennessee to Rome, Georgia. He was perfectly familiar with the road, as it was one the soldiers had used many times.

In his dream, he suddenly came to a fork in the road, and was undecided as to which road led to Rome. Then, he was amazed to see Brigham Young standing in front of a large tree in the fork. President Young told him the right hand led to Rome, but if he would take the left hand road, he would have an experience that would give him a strong and abiding testimony of the divinity of the Book of Mormon.

He asked Mrs. Heywood what she thought of the dream. She replied that she believed the time would come soon when he (John Morgan) would join the Church. In due time he would be called to do missionary work in the Southern states. She thought that in the work, he would be following the road, and would arrive at the fork he saw in his dream. President Young would not be there; but she counseled John to remember his instructions, and take the road that led to the left.

John Morgan thanked Mrs. Heywood, and soon forgot about the experience. A year later he joined the Church and was baptized.

Ten years later, while traveling as a missionary from Chattanooga, Tennessee, to Rome, Georgia, he came to a fork in the road, which confused him and caused him to stop.

He was undecided as to which road led to Rome. As he pondered, he suddenly realized that the fork that lay before him was the identical place he had seen in his dream, while residing at the Heywood home. The large tree in the fork was there. But as Mrs. Heywood predicted, President Young was not there. He then vividly recalled the counsel given in the dream not to take the right hand road, which he said led to Rome; but to follow the left hand road which would lead him to a remarkable experience. He would gain a greater testimony of the divinity of the work he was engaged in, and a pure knowledge of the divine teachings of the Book of Mormon.

Thrilled with the remembrance of the dream he had experienced, he took the left hand road and continued his journey. After an hour walk, the road led him to the rim of a beautiful valley in northern Georgia. From a passerby, he learned that the name of the place was Heywood Valley, having the same spelling as the Heywoods in Salt Lake Valley. He was told that the valley had been settled, and was owned by some twenty-three prosperous families.

In high spirits, John traveled on. He called at the first house he came to, where he was received with true Southern hospitality. Filled with the spirit of his mission, he spent the entire evening in gospel conversation. Three hours were engaged in his effort to explain the first principles of the gospel to his new friends.

As the evening came to a close, the head of the house brought out the family Bible. To Elder Morgan's amazement, he found that many of the scriptures which he had used in explaining the principles of the gospel were underscored. He asked the family who had done this.

Ten days before, the man said, a kindly looking man in tidy clothing, and seemingly possessed of great intelligence, had come to their home and had, with their permission, marked the Bible. He explained to them that in a few days another man would come. He would teach them the meaning of the marked passages, and explain in its completeness, The Great Plan of Salvation.

They knew not who the stranger was. He did not give his name. They knew not from whence he came, or where he went.

During the next six weeks, Elder Morgan called successively on each of the families in Heywood Valley. In every home where the stranger had called, the family Bible was marked. He had told each family that a man would follow after him, and explain the scriptures in their fullness.

John Morgan was successful in converting and baptizing all the Valley inhabitants except for three families. Among those converted was a Methodist Pastor, who was made the presiding Elder of the Heywood Branch. The building previously used as a Methodist Church now became a Mormon meeting house.

John Morgan's dream had come true. In his heart he always believed that he had gained as a missionary companion none other than one of the three Nephites.

On Saturday morning, 1 June 1878, while a guest at the home of his first converts in Heywood Valley, Elder Morgan began the writing of an epistle to the Saints in Georgia, and Alabama in particular, and to the world in general, setting forth clearly and convincingly, the answers to three weighty questions which have addressed themselves to thinking people since the dawn of time: Where did we come from? Why are we here? Where do we go from here?

He walked 10 miles to Rome, Georgia, where he visited the Mosely Printing Shop, to whom he awarded the printing job. It was then he decided to change the designation of his writing from epistle to tract.

He gave it the name 'The Plan of Salvation' which his mysterious missionary companion had used.

Submitted by John Morgan, descendent of John Morgan
Pages from a family journal

Claudia's Baptism

Journal Entry: June 30, 1997, Tujunga, California

Wow!! Yesterday was one of the best days of my whole mission. Where do I start? There is a part member family here in the Tujunga Branch; the Valadez family. Both of the parents have been members for about a year. Their children; four daughters, and a son, seven years old, were not members.

When I first arrived in this area I thought that was strange. I immediately wanted to go visit this family. I was told that the key to helping the whole family become members of the Church was to help the oldest daughter, Claudia, gain a testimony that the church was true. If she would join the Church her sisters would follow. I was also told that it would not be easy.

I did not get it. Claudia would come to church every Sunday with her sisters. They would participate, and they seemed to be good young people. Since I arrived here we have seen her about once a week, taking different messages to share. The Spirit was always strong, but Claudia would never open up to pray, and ask God if the church is true.

One day she let us know that she was a bit tired of our continued visits. I asked her if she would pray to know if Joseph Smith was a prophet of God, and whether the Book of Mormon was true. She looked at me and said "NO! I won't. I will never believe either of those things. Why don't you quit wasting your time?"

At that moment the Spirit came over me like a warm rush of air. It caused me to tell her something that I could not believe I had said after it left my mouth. "Claudia," I said, "not only will you come to believe these things, one day you will be telling others as I am telling you, that these things are true!"

When I told her that her whole countenance changed. The Spirit was in the room. I explained to her that what she felt was the Spirit of the Lord testifying to her that what I was saying is true. We said a prayer and left.

After that experience Elder Guerra and I knew we were making progress. Now to what happened Saturday. We decided to teach her the third discussion on the apostasy and restoration. It went really well. She became receptive and began to ask questions having to do about some of her doubts about the three degrees of glory, temple marriage, and baptisms for the dead.

All those principles are in the fourth discussion. We went on and taught her that discussion. The Spirit was really strong. The difference this time from the other times, is that when we asked questions like, "How do you feel to know God loves us enough to send us a Prophet to lead and guide us?" She said, "good" instead of like before when she would say, "I don't know."

We then asked her to pray and ask Heavenly Father to let her know if she should be baptized. She said her prayer sincerely!! We were so happy because we knew if she did that she would get her answer. Claudia told us that she would let us know her answer the next day at church.

We were planning baptisms for her brothers, Richard and Berto, with great faith that Claudia would receive her answer. The next day at church, Claudia bore her testimony about the pioneer trek that she went on, and how she received a card from her mother telling her how much she wanted Claudia and her sisters to be members of the Church. She also told about Diana, one of the young woman on the trek, getting up to bear her testimony of how much she loved the Church, and that she hoped Claudia would become a member. Claudia said this made her feel special.

It was good to hear her bear her testimony. After sacrament meeting we did not get a chance to talk to her, nor after Sunday school. But when the meetings were over, I saw her and went to talk with her. I asked her how her prayer went. She told me she got her answer but wanted to wait. She did not want to regret anything. I asked her what answer she had received.

She said she felt the Lord telling her she needed to be baptized, but that she was still nervous. Elder Guerra and I were so happy. We shared with her the Doctrine and Covenants, section 6 verse 23, how her witness came from God and that she did not need to fear. She decided she would be baptized, but wanted to keep it a secret from her mother.

We went to eat dinner with the Antillons like we do every Sunday after church. We brought Claudia with us. Presidente Barrias called Sister Valadez and asked her to give a talk at the baptisms for Richard and Berto.

That evening we went to the baptisms and Hermana Valadez was there but looked kind of sad. I think she believed Claudia would be baptized, but when she did not see her there she lost hope. Claudia was waiting in the girls bathroom, dressed in her white clothes.

First I baptized two wonderful brothers, Richard and Berto. (There were 40 or 50 people from the branch who had come to the baptism. It was so cool.) When Claudia walked down into the water it was such a surprise to everyone, we heard gasps of air. The best part was seeing the reaction of Claudia's mom. She put her hands over her face and burst into tears of pure joy.

After Claudia was baptized her mother bore a wonderful testimony, but that's not all. Claudia's sister Nancy was angry at first, because Claudia decided to get baptized without telling her. But that night, after they had a Stake young women's camp meeting, when they were walking out I went to tell them goodbye, and they asked if it was too late to baptize Nancy. I was so happy. I said, "Of course not."

We called everyone back for Nancy's baptism. The rest of the family will be baptized next week.

I love my Heavenly father and am thankful for the opportunity I had to play a small part in the conversion of Claudia. I know this is the Lord's work. Days like this fulfill the part of my patriarchal blessing where it states that my mission will be a golden time of my life!!

The Rest of the Story

Claudia is now married to President Barrias' son Humberto. They were married last December in the Los Angeles Temple. Claudia has shared her testimony with many people. She has been an instrument in the Lord's hands in helping people gain a testimony of the Prophet Joseph Smith, and the restoration and the Book of Mormon!.

She plans on serving a mission in her later years. I will never forget when the Spirit prompted me to say that she would one day be doing exactly what I was doing: preaching the gospel of Jesus Christ. She has never forgotten it either. We must always follow the Spirit when prompted. A promise made by anyone under the influence of the Spirit will come to pass!

Submitted by Justin D. Robinson

The Gift of Tongues

I was born in London, England, in the mid 1960s. I was the only daughter; I had five brothers. My first thirteen years were spent living in London, England. In the late 70s we emigrated to Ontario, Canada. This is where the missionaries found us. They taught us the gospel, and we were all baptized. We have always had the priesthood in our home, as my father was baptized after the 1978 revelation.

For the next ten years I lived in Canada. After graduation from high school, I attended the University of Western Ontario for two years. I then returned to London, England, where I was accepted and able to get a degree in Physical Therapy at the Middlesex Hospital School of Therapy. Following that I had a great desire to serve a mission, but the Lord had other plans for me at that time. He seemed to want me to consolidate my degree by working as a therapist at the Hospital, which I did for two years.

While there I served in the Hyde Park ward as the Young Women's President, and later as the Gospel Doctrine teacher.

After two years I returned to Canada to be with my family. I was immediately called on a mission to Tennessee. I served there from 1992 to 1994, under President Serge B. Woodruff, and then under President Josiah Douglas.

The experience I wish to share with you occurred during the latter part of my mission under the guidance of President Douglas. It is an example to me of how the Lord was much engaged in what was going on. Through His inspiration I was able to receive the gift of tongues, and thereby save my life and the life of my companion.

I had been transferred to Hopkinsville, where I felt privileged to serve. On this particular morning, after breakfast, prayers, and study, because we had no appointments, we decided to find the address of a family who had requested the 'Family First' video.

Not having been in the area before, we decided to rely on a map of the city to help us find the street and the address. Looking around, it came to us that the neighborhood we were in was not a very good one for two young women to be in alone.

It was 10:30 A.M. as we drove slowly down the street keeping an eye out for the street we needed to find. There were very few people outside, so we could not ask for help finding the street.

Suddenly a car came up. Looking in the rear view mirror, I saw the occupants of the car, and knew they were dangerous. I had the thought that they could be intent on doing harm to me and my companion.

They pulled alongside us. It was hot and all the windows were down in both cars. Because of the way we were driving, and using a map, they assumed we were lost. And of course this made us more vulnerable.

Because I was black, I was afraid they would find me "cute" and desirable. My British accent would also be very amusing to them. The Spirit distinctly told me that they were up to no good, and we were in danger. While on my mission I had decided that I really did not want to pick up the Southern drawl. I wanted to keep my own British accent because it was part of who I was.

The Spirit emphatically told me, at that instant, that I needed to play the role of a Southern religious fanatic. I did not question what the Spirit said. I didn't think twice about the instructions.

Later on, after the event was over, I realized from what I had seen that these young men were probably drug dealers. Their new car had mag wheels and was all souped up. They were young men, in their early twenties, not at work at 10:30 in the morning. They were just cruising around with loud music blaring. The feeling I got through the Spirit was that they had been raised in a church, they may have turned away from it, but they still had some respect for their God. They had respect for their mothers and grandmothers, and would probably respect a young woman who was an obvious religious fanatic.

The young men said that we looked lost and wanted to know if they could help us out.

"All right," I said to the Spirit. With that, I asked my companion to pass me a Book of Mormon. The look on her face told me that she thought I was insane. Her eyes got real big. She was obviously thinking, "Sister, these young men are not going to listen to a gospel message." But she handed me the book.

I got out of the car, waving the Book of Mormon, and pounced on them. I opened the book to the first page, and asked them if they had ever heard of the Book of Mormon. But the way the words came out was not the way I normally spoke. Every word was in a down home Southern drawl.

"Have y'all evah hear tell of de Book of Moahmon? Have y'all evah heard of Lehi? Now, jist listen heah, I'm goin' to tell y'all somethin' impotent to yo sal-va-shun. Six hundret yeahs befo' Christ wuz bone, Lehi took his fambly, he wuz instructed by de Lawd to do dis thing. Now, y'all member he wuz a prophet, see? Him and his fambly wuz the vehy fus fambly to come to dis heah con-ta-nent." I just went off on this tangent about Lehi and Nephi, and how they had built a ship and come to the Americas all the way across the ocean. I didn't allow them one word edgewise. I talked about how the Lord had blessed them on their voyage. And then started to tell about those blessings.

I could see their eyes begin to glaze over. And then their countenances changed.

"Tell us again, what's the address you guys are lookin' for?" One of them spoke like he was in a trance. I guess my ranting on in the hot sun was putting them to sleep.

We gave them the address.

"Follow us, we'll take you there," one of them said.

I got back in the car and we followed them. They escorted us to the proper street, and the proper house number, which we had spent considerable time trying to get to. They pulled away. We were so shaken up. It is doubtful that our legs could have held us up if we had tried to get out of the car. We made no effort to deliver the video. We waited until the car of the young men was out of sight, then we left; going the opposite direction as fast as the speed limit would allow.

We drove to another area that we were more familiar with. We stopped the car and had prayer. We thanked our Heavenly Father for delivering us from a bad situation. At that time, and in that place, if they had discovered that I was a foreigner, we could have been in mortal danger. I thanked the Lord for putting into my mind what I needed to do in order to keep us from whatever harm those young men intended.

It was the Lord's idea to make me seem as though I was a local. He showed me the way that I could gain the quickest respect, and maybe repulsion from these young men, in the shortest amount of time, in such a way that we were preserved.

I have since discovered that I have been blessed with the gift of tongues. I studied French and picked it up, with the proper accent, in a short amount of time. In my job as a physical therapist at a Salt Lake hospital, I meet many people who speak different languages. I have received the gift of being able to communicate with each one, enabling them to understand my instructions.

I bear my testimony that I know the Lord works with us in mysterious ways, and if we will listen to the still small voices that come to us on a daily basis, our talents will magnify; and as we obey, the still small voice will become louder: more easily discerned.

The Lord will take care of us in our hour of need, he has always a plan for us to escape the tempter. He knows what needs to be done for His work to progress. He wants us to be kept safe.

In the experience I have related, I know without a doubt that the gift of tongues works. The Lord can bless you in your life, to speak Russian or Cambodian, whatever the need, that we may carry forward His work.

Submitted By Muriel MacIntosh Lee

We Will Do What You Want Us To Do

I was an educator during my working years. My wife, Annetta, worked as a nurse, also teaching classes at University Hospital. We had always planned to serve a mission for the Church when our children were grown and we had retired.

In September of 1990, we put in our papers and were called to serve in Sofia, Bulgaria. Elder Russell M. Nelson asked us to come and see him before we left. When we were seated across from him in his office, he leaned back in his swivel chair and asked what we were going to do in Bulgaria.

"We are going to teach the GRE (Graduate Record Exam) and TOEFL (Test of English as a Foreign Language)," was our reply.

"No, you're not," he said. He sat up straight in his chair, and the chair shot forward. He put his arms on the desk, and leaned towards us.

"You are going to baptize people and organize the Church in Bulgaria."

"Can we baptize?" Sister Mower asked.

"People will ask you about the Church. Yes, your husband can baptize."

Six weeks later we finished the first week with our GRE class in Sofia. We had sixteen students. They all spoke English and were well-educated people: a judge, a math professor at the University, a physics professor, a dentist, an architect, etc.

That weekend President Dennis Neuenschwander, the Austria Vienna East Mission President, came to see how we were getting settled. During the visit he suggested that we hold a fireside.

Sister Mower and I were a bit stunned. "Who do we invite?"

"Your class," he replied.

At the end of our afternoon class on Monday, we extended the invitation.

"What is a fireside?" they wanted to know.

That evening twenty-four people came to our tiny apartment. They met President Neuenschwander who encouraged them to seek scholarships, and to continue their education in England, Europe, and America. He also told them the Joseph Smith story, and cited Alma's story of planting seeds in the hearts of those who were seeking truth.

At the beginning of the Tuesday class, I was excited to get their reaction to the fireside. Daniele, a masters level student, raised her hand and said, "Elder Mower, it would be nice to believe what your President Neuenschwander told us, but that is like believing in a fairy tale." I did not seek out any more responses.

The class ended. As students were signing up for books to take home, the dentist, Mirella Lazarova, who had come to the fireside with her husband, Vensislav, said, "Elder Mower, we would like to know more about your church."

They were in the first group of six to be baptized in Bulgaria. Her mother was in the second group. Later the grandmother was baptized and sealed to her husband who had died. The Lazarova's young sons have also been baptized.

We went forth to try and obtain legal recognition for the Church in Bulgaria. This was no small thing. Under Communism in Bulgaria it was risky to even admit that you were a Christian. After much fasting and many prayers by the members, it finally happened: the Church received official recognition by the Government. Venisislav's name appears on the legal document.

A few days later, two branches of the Church in Bulgaria were organized. Vensislav became one of the Branch Presidents. Mirella was called to serve as the Relief Society President.

The Rest of the Story

Eventually the Lazarova's came to Salt Lake City. Mirella helped translate the Temple ceremony in Bulgarian. She obtained a scholarship to study at BYU and earned a Ph.D. in chemistry. During these years Vensislav gave countless hours of assistance at the Fourth Street Dental Clinic in Salt Lake City. He also served in an elders quorum presidency, and as a counselor in a student ward bishopric.

They now live in California where Mirella works in a lab doing DNA research. Vensislav is at a dental clinic awaiting admittance to a dental school.

Elder Dallin Oaks, in a fireside chat in Calgary, Alberta, Canada, cited examples of modern-day miracles. In this case it was the gift of tongues. He said that when he was in Sofia, Bulgaria, Mirella had translated for him. He spoke on a gospel subject that she was not familiar with. While translating, she had words come to her that she did not know, or understand.

Sister Mower and I were impressed to have a Prophet of God tell us that people in Bulgaria would ask after the Church, and surprised at how quickly they did. The Bulgarians have been greatly blessed since hearing, believing, and trying to live the gospel. We are still amazed at the growth of the Church there because of a few good people who were touched by the Spirit.

Annetta and Morris Mower

Spiritual Communication in Jacksonville

My sister Nadyne and I were called to serve missions for The Church Of Jesus Christ of Latter-day Saints. We were called to serve at the same time and to the same mission, the Southern States. Nadyne's first assignment was to be Secretary to the Mission President in Atlanta, Georgia. My first assignment was to proselyte in Orlando, Florida. This was before the time of Disney World.

I served in several cities with different companions. My last assignment was in Jacksonville, Florida. Although this was a fruitful area where several persons joined the Church, it was decided that my companion and I would be moved to another location in the city.

During the months of September, with two weeks left before moving to our new area, we continued the work of knocking on every door we came to, in order to spread the gospel message.

As we entered a new area, we came upon a trailer house parked on a corner lot in a residential area. We walked across a lovely green lawn, and knocked on the trailer door. An attractive young woman answered out knock, and we were invited in.

We introduced ourselves as missionaries representing The Church of Jesus Christ of Latter-day Saints. She told us that she had been baptized a "Mormon" but she was not active. She told us she had married a non-member, she had two children. Her husband was a U.S. Naval Air Force officer. He discouraged them from attending church services.

Sister Kersey then dismissed us because she thought her husband might come home and find her talking with us. This would cause him to be angry. We left three copies of the Book of Mormon with her; one each for her children, (a boy age 8, and a girl age ten) and one for her. Two weeks later we moved from this area to our new assigned location.

Six months had passed since I was first assigned to Jacksonville. I had worked with two other lady missionaries; now I was to have yet another companion. This was special for me. It was own dear sister, Nadyne. We worked beautifully together.

Time was passing fast now. There were only six weeks left before the completion of our missions. We faithfully proselyted every day. The Florida sun is hot in March, but we continued our labors.

However, one morning as we began our tracting, an impression came to me that we should go and visit again the family in the trailer. It would be a two-hour trip by bus to reach that location. I quickly pushed the "impression" from my mind. Perhaps I was just trying to avoid having to go back out in the burning sun knocking on doors. I told Nadyne about the thoughts I was having. The impression came for the third time. I ignored it. We began working in our tracting area. When the thought came again, Nadyne and I talked about it, and decided that we should go.

We had no available address book of the location, but I felt I could remember where the trailer was. We caught a bus to downtown

Jacksonville, and made the two-hour trip. It was now early afternoon. The sun was high in the sky. It was very hot and we were tired and thirsty. We began the search, walking up and down one street after another. Another hour passed. A feeling of guilt came over me, thinking we had wasted a good day. Nevertheless, the impression came for us to continue on, and this impression was stronger than ever.

We kept going. At the next corner there was the large green grassy lot with the trailer parked on it. We crossed the lawn and knocked on the door. No answer. We knocked again. No answer. Then came a call from the house next door. Sister Kersey exited the house and ran towards us, calling out: "Sister Nickle, Sister Nickle."

Sister Kersy opened the door of her home for us, and invited us to go inside. She said she would be right back with her children. Soon the three of them returned. They sat across from is. Each one held a copy of the Book of Mormon that my companion and I had left with them.

"Let me explain," she said. She then told us that after we left, she and the children started reading their books when the father of the house was gone. Then Sister Kersey said she began praying that her husband's heart would be softened towards the Church. Finally, she approached him with her petition. Her prayers had warmed his heart. He gave permission for the children to be baptized if they so desired.

Not knowing how to locate us, the mother and the children knelt in prayer, and asked Heavenly Father to send us back to them. Thus the impressions: the spiritual communication of God. Tears ran down all our faces. We met with them and taught the children, and the mother. We asked the Elders to meet with them and make arrangements for their baptism.

With only two weeks left in our missions, we were blessed to see these two young children go into the waters of baptism. The father attended the services. The mother and the children cried again as they heard, realized, and acknowledged that the Lord had heard their prayers and answered them.

When we bid them goodbye, we learned the Elders had made an appointment to meet with the father, to also teach him the gospel.

As for Nadyne and me, we pray and receive "impressions." We follow guidance from the Lord; by so doing, our blessings have been legion.

Submitted by JoAn Nickle

Mirror! Mirror!

I had many great experiences as a missionary. I had many opportunities and challenges that enabled me to grow. Toward the end of my mission in Spain, I learned a great lesson. I had a companion who happened to be a native of Spain. I knew that he loved and respected me. He often told me how much he admired my work ethic.

However, in street contacts, and visits with possible investigators, he often interrupted me. This irritated me because I felt that he wasn't respecting me. I talked to him about it. After some discussion he divulged that he simply felt that others wouldn't trust me because I was American. This hurt my feelings. I felt that he supposed I was limited in my ability to help others come unto Christ because of my nationality.

After a couple of difficult days in which I perceived continued arrogance from my companion and saw my own effectiveness decline, I entered the following in my journal:

"I am continuing to struggle but I'm learning some important lessons. However, I am still letting things bother me. I am actually looking for further reasons to be upset with my companion. I need to change. I cannot let this dominate my thoughts. I was recently praying and I saw in my mind's eye a man standing. I then saw a mirror pass in front of this man from head to toe. I took this to mean that I needed some introspection. I understood the mirror to be the spirit which helps us see ourselves as God sees us.

As I look at myself, I see bad feelings and a bad attitude. I also see myself dwelling on little irritants and actively searching for other irritants. I am not happy. I am not useful. I feel like I am losing an important spiritual battle in a crucial moment of my mission. Even knowing this, I feel too weak to change. I need to get back on my knees. After praying and meditating, I know that I need to change and get the spirit back. I need to release myself from the yoke of anger that I have placed on my own shoulders. Though I felt unworthy, I knew that like Enos, I could receive comfort from the Lord and then I would be in a position to love and help my brethren. As I ended my prayer, I asked my Heavenly Father for a reminder of how much he loves me. He sent his spirit in such abundance that I could tangibly feel myself wrapped in his love. This brought tears of gratitude to my eyes and I knew that I had taken important steps on the road to recovery."

The Lord answered my prayers and healed my soul. I learned that all I needed to be happy was a knowledge of my Savior's love for me. Nothing else seemed to matter. I also found it much easier to have patience with, and love for my companion, even though I felt he was imperfect. After all, the Lord loves me in my imperfection. Our companionship mended and we were able to help the Lord perform miracles in the hearts of those we taught. That area turned out to be the happiest and most productive of my mission.

Another spiritual experience that I later had in the same area, though with a different companion, came in teaching the gospel. My companion and I had been teaching the discussions to a woman named Maricarmen. She and two of her children seemed to love the gospel. She had taken the discussions before and she even had a sister who was a member of the Church. In spite of this, she repeatedly refused to be baptized. She just felt that she wasn't ready. One day my companion and I had invited her son to a youth activity in the ward. When we dropped him off at his home, we stopped to chat with the whole family for a minute. After exchanging pleasantries I asked if I could share a spiritual thought with them before we left. She agreed and I continued. I don't remember what scripture I was reading, but I do remember that the thought that I should again invite her to be baptized entered my mind. I was going to dismiss it as I had asked her just a few days previously, but the Spirit confirmed to me that I should ask. I stopped reading the scripture and simply asked Maricarmen if she was ready to get baptized.

She looked at me, smiled, and said that she was. A couple of weeks later, she and two of her sons went into the waters of baptism, and made eternal covenants with the Lord.

The Lord knows when people are ready. I am grateful that I was sensitive to the spirit when an impression came.

Submitted by Brett Robinson

Golden Prints of Light

One day we took Luke, our new puppy, to the mall. It was spring-time in Phoenix and very hot. Kathy, my twelve-year-old daughter, went into the ice cream store to get water for Luke. A lady working there said she was just leaving on a break, she would bring some water out in a cup.

When she came out, Kathy noticed that she was pregnant, and she was smoking. She said to the lady, "Smoking is not good for your baby."

The lady said she knew that. As soon as the baby was born she would stop. Kathy explained to her that it was not healthy for the baby now, and told her about the Word of Wisdom.

The lady said she wanted to stop smoking. She had tried but could not.

Kathy said, "Just do it one day at a time. Don't smoke one whole day. Then try to do that the next day until you are able to quit." Kathy also talked to her about the Church and the gospel principles.

When the lady went home she tried what Kathy had told her. She found the strength to quit smoking. She had been impressed with Kathy and her knowledge of the gospel at such a young age. She thought she would like to have a child like that, and wondered about the church Kathy had talked about. She wanted to know more. She prayed about this church, wondering where it was, and what it was called.

Two men dressed in slacks, wearing white shirts and name tags knocked on her door. Her husband answered it. The young men introduced themselves as representatives of The Church of Jesus Christ of Latter-day Saints. The man said he was not interested and closed the door.

His wife called "Wait," and ran to the door. She opened it and invited them to come inside. They talked for a while and she noticed that everywhere the Elders walked they left golden shoe prints of light. She was the only one who could see them. She took the Elders into every room in her house because she wanted the light in every room.

She made arrangements for them to come back and teach her, and her husband. But she wanted to make sure it was the same church Kathy had talked about. We went to the mall again. The lady had been watching for us. She came running out when she saw Kathy. She told us all that had happened, about the smoking, and about the Elders, and the prints of light. She asked if that was the right church. Kathy told her that it was. She and her husband took the discussions and were baptized. It began with a puppy needing a drink of water.

Submitted by Jan Johnstun

Little Zions

At the time of this writing (2004) I am serving a mission in Santiago, Chile. The following experience has helped me see that the Lord has a plan for the way He wants us to do His work. My companion and I were having limited success knocking on doors, and trying to share the gospel with people in the streets. It isn't because they are bad people, but they feel a lack of trust. We are foreigners. We bring new ideas. We look like salesmen. I kept thinking there must be something we could do so the people would want us to teach them. If they only knew what we had to offer they would stand in line for baptism.

With these thoughts in mind, I prayed for divine direction.

A short time later, we attended a conference with the zone leaders and the Mission President. They shared news of a meeting they had just attended where a member of the Area Presidency spoke. Years ago he had served as a missionary in Chile, and ended up baptizing more than one thousand people. He said that quite a number of the people he baptized have gone to the temple, and are still good members.

One of the ways he had so much success was that in the sector where he served, he felt impressed to choose a certain area consisting of a few streets. He called this area his "Little Zion." He and his companion spent some time there every day. They became friends with the people, without mentioning the gospel.

Once trust was established, the people wanted to listen. They even asked the Elders to teach them. He said he came to care about the people and they could tell. That was why they opened their hearts to hear the gospel. Not surprisingly, most of his baptisms came from these various "Little Zions."

My companion and I were very impressed with this story. I felt it was the Lord's answer to my pleas for help. We prayerfully chose an area in our sector. We began to greet people in their yards, give cheerful waves as we passed by, and pausing to play with the children. This new approach felt immediately more comfortable than the old method. I have developed a greater love for the people. Chatting with them is pleasant. We do not think of them as investigators. We are developing friendship bonds.

The other night, as we said good-bye to a man is this area, he told us we should visit him again, but next time we would talk about God. We are having other experiences like this. We don't have to push the gospel. The people invite us in to share what we have to tell them. The Spirit still prompts us to invite, to challenge, or even to find those we would not think of. Following His prompting, he blesses us as well as the people we meet.

I love being a missionary, especially after finding this new approach. I like connecting with the people—first with love, and then teaching them the gospel. After they feel of our love it is easier for them to feel the Spirit, and recognize gospel truths. I appreciate the way the Lord answered my prayer, and helped me learn a better way to share the gospel. Dedicating my life to Him as a missionary is the best thing for me to be doing at this stage of my life.

Submitted by Elder Devin D. Robinson

"My Preaching Will Be To Those In The Spirit World"

Christmas Day 1939 was the nineteenth birthday of my brother, Kay Baker Robinson. Our parental home was in Oakley, Cassia County, Idaho. I was then living in Salt Lake City, as did my sister Maurine Simmons. Kay, and our sister Arva, were living in Pocatello, Idaho, where Kay attended school, and Arva was teaching. Our oldest brother, Merrill, was on a mission in New England.

Our family numbered twelve: our parents, and ten living children. The other five children were still at home.

To celebrate Christmas, and Kay's birthday, we all went home.

Christmas Day happened to fall on Sunday that year. The entire family went to sacrament meeting in our ward. The bishop asked Arva, Kay, and me to say a few words and bear our testimonies. There were other young people home for the holidays. The bishop asked some of them to speak also.

Most of us complied with the bishop's request. However, my brother Kay's response was a most unusual one for him. He declined to speak to the congregation. He indicated that he would do his preaching in the spirit world. All of us in the family wondered about his saying that. We did not learn until later that he had related to our mother a dream he'd had the previous night that troubled him. Kay was a pole-vaulter. He never opened a gate, he jumped over it. His dream was very vivid: he had tried to jump a fence, but his legs got tangled in a wire and had to be cut off.

The next day I was to return to Salt Lake City. Kay, with my brother George, and Arva, drove me to the bus depot in Burley. I had an uneventful trip back to Salt Lake City. I was met by my sister Maurine, and her husband, Ray Simmons. Maurine was crying and I wondered why. Through her tears she told me.

On the return trip from Burley to Oakley, there had been an accident. My brothers and sister were hit by a drunk driver in a flat bed truck. Kay was killed instantly. Arva was scalped. George was thrown into a deep barrow-pit covered with sagebrush. The two of them recovered. Arva's life was saved because the next car to come along was driven by the Oakley doctor.

Religious tracts that Kay had in his coat pocket were well-worn, and had been underlined in some places. The tracts had to do with teaching those who are in the spirit world. One day after saying he would do that, he was there; on the mission he had talked about, and obviously studied about.

While I was serving on a mission to the Central States, I had a very real dream. I have never forgotten the smallest detail of it. In the dream, I entered a building and I found myself in a room like a cultural hall. A large group of people were gathered there. They surrounded a man who seemed to be teaching them. I looked closely. The man was my brother Kay.

He looked up and saw me. I expected him to leave the group, and come to welcome me. Instead, he smiled as if to say hello, then he turned back to the people he was teaching. As I awoke I heard a voice say, "Yes, he is preaching to the dead."

Submitted by Byron B. Robinson.

Harker Island Missionary

Dear Elder Joe:

I promised you some stories from my mission in North Carolina. My companion, Elder Ewell, was going home. His uncle got permission to pick him up, and also to take us to Harker Island, where he had served his own mission. He told us that the early day missionaries were spitefully abused by people on the island. One day, a mob formed against the Elders, and drove them out into the ocean expecting them to drown, for they would not allow them to come ashore. The Elders swam and tread water, trying to stay afloat. A fishing boat came by and picked them up.

A small girl on the island was restricted to a wheelchair. She had contracted polio. She was unable to walk, and her hands were drawn and twisted out of shape. She liked to read the Bible. One day she read the passage from scripture which says, "If there be sick among you, call the Elders so the prayer of faith can make you whole." The girl asked her mother to call the Elders so they could pray over her.

Her mother said, "We don't have Elders in our church. But there are a couple of Elders who come on the island from time to time. When I see them again I will ask them to call."

The next time the Elders came, she sent for them. They anointed the child's head with oil and gave her a priesthood blessing. They visited for a while and left. Later, the girl's mother was out hanging clothes on the line. Her daughter called to her, "Mother, come quick." Thinking the child had fallen out of the wheelchair, the mother ran to the house. Her daughter was beaming. She sat in her chair flexing her hands and stretching her legs. She had been made whole. This mother and her child were the first people on the island to be baptized.

The Church began to grow. They obtained a small house in the woods for a church. Hatred for the Church was still very strong. One day, during sacrament services, a man went to the beach and picked up a large conch shell. He threw it through an open window into the congregation. The shell hit an elderly woman in the head. She received a large contusion. She was taken to the hospital where she developed an infection, with a high fever.

The man who had thrown the shell made a hasty retreat through the woods. A tree had fallen across the path with the stub of a broken branch sticking up. When he jumped over the fallen tree he struck his knee against the knot. This caused such an infection that the man's leg had to be amputated. His hatred continued until it nearly consumed him. He decided to get even. On another Sunday while the Saints were meeting, he went again to the beach, picked up another conch shell and threw it through the window. This time the shell hit a baby. The baby went into a coma and was hospitalized.

The man, using crutches, made his way along the same trail. He fell over the fallen tree, hit his good leg against the knot, and got another infection. His other leg was eventually amputated also.

The Methodist Church was the most prominent one on the Island. They had a large and beautiful building. One day a group of them got together, went into the woods and burned down the little building the Saints met in. The Elders went over to the Methodists and prophesied to them that where their church now stood, our church would one day stand, and it would be the largest church on the island.

Shortly thereafter a storm arose. Lightning came down from heaven, struck the church, and it burned to the ground. The property was purchased by the Latter-day Saints. Today it is the largest and most prominent church on the island.

When I was serving on my mission a sister told me the story of how her grandmother had received her testimony that Brigham Young was to lead the Church after the death of Joseph. She was ten or eleven years old when the Saints were called together by the Apostles. It would be decided at that meeting who should be the Prophet. People were still mourning Joseph. He was the only prophet they had known. When Brigham Young stood up to speak, his countenance changed. He spoke and looked like the Prophet Joseph. All who were there gained an immediate testimony that Brigham Young was chosen to be the next Prophet of the Savior's Church.

I am so grateful to live in a time when the gospel has been restored. We (our family) has seen so many miracles by faith, and by priesthood blessings. It is a comfort to know we can have the Holy Ghost as our constant companion, and be directed in our daily lives.

Love you much,
Your Dad

Written by Alma Johnstun in 1991 to his missionary son
Submitted by Jan Johnstun

Swimming Against The Tide

This miraculous happening took place in Torreon, Mexico, in July, 2003.

There was a man that different missionaries had taught many times over the years. His wife was a member before they were married. But the husband had never been interested in the Church. He supported her in her church service. She held many callings. Her life was a testimony of her belief. But this did not change the mind of her husband.

About 7 months ago the Elders called Kurt Alexander, the Mission President, and asked him to go with them to this man's house. This time he had made a request that the missionaries come and see him. Since he had never shown any interest before, and because he was a wealthy man, with high standing in the community, I think the missionaries wanted spiritual support from their Mission President. They wanted him to testify about the gospel.

When Kurt got there, the man was ready to accept baptism. Kurt asked him what had happened to change his mind so suddenly. The man told him about a recent dream he had had. In this dream the man, his wife, and their three small children were in the middle of a large lake. His wife and children started to swim to shore and were making good progress. But as hard as the man swam he never moved any closer to the shore. He stayed in the same place. Finally, his wife and children reached the shore line, and were climbing out of the lake. The man had a horrible feeling that he was losing his family. The dream was so powerful that he woke up sobbing. He had the impression in his mind that if he didn't take his family to the temple he really would lose them.

He was taught and baptized that week. We just saw him at Stake Conference a week ago. His wife's sister, Loraina, is in our ward. I go there visiting teaching. Loraina is in the same situation her sister was in. She has three children and her husband is not a member. He has been to church many times and has had all the missionary discussions several times, but is not interested in getting baptized. It would be wonderful if we could see the same miracle happen in Loraina's life. We are praying for that to come to pass.

Submitted by Kathy Alexander
Wife of Torreon, Mexico, Mission President

Missionary Service in East Germany

After the wall was erected between East and West Berlin, our lives were changed forever. Gone was our freedom. In school the children were taught to worship, and pray to Joseph Stalin. Kindergarten children began learning songs that praised this man. All school children must declare their devotion and admiration to the dictator of our shrunken world. What Adolf Hitler was to the Germans, Joseph Stalin was to the Russians.

I remember the day Stalin died. My sister and I were in a large state-owned department store. Over the intercom an announcement came saying that the "Great Leader of the Soviet Union was dead." The store manager asked the people for a moment of respectful silence. Obediently, all the people stopped what they were doing, and stood in silence. No one moved or said a word. This was too much for my sister and me. We kept on walking and talking like nothing had happened. This is the way we were. Our poor mother lived in constant fear for our safety.

Once I was asked to become an agent, a spy for the west. I refused because I did not want to bring harm to our Church. The policy of The Church of Jesus Christ of Latter-day Saints is that we members support the government by obeying the laws of the land.

Our young men were also encouraged to do their duty and serve two years in the military. They were drafted and had no other choice but to go and serve their two years. This was the reason for the East German government to look favorably to the members of the Church, because in spite of the terrible conditions in which we lived, we were good and honest citizens; and reliable workers who did not smoke or drink. That was also the reason why we could hold our meetings, and some other activities. But every meeting had to be planned and reported in advance to the police. We had to report who the speakers would be, and what they would talk about.

Missionary work was permitted only by our own people, and within the country of East Germany. I was called to serve a mission from 1956 to 1958. I served for 33 months. Sometimes the Elders would be taken to a police station and told we could not go on proselyting. But we were not so easily intimidated by the police. We would remind the officers that our State Constitution guaranteed us freedom of religion. I would then ask them to give us a written statement forbidding us to do our job as missionaries. But, of course, they could not do that.

I was the last missionary to be called from within our country. After that no missionary work was permitted. We knew that the local government officials watched us closely; they were looking for any kind of a reason to close our Church doors. Members had to be careful of what they said and did.

When we had baptisms they were performed in public lakes and rivers. We had no baptismal font in our chapels. At a town in Thuringia, while I was serving my mission, we had planned the baptism for a young man, his mother, and an elderly woman. It was November and very cold. This part of the country was called the Harz. It was near the city of Quedlinburg. The river we must choose came down from a snowy mountain called Brocken. On Saturday morning, before the baptism, I walked into the stream to test the depth; looking for the right spot. The freezing water shocked me. I rushed back to the river bank.

On Sunday, the next day, we went ahead with our baptism as planned. Some people who were not members stood and watched us. The elderly woman had asthma and a weak heart. If anything went wrong with her that would be the end of our little LDS ward there. But we trusted in the Lord, and prayed for Him to sustain those who were being baptized. All went well. Some times, there were baptisms where we had to chop a hole in thick ice to make an opening for the elders, and those being baptized.

One very sick woman we had to carry down into the river. After the baptism she walked out by herself.

I was transferred to the city of Bernburg, also in the country of Thuringia. There I met an old woman who told me her husband was also a prisoner at the same Russian concentration camp which I had escaped from. Her husband was allowed to go home because of sickness. He told her that of the two thousand prisoners shipped to Siberia, only eighty survived.

I was honorably released from my mission.

Submitted by Werner Klein from the pages of his journal

Prayer

Before the first generation of mankind had passed away, men began to call upon the name of the Lord. Blessings require work or effort on our part before we can obtain them. Prayer is a form of work, and is an appointed means for obtaining the highest blessings.
(Bible Dictionary, Page 753)

The Night My Father Died

My dad died when I was 15 years old, the oldest of eight children in our family. My dad was a pharmacist who routinely closed up the drugstore where he worked. The store closed at 9:00 PM. By the time he counted the money, cleaned up and did all the other necessary tasks, it was usually 10:00 PM before he started the thirty-minute drive home. It was not unusual for him to arrive home at ten thirty or quarter to eleven. On the night that he died of a massive heart attack, he was closing up the store, and was there alone.

After suffering the heart attack, he was able to reach the pharmacist's phone under the counter where the prescriptions were filled, and call 911. Around 11:00 PM, the doctor called my mother and told her what had happened. He instructed her to go to the hospital where they were taking my dad by ambulance. As I was the oldest child, she woke me, told me what happened, and asked that I take care of the younger children.

After my mother left the house, I remember sitting on the sofa in the living room, in the dark stillness of the night and feeling very frightened, alone, and overwhelmed with questions that couldn't be answered. All I could think to do was kneel there and pray for Heavenly Father's help to keep my dad alive. I did so, and immediately felt the most warm, calming, reassuring spirit in my heart—a definite message to me that everything would be OK, and there was nothing to worry about. I felt so reassured that I lay down on the sofa and fell asleep, not waking up until some of the younger kids woke me the next morning.

It being a Saturday morning, we were all gathered watching Saturday morning cartoons when my mother returned home. She came into the house and had obviously been crying. She looked at me, shook her head and said, "He's gone."

I couldn't believe my ears. What had happened the night before when the Lord had reassured my heart that "everything would be okay"? In my mind, there was no mistaking the positive, calm impression I had received. But my dad died. It was hard to reconcile the two events.

I have since learned that our Heavenly Father knows what is best for each of us. He gives us what we need, and sometimes we do not interpret those answers in the correct way; but as time goes on we gain a greater understanding of what the answer really meant.

I interpreted the calm reassurance I received after praying that my dad would live, and that all would be well in our family. What I really received was a blessing of comfort for myself in my hour of need. Although my dad was called from this life to perform work in the spirit world (as I have been told in my patriarchal blessing), and I have missed his influence in my life, I have received great blessings and growth opportunities over the years due to his absence. It has taken many years, but I have truly come to know that the answer to that prayer had not only immediate, but also long-term benefits for my life. And things have turned out "OK!"

These other experiences are not as succinctly described, but they left strong impressions on my heart.

I worked for the same company for 21 years in San Francisco. It was a wonderful company to work for, with great co-workers and a definite environment of "family." Unfortunately, that all came to an end in 2000 when our parent corporation in the U.K. decided to sell. The company we were so fond of was broken into several pieces and sold. For many of us, who had been together a long time, it felt as if our "second family" had been torn apart.

After having had the stability of 21 years at the same company, the past three years of my life have been chaotic, to say the least. We moved from San Francisco to Olney, Maryland (suburb of Washington, D.C.) for eighteen months, then to Milford, Connecticut for another eighteen months, and are now preparing for a third move to Overland Park, Kansas. Each of these moves has been precipitated by a change in employment. And each move has had its share of trials and challenges in the transition.

But the most interesting thing to me is that with each move, in spite of the trauma and challenge that moving brings, I have felt a calm reassurance through prayer and fasting that this is what the Lord wants us to do, that He has prepared the way and guided us in that direction. And we have been so abundantly blessed. Each move has brought us a new circle of friends, especially within the Church, that has enriched and touched our lives for good. There are numerous examples of opportunities we have had to serve—and to be served.

Someone could look at this history and say that it's all pretty random and coincidental. But I believe that we have significant control over what we experience in life—the "glass half empty" versus the "glass half full." We can look for the positive, or look for the negative, and support either view through our experiences and surroundings. I have no doubt whatsoever that if we do as our leaders and the scriptures teach—place our will on the altar of God and allow Him to direct us—we cannot fail, and in fact we'll be blessed beyond measure. I am overwhelmed and humbled by the goodness that my Heavenly Father pours into my life, and know that He will do the same for anyone and everyone who seeks His guidance and direction.

Submitted by Jerry Okabe

The Death Of A Child

My child, Robertje Peter Inthout, was born 23 April 1963, in Los Altos, California. He was born in seemingly perfect health. He was a beautiful, big baby of almost ten pounds. Soon after his birth, it was discovered that the nervous system for his intestines was missing. The doctors told members of the family that he would probably only be able to live by artificial means. However, they wanted to do more testing. The doctors asked our permission to take him to the San Francisco hospital where more advanced technology was available.

We signed some documents, and a nurse brought Robertje into my room so I could hold him and say goodbye. (I was being confined to the hospital for six more days due to complications from the birth). At this time I had no inkling that I would never see my baby boy again. I am, and will be forever grateful for that one last opportunity to hold him.

Just after midnight of the day I came home, we received the indescribable phone call that Robert Peter had passed away. While in the hospital he had caught pneumonia and was gone. It was a shock for which we were totally unprepared. For nine months I had carried this little baby, filled with anticipation of the day he would make his entrance into this world. Now, so suddenly, he was gone. I simply could not understand why God would take him from us.

I cannot describe the anguish I felt. It took a long time before I could get over it. Janny (we called her Gini then) was only five years old. She had been excited and was looking forward to Robertje's arrival in our family. She asked a thousand questions: could she hold him?

could she kiss him? could she sing to him? would he sit on her lap?

Now, she was confused. She had not seen him. He would not be coming home. She kept asking why Robert was gone. Ricky was only two years old—too young to know what had happened. I picked up my duties as mother and homemaker, and even managed to play with the children. But there was a gnawing void inside me. I needed to talk about Robertje. But when I brought the subject up with my husband, Henk, he turned away. He would not discuss Robert's death.

Our minister came by. The only consolation he could give me was the remark, "Oh, well, someday you will have another baby."

I was desperately worried about Robert Peter having died without the opportunity of baptism. Did this mean that his soul was lost forever? When I expressed my distress about this to my minister, all he knew to say was that I must not dwell on it. I should just leave it be.

However, I did dwell on it. I had been taught that a child must be baptized in order to be "saved." I blamed myself for not having Robertje baptized before he was taken to San Francisco. He had been whisked away so quickly that the question of baptism had not even come up. I had been too sick to think clearly. Of course, we had fully expected to have our baby back after he had been tested.

The emptiness was huge, and could not be filled. Our doctor had recommended that we not have any more children. But I prayed hard for another baby, believing that only holding another baby would help fill the void. Lydia's arrival one year minus three days after Robertje's birth created tremendous joy. The family fell in love with her instantly. We had her baptized right away. Again, remorse gnawed away at me that Robertje had left life without this blessing, and that he was lost forever.

Looking back on those years after Robertje's passing, I can see clearly how, through his death, I began thinking about things I had not considered before, trying to obtain an understanding. I struggled with the question of why this beautiful, seemingly healthy and perfect baby had come to earth. There must have been a purpose for his brief stay, but what had it been? I was convinced that he had not come just to submerge us in grief. For the brief week he was with us, and for the few moments I was able to hold him, he had deeply touched me, and then left. I felt as if I had lost a part of myself. Why did it have to be this way? Life went on, highlighted by Lydia's arrival, but the questions kept gnawing at me, and the answers eluded me.

It was nine years before we discovered the LDS Church. We took the missionary discussions after a trip to Utah in 1973. For the first time we learned of the Plan of Salvation, and of the opportunity all of us have to be an eternal family. Suddenly, my perspective changed completely. I knew I had found the truth I had searched for during all those years. Henk said that he felt likewise.

Robertje had not been lost at all. He had returned to the highest realm: the celestial kingdom, as described in 1 Corinthians, where the Apostle Paul speaks of the three glories. That is where children go who die before the age of eight—the age of accountability, when they are baptized.

We learned that, whereas in all likelihood, because of physiologic problems, his life would have been difficult and miserable, the Lord had mercifully taken him back, giving him the opportunity to do missionary work among the dead. I finally understood that, even though he was not to stay, there was a need for him to come to our particular family.

The Lord had sent him to us as His emissary in order to open my eyes as to the purpose of our lives here on earth. He has given every living soul the freedom of agency to make choices while here. He has placed us here to learn certain lessons, and given us the opportunity to grow. Robert had not needed to learn those lessons; his was a higher purpose: to influence our lives for good, and to do missionary work for the dead. There was no need to mourn for him; he was home.

I also learned that if we make the right choices, and live righteously, we will be reunited with those family members who have gone before us, fulfilling certain required ordinances. My lingering despair changed to great joy. If I made the right choices, I would have my little Robertje back. This new knowledge took the sting out of death.

We were baptized on 15 December 1973. Our family was sealed for time and eternity in the Oakland Temple. Robert Peter was sealed to us by proxy. Since that time I have had complete peace of mind, knowing that if we live worthily, we will see our boy again. What a reunion that will be! Robert Peter is always in my thoughts, but now they are calm, peaceful thoughts.

Unfortunately, Henk shared none of the same thoughts with me. Even though he participated in our family baptism and sealing, I do not believe that he had a real spiritual understanding of what these actions meant. In time, he came to resent the Church and our activities in it.

Robertje's brief stay may have done nothing for him, but it has influenced the lives of the rest of us for good. The children have attended LDS colleges, gone on missions, found fine, faithful spouses to be married and sealed in the Temple.

As for myself, Charles Shutter and I found each other and were sealed in the Temple. I believe that if Robert Peter had not come, all of our lives might have been entirely different. They may have been "goodly" lives, but without the knowledge, purpose, and depth we now have. In essence, that little baby was our first missionary. How he must have rejoiced in Heaven when we were baptized, and a year later, sealed to him.

Submitted by Maryke Shuttle

The Power Of Prayer

I have been in the practice of doing a pilgrimage to a sacred site each year at the same time for a period of five years, following a Huichol Indian shamanic tradition.

The story to follow occurred fifteen years ago when I was visiting sites in the Southwest (Sedona, Chaco Canyon, and Bandolier National Monument). I had left Sedona and went to Chaco Canyon for a few days of camping, exploring, and ceremony. While camping there, a man in a white van camped next to me and I started to run into him at various remote places, at various times of the day. We left the camp at separate times and had not talked about our plans, so it was pure coincidence to meet everywhere we went. We eventually laughed about it and began to talk, and sometimes explored the areas together.

My next stop was to be Bandolier National Monument. When I mentioned this plan to the man one day in camp, he asked if he could join me there, and I told him to follow me the next day. I had heard of a shrine in the wilderness that was still used by Native Americans and wanted to find it to do a prayer ceremony there. I found out it required a rigorous nine-mile overnight hike into the back country so I welcomed my new travel companion's company.

Off we went with just sleeping bags, water, snacks, and my offerings. After many hours of hard hiking we found the shrine. The power of the place was awesome . . . the mana (mah-nah—native Polynesian term—a supernatural force to which certain primitive peoples attribute good fortune) was palpable. Two stone lion figures were surrounded by a large circle of antlers piled high. I immediately got ready to do my ritual . . . set out my offerings and commenced to pray for my life and those in it.

As I was praying, I noticed my friend standing and watching a respectful distance across from me, on the other side of the shrine. I wove him into the prayer, noting how mysteriously he was led to me, and asking that he receive whatever he needed in his life at this time. When I was finished we set up our sleeping bags as the sun set.

It was getting dark. We talked. He asked me if I did anything regarding him when I was doing my ceremony. I said, "Yes, I prayed for you." He then proceeded to tell me that he intended to kill himself at some point on this trip, but as he watched me doing my ritual he felt something change. He no longer wanted to die. He told me he had been despondent because a few years earlier his wife had died in a car accident.

Shortly thereafter he had been diagnosed with diabetes. During my prayers he began to feel a new life force come into him. He felt hope for the fist time since the death of his wife.

When he first said he planned to kill himself, a wave of fear washed over me. Here I was in the wilderness with a total stranger. I knew nothing of his background. Why had I not thought of this before? (Youth and naiveté.) I then thought, "What if he kills me and himself? I will never be found. No one in my family knows I am here." As soon as this thought came over me, I felt a whisper of something that said, "Trust in the moment. You are on a dedicated pilgrimage. You will be protected." The Spirit arranged for our paths to cross because I could be of help. That help was in the form of a simple prayer! I felt the Divine Presence at hand.

Submitted by Gyongyi (Momi) Szirom

Locked Out

My name is Brooke. I am eight years old. When I was six, I came home from school one day, and the front door was locked. My mom was gone. No one else was home either. I opened the gate going into the back yard. I hoped the back door was unlocked. It wasn't. I decided to go back to the front of the house to wait for my mom. But when I passed through the gate it had locked tightly behind me. I was too small to climb the fence and reach around to open it. I felt trapped and alone. I began to cry. Then I remembered what my parents had taught me; do all you can do, and then pray for help.

Sitting on the back porch, I bowed my head and asked Heavenly Father to help me not be afraid. Just as I said "Amen," someone called my name. It was Sister Martell. She lives on the street behind us. Our back fences are together.

"Brooke," she called, "are you alone?" She had seen me at the moment I said my prayer.

I answered back, "Yes, no one is home. I can't get in the house."

"Would you like to come to my house and wait until your mom returns?"

"Yes," I answered with relief. I didn't feel trapped and alone any more.

Sister Martell helped me over the fence, and took me inside her house. She shared some popcorn with me. "I happened to look out the window. I thought you looked like you might need some help," she said.

When my mom came home, I told her that Sister Martell was an answer to my prayer for help.

Submitted by Brooke Robinson

Keeping the VW Running

In 1969 I found myself in a most unexpected life situation. I was a divorced mother with three children. I had an elderly Volkswagen to drive. It kept testing and trying the faith of everyone in the family. For several months, the car would not start when we got into it with the idea of going somewhere. This became such a frustration. Especially when the time eventually came that the car would rarely start.

One day I thought about the brother of Jared, and his going before the Lord with a handful of stones, expecting the Lord to touch them so they could have light in the dark ships on their long voyage. If the Lord would do that for His people of an earlier day, I rationalized that He could therefore touch my car and make it run when we needed to go somewhere. He is the same, yesterday, today, and forever. I talked to the children about this. I told them we needed to exercise faith.

After that, whenever the kids and I wanted to go somewhere, we would get in the car, bow our heads and pray for the Lord to reach down His finger and touch the car so it would run. I would then turn on the ignition. Miraculously, the engine would start. If we did not pray, the car would not start no matter how many times we tried.

Several times our prayers did not work. When this happened we went back into the house, knowing that we must wait for something. Invariably, the phone would ring with an important, unexpected call. When we returned to the car, we had our prayer, turned the key, and the car never failed to start.

Submitted by Jan Johnstun

Enduring All Things Well Until The End

My grandmother, Blanche Lafern Devey Bennet, died in December, 2003. She was one month shy of her 99th birthday. To our family, and others who knew her well, she became a living testimony of enduring well what life hands you. My grandfather died in 1982. They both died in the house at Alpine where they had gone to live as newlyweds. The house had high ceilings, tall cupboards, and steep narrow stairs without a railing.

Grandma Bennett was a small woman. She had a footstool that she used to reach into the cupboards. Her storage was in the attic, up the steep stairs. Many times every day she went up those stairs, until she lost the strength in her legs, then she crawled up the stairs.

She became a Temple Ordinance worker shortly after the Jordan River Temple opened. She worked there three days a week until 2001, just before her 97th birthday. She then did endowment work three days a week until January of 2002.

In February of 2003 I went to visit her. I was glad to see that she was happy, with brightness in her eyes, and good color to her skin. During the summer, her legs had developed ulcers which were not healing. She had to be in a recliner with her legs up. After leading such an active life, being sedentary depressed her.

In January of that year, someone had called every member of our family, asking us to fast and pray for Grandma, because of leg ulcers, and because of her depression. We had all done this about two weeks before my visit.

I told Grandma she looked happy.

She smiled and responded, "When my legs became infected last year, I was very discouraged. I didn't see how I could live this way. But then, I read in the newspaper several days ago, about a man who was repairing his car when it slipped off its supports and fell on him. He is paralyzed from the neck down. His mind is still sharp but nothing else works. I realized in that moment that I could be a lot worse off. I gave thanks for what I have."

I was amazed; not only because of her words, that she had chosen to accept her situation, but also because her change of heart came on the heels of our family fast. Her new attitude reminded me of the following scriptures: "I have learned, in whatsoever state I am, therewith to be content," and two verses later: "I can do all things through Christ which strengtheneth me" (Philip 4:11,13.)

The last day of Grandma's life was very sweet to our family. Since August, when I had been diagnosed with a rare, life-threatening illness, I had not been to see her. With a weakened immune system, except to take care of necessities and attend Church meetings, I had remained home as much as possible.

I began feeling better in early December and made plans to visit Grandma on the 5th. The evening of the 8th, my mother called to say she did not think her mother would last that long. We changed our plans and made our visit the next day.

My three youngest children (Caleb, Brooke, and Veronica) were able to come too. Each of them sat on their great-grandmother's bed, squeezed her hand, and embraced her. I sat with them.

Twice she said to us, "I will be up tomorrow." The second time she said, "I will be up tomorrow morning." She spoke with conviction. Each time she spoke, the thought went through my mind, "Tomorrow she will be up in heaven."

The following morning, as I read my scriptures, I turned randomly to those words in Alma 40:11, "Now, concerning the state of the soul between death and the resurrection . . . Behold, it has been shown unto me by an angel that the spirits of all men, as soon as they have departed this mortal body, yea, the spirits of all men . . . are taken home to that who gave them life."

My thoughts were there with my grandmother. I could not help but wonder if she had already passed on. (That was between 7:30 and 8:30 a.m.) Later, I received the call that told me her spirit had left her body between 7:00 and 7:30 a.m. She was indeed up that morning—up in heaven with the God who had given her life; and other beloved family members.

I took comfort in the final moments given me to be with her.

Grandma knew of my health condition. My mother told me that she prayed for me every day. This was so touching to me. At age 98, and with many health problems of her own, she was praying for me. I cherish this thought. It tells what Grandma was about.

Grandma had some porcelain plates that belonged to her great-grandmother. They had somehow survived the 1,300-mile trek west by an oxen-pulled wagon. She kept them on the highest shelf of her china cabinet. There must have been divine intervention to preserve those plates. They were in a wooden box, jostled each day by thousands of ruts on the trail. Day after day, children and adults rummaged through the boxes. When they finally reached the west, the plates stayed in boxes for a long time. There were no china closets to put them in.

If even feathers from a sparrow's head are watched over, perhaps the Lord sometimes looks after porcelain plates, and other small details in life, when the owners are obeying, and following after him.

At Grandma's funeral, the bishop said, "enduring to the end is continuing in the commandments until the last day." To me, it also means continuing in hope until the end, (rather than in discouragement, or impatience.) Hope is made possible through faith in Christ and his Atonement. It includes hope for the future. It implies hope in life's daily experiences.

I believe that by coming to Him in daily, sincere prayer, with a heart ready to listen, He will enlighten my mind, whisper peace to my heart, give solutions to problems, answer my questions, and help me cope with life's toughest situations.

As Grandma Bennett wrote in her final testimony; "The Gospel is definitely true, and the Savior is real. Thus, there is hope for all mankind."

Submitted by Jennifer Day Robinson
Written as a memorial tribute to Blanche Lafern Devey Bennett

Alma's Eyes

In November of 1997, my husband, Alma, had been diagnosed with metastatic nasopharyngeal carcinoma. The doctors had found numerous tumors in the nasopharyngeal area. We were told that it was a slow growing tumor. In reality the tumors metasticized and grew very fast.

Alma was in continuous pain. But he was not a person who complains. He decided to hum instead of moan. I believe he knew from the beginning that he would die from this cancer. But he tried to protect me from the knowledge, knowing that I needed to have hope and belief in his recovery.

During the last weeks of his illness, he kept asking me who the man was who sat at the foot of his bed. He wanted Alma to go with him. I said no, Alma could not go. I felt sure his mother would come for him when it was time. I didn't want him going off with a strange person I did not know.

On a Sunday the children and grandchildren came for their final good-byes, and for blessings, and counseling from Alma.

On Tuesday, we spent the day alone. Alma was in terrible pain. I got him into the wheelchair and we headed for the bathroom. As I tried to help him, he reached out for the towel bar, to help lift himself. His hand went out and then dropped. He fell from the wheelchair and I went down with him. I thought he had fainted. I pulled myself out from under him, reached for him and realized that he was not breathing. His eyes were open. I looked into them and saw that the light was gone. I knew then that his spirit had left his body.

The paramedics arrived but it was to no avail; the time had come for him to return home. Alma's eyes had always been so beautiful. They were an intense bright blue, with a special gift for seeing deep into another person's soul. I knew the spirit could be seen from the pupil of the eye, but until then I had not realized that the spirit is what gives light to the rest of the eye. It was plain that Alma's spirit did exist, and was now gone from his body. I knew it wasn't coming back either. I called for him to come back, but I knew he couldn't. His body was too broken to be used anymore.

One week after Alma's funeral, I was sitting in Sunday school half-listening to the instructor, when I saw this man dressed in white, standing a short distance from me. He resembled Alma. He smiled and waved. He was younger than I had ever seen him. He had a full head of hair. He no longer wore glasses, and his teeth were perfect. I did not recognize this person, but he was clearly waving to me. I looked closely. The knowledge came to me that it was Alma. I recognized him by his eyes.

I thought, "that's Alma." At my recognition he immediately disappeared. Before his death, I asked him to promise that he would come back and see me afterwards. He was most reluctant because he thought Heavenly Father would not like him to make such a promise. I said that if he made the promise, then he would be allowed to keep it. I am glad to have been right about that. His appearance assured me that the ravages of his disease were gone. I remember him now as I saw him then.

Submitted by Jan Johnstun

Little Girls Lost

A parent's worst nightmare is the loss of a child. One morning recently, my neighbor knocked at my door. Her daughter, age five, and a friend the same age, had gone out in the yard to play. She called them to come in for lunch, and to get ready for the afternoon kindergarten bus. Neither child could be found. She had walked up and down our street looking for them. By now she was frantic. I have a daughter the same age. They often play together; but I had not seen the children that morning. I suggested that she get in the car and drive around the block looking for them.

She returned in more of a panic than before.

"They are nowhere to be found. Shall I call the police?"

An answer came into my mind; "Go inside your homes and pray. The Lord will know what to do." I suggested this to her. We immediately followed through.

After kneeling to pray in my home, a sudden feeling came to me that the little girls had gotten on the wrong bus. I called my neighbor whose child attends morning kindergarten. She explained that a substitute driver was on duty that day. He had let her child off at an odd time because he did not know the route. A feeling of peace came over me. I headed for the house of my friend with the lost children. She met me in the yard.

"You know what?" she said, "After my prayer, I had the thought that they went out and got on the wrong bus."

We took comfort in knowing that we had received the same answer. We called and alerted the school, then waited outside. Soon a bus turned the corner. The two little girls were sitting side by side, contentedly looking out the window.

With the Lord's help this terrifying hour turned into a faith-promoting experience. The mother and I happily parted company. We both expressed the thought that there was one thing left to do. We must go inside and thank the Lord for this blessing.

Submitted by Jennifer Robinson

An Angel Watching Over Him

Summer vacation was coming to an end. The time for my son Michael to begin his school year at West Canyon Elementary approached. Michael became more and more unsettled, and nervous about making friends; and he worried about the 15 mile bus ride to school. In an effort to calm his fears my wife, Carolyn, suggested that Michael ask me to give him a father's blessing. They then planned a special family home evening around the giving of that blessing.

At the appropriate time Michael was given the blessing. I promised him he would enjoy his school year, he would make friends, and he would enjoy what he learned that year. I prepared to close the blessing when I was prompted to bless him that angels would watch over him, and protect him as he traveled to and from school. Then I closed the blessing.

On October 17, 1977, Michael boarded the bus as he usually did and headed for school. At the same time a convoy of county dump trucks was coming from town in the opposite direction from the bus. The bus met the convoy on a curve of the road. One of the trucks swerved wide on the curve and struck the side of the bus. The results were catastrophic.

The entire side of the bus was ripped off, killing four of the children, and seriously injuring many. Michael was seated on the bus in the very center of the impact area, next to one of the boys who was killed. Everyone around him was either seriously injured or killed.

In telling us what happened to him, Michael said, "I felt as though something plucked me out of my seat and moved me across the bus." His only injuries were a small cut on his right cheek and a bruise on his shin.

We do not know the missions Heavenly Father has in mind for us, or for those who lose their lives, but we firmly believe in the power of promptings and prayer.

A Father's blessing has since become an important part of our family tradition. We are most certainly thankful for the angels who watch over us.

Submitted by Ray Hendershot

Written in memory of Stephen J. Hennis, who was seated next to Michael on the bus, and died in the accident.

The Little Red Car

A few years ago, we began looking for a car for our older children to drive to work and school. I remembered a little red car for sale in the parking lot at work. I'm cautious about used cars. I usually take them to a shop for testing before deciding to purchase. At this time one of our other cars was already in a shop for repairs. Time was of the essence. The price was reasonable, and it was easy for me to negotiate a deal with someone who worked in the same building. I bought it without the usual test procedures.

I barely got it home before troubles began. Our son called from a pay phone a few days later. "I was driving around a corner, and the car stopped running." This scenario repeated itself five or six times over a short period of time. The car would die, be abandoned on a side road, then a telephone call. Sometimes the car would start after a rest. Other times we towed it home. It was like playing Russian Roulette. No one drove it more than a few miles from home, not knowing when it would refuse to run.

We took the car to two different shops, but they could not detect the problem. One garage man referred us to a shop that specialized in electrical problems. We left the car with him for a week. He thought he had solved the problem, but the car died on the way home. We really needed this car. I thought of selling it, and using the money to buy another one, but in good conscience I could not dump the car on someone else.

We decided that the family should make this a matter of prayer. The next day a thought came to me that the car's computer must be bad. What did I know about car computers? Very little. There was no way to know if my impression was correct. I didn't want to spend a lot of money on a part that would not solve the problem. I felt to call a few wrecking yards. At the second one I called, a man said they had a car of the same year and make as ours. Tools in hand, I entered the yard, prepared to find and retrieve the part. I was pointed in the general direction of the car. I felt a bit like Nephi going back for the brass plates, not knowing beforehand what to do. Could I locate the car in the midst of acres of wrecked cars? If I found it, would it still have a working computer, or would some other needy person have already purchased it?.

After twenty minutes of wandering, I spotted the car sitting on blocks. It had been stripped of nearly everything usable. Where the motor should be, there was one small part left—the computer. It was sitting on a fender with no wires attached. It looked as though someone knew I was coming, and had placed it there only moments before.

All I had to do was pick it up, pay a few dollars, and take it home. In the garage at home, I replaced the old computer with the "new" one. I got in the car, turned the key, and to my joy and amazement, the engine sputtered to life. A year and a half have come and gone since that day. The car never experienced the same problem again.

At first, I was proud that I fixed a problem no one else could diagnose, and several hundred dollars could not fix. Then I realized it wasn't me. I had been impressed by the Spirit as to what was wrong, and where to go. These blessings came from a heavenly sphere; they were not just lucky hunches for which I could take credit. I was humbled and thankful, that even in the small things of life, the Lord can be here for us.

Submitted by Warren C. Robinson

A Call For Help

15 April 2000, I was on the freeway with members of my family in my BMW. My daughter Kathy, and her husband, Don, were with me. I was taking them to my son Rob's house to pick up a truck and trailer. We were ready to leave and my car would not start. The red battery light was on. Don used jumper cables connected to the truck and my car battery. It worked. The car started. But on our way home the car stopped and would not start. The red battery light was on again. Don used the cables and jump started it again. The light went off. The car started. I took off, looking for an auto parts store.

On the way down 7800 South, the car began to die again. The red battery light came on. The car got slower and slower no matter what I did. Just then, my daughter, Kathy, called out to her father, "Dad help us." Immediately, off toward the northeast we saw a very wide double rainbow; the promise to remember.

The car immediately started to run again. The battery light went off and stayed off. We continued a few blocks further when we saw a Checker Auto Parts sign. Tests were made, and it was determined that the battery was completely dead.

Kathy and I knew that my husband, Alma, who had died the year before, was watching over us and helping us; but the greater help came because we asked for it. I was amazed at what we were witnesses to. The infinite laws of heaven supersede the finite laws of our mortal existence.

Submitted by Jan Johnstun

80

Faith and Belief

Where is your faith? Where is your confidence in God? Can you not realize that all things were made by him, that he rules over all the works of his hands? Suppose that all the Saints here should lift their hearts in prayer to God, that the way might be opened before us, how easy it would be for him to cause the ice to break away, so that in a moment we could be on our journey.

(Lucy Mack Smith)

A Thin Veil

It was April 1975. I was expecting my 7th child. This pregnancy was different. I became extremely ill. Among other things, I had kidney and bladder stones, with serious blood pressure problems. The doctors did not expect me, or my unborn child to live. I was in the hospital for 9 days. Friends and family prayed and fasted for me.

My grandmother was Mina Jensen Olsen. She had been praying much concerning my welfare. Grandma had health concerns of her own, including a recently broken arm. One afternoon she was in her bedroom resting when a vision appeared to her. It was a little girl. The child told Grandma not to worry because both I and the child would be all right. Grandma told members of the family about the answer she'd had to her prayers, that the child had come to see her.

In the hospital, during that same time frame, the doctors could not detect my baby's heartbeat and thought it had died. But 15 minutes later, the baby's heartbeat resumed. I always thought my last child was going to be a boy but Grandma insisted I was having a girl because she had seen and talked with her.

One of the most precious experiences I've ever had was during this illness. When my blood pressure dropped to 70 over 30 I was taken to the Intensive Care Unit. From the second I arrived, to the second I was wheeled away from Intensive Care three days later, my mother (who had passed away a year prior to this) was my constant companion. When my dad and sisters came to see me, they could feel and recognize my mother's presence as well. The first question they asked was if Mom was there to take me home. I said no, she was there to lend her love and support. I would live.

Eventually I was able to leave the hospital, confined to bed rest for the remainder of my pregnancy. The doctors still did not expect my baby to live. They said that if, by some miracle, the baby should survive, the probability was that it would be born blind, deaf, mentally retarded or a combination of those things. They told me I would be sick a long time before recovery, but there was little they could do to save my baby.

I was greatly concerned that the doctors might be right until my father visited. Dad said, "You've had a witness from your grandmother that the baby will be fine."

I answered that I had.

"Who are you going to believe?" Dad asked. "You can trust in a higher source, or you can lean on men's understanding."

I knew he was right. I was comforted by my faith.

Three months later I was back at the hospital where I gave birth to a perfect baby girl. We named our newborn daughter Jennifer. When Jenny was about four years old, Grandma told me that this was the way the child looked when she came to see her.

I've lived to see my children grow, including Jenny. Some have served missions and we've had marriages in the temple. My husband and I have been privileged to serve a mission, and are currently ordinance workers in the Ogden Temple.

The veil is so thin. The bonds we share with our loved ones are eternal. When my mother passed away we could feel and recognize her father in the room waiting to help her make the transition from this life to the next. When my sister Anna was married in the Salt Lake Temple, I could feel my mother's presence and I knew where she was standing. Patriarch Edwin Owens came up to me and said he saw her there. He pointed to the spot where I knew she had been standing.

I've since felt Mom, Dad, and my sister Roselyn, who passed on, at family weddings in the temple. Mom, Dad, and Rose were there when my younger sister Krysty graduated from college a week after my dad died.

These are experiences I seldom talk about. But I have a strong testimony concerning the unity of eternal family bonds.

Submitted by Elizabeth Joannah Olsen Williams

Those Who Care In Life, Care In Death

When Joseph Sharp was born, little did anyone suspect that after generations of living in Clackmanan Shire, the Sharp family would uproot and move to the other side of the world, thereby lengthening the life span of all who left. Coal mining was what they did to stay alive. Entire families worked in the mines—parents, grandparents, children— until they died of causes incident to the hazards of the work. Children began working in the mines as soon as they were strong enough to lift buckets onto back harnesses that workers would load with coal.

Joseph, lawful son of John Sharp and Mary Hunter, was born 8

July 1830. A few days after his birth he was christened. It had become the custom at christenings for the Coal Master to get a contract, witnessed by the minister, which was for the sale of the future labor of children. A meager sum was paid to the parents for this promise of their child's work for a lifetime. The families in the shires agreed to this practice because they needed every small farthing to survive.

Instead of going off to school each morning, these children went down into the dark pits of the mines when they were six or seven years old. They were usually walking in muddy water up to their calves and breathing black damp air that was certain to kill, if an accident didn't happen first.

Generations of people in Scotland, thousands of them, lived and died as slaves to mine owners. Year in and year out, they saw natural light only on Sunday, their one day off. They went down into the mines before sunup and came out after sundown.

In the 1840s a young Scottish man, Alexander Wright, emigrated to Canada. He joined The Church of Jesus Christ of Latter-day Saints. He wanted to share his new religion with his family, so he sent a copy of Parley P. Pratt's book, *A Voice of Warning*.

From this small beginning the Church began to establish root. Alexander was called, with another Scots lad, to preach the gospel in Scotland.

Elder William Gibson brought the gospel to the Sharps in Clackmanan in 1847. John Sharp was baptized 2 May 1847. He was ordained an Elder shortly thereafter. In 12 months he taught and baptized 105 people.

Baptized Saints began to leave Scotland for America by the thousands. An account is written by a woman who remembers being taken by her father, in the early morning, to the top of Clackmanan tower. There, as the sun was coming up, she saw the Mormons with their donkey carts stretching out for two miles or more on the trail from Sauchie, on their way to Glasgow. The distance was 35 to 40 miles.

There were no bag pipes playing farewell; the only sound she heard was the donkey's feet, and the creak of axles. People walked beside the small carts that held what little they could take with them. When the Sharps pulled out of Sauchie in 1848, a new life opened before them. They left forever the mean existence that life had forced upon them.

They arrived in St. Louis, Missouri, 6 November 1848. All were well and in good health. The men got employment immediately after their arrival. They needed money for the wagons and supplies that would take them 1,300 miles to the valley of the Great Salt Lake.

Joseph, who had been born and christened at Clackmannan in 1830, was now 18 years old. On the trek west, he became a strong and capable teamster. He was so strong he could hold fifty pounds at arms length for one full minute, and shoulder 150 pounds of wheat with his feet together.

The Sharp family prospered in Salt Lake City. Joseph made trips from west to east and back again, hauling needed freight. In 1864, he was preparing his wagons for another trip east. Brigham Young asked him to take only a skeleton crew, and let some of the new Danish immigrants go with him as drivers, then they could return with their families who were waiting to come west.

Joseph agreed to do it against his better judgment. He could foresee trouble. A 1,300 hundred mile trip with unskilled teamsters was courting disaster. He was right. The train moved slowly with much wandering and straying from the trail.

At Willow Springs in Wyoming, one of the drivers allowed his wagon to get off the trail. The rear wheel of the wagon dropped into a deep mudhole. Five men tried to lift the wheel clear of the hole, but could not budge it. Joseph brushed them aside, placed his shoulder against the wheel, grasped two of the spokes, and lifted the wheel clear. The oxen pulled the wagon ahead.

Joseph died the next morning of a ruptured blood vessel. He was 34 years old.

After Joseph's death, his young son, Joseph C. Sharp, tells this story of when he was a boy: "I was out herding sheep in Rush Valley. I had lived so much of my life outdoors that I got used to cold weather. I never wore an overcoat, even in the middle of winter while herding sheep, or thereafter during my life time.

"Once, in early winter, a heavy fog came over the area and I got lost. For three days and nights I wandered, trying to find my way back to the sheep camp. At the point when I was about to give up, a man appeared out of the fog and asked, 'Do you know who I am?'

"I was quite puzzled. I had never seen this man before in my life, and I told him so.

"The man said, 'I am your father.'

"I was more than puzzled by his reply. 'How can you be my father?

He died when I was three years old.'

"The man responded by showing me a scar on his body. He said, 'when you get back to Salt Lake, tell your mother about the scar.' I then looked very closely at the man, and was able to accurately describe him later.

"The man asked me to follow him and he would lead me to the sheep camp. In a short time we were there. The fog began lifting. The man who was with me tending the sheep, saw us coming and rushed about to prepare food. I had been gone so long he knew I would be hungry.

"But when I walked into the camp I was alone. The man who rescued me had disappeared. We walked all about, calling and searching for him, but he was gone.

"When I returned to Salt Lake, I anxiously described to Mother what had happened. I told her about the man, and the scar, and all that he had said."

"There is no doubt," mother said, "that man was your father."

Even after death, Joseph Sharp was watchful over his family. We may wonder about events such as this. But we can only wonder. We do not have the answers.

Submitted by Bonnie Barker Rice

Bring Many Souls Unto Me

We read in the 18th Section of the Doctrine and Covenants:

"And if so be that you should labor all your days in crying repentance unto this people, and bring, save it be one soul unto me, how great shall be your joy with him in the kingdom of my father! And now, if your joy will be great with one soul that you have brought unto me in the kingdom of my father, how great shall be your joy if you should bring many souls unto me."

It was the early 1900s; the location was the resort town of Eureka Springs, Arkansas. Two missionaries had been assigned there to preach the gospel. When one of the missionaries became ill and sought medical help, the doctor asked if they were "some of those Mormon missionaries?" He pulled out a gun and told them to "get down those stairs, or you'll have to be carried down."

Soon there was an uproar in the town. When the missionaries returned to their hotel they found their luggage on the porch. The manager of the hotel was certainly not going to be found harboring "Mormons."

Our uncle, F. C. Nickle, a resident of Eureka Springs, found the missionaries, and invited them into his home.

These were the first missionaries my Uncle F. C. and Aunt Nellie had in their home. Soon the one who had been ill was sent home. Another missionary came in his place. The Nickle home became a place of refuge for these outcasts from society.

In the year 1913, two of the missionaries asked F. C. if they could hold a meeting in his home. He agreed to this. At the meeting, the missionaries were seated with their backs to the large front window. F. C. (also known as Clem) was seated across from them. At one point, Clem, looking over the Elders' shoulders, saw that a mob was gathering in the front yard. He excused himself, nodded to his eldest son, Jim, and the two of them exited through the back of the house, picking up their guns as they left.

They walked around to the front porch. They stood facing a large group of their neighbors and townspeople who had begun calling out for the Mormon Missionaries. Clem, a tall, strong man with an authoritative voice, said, "You'll have to go through me to get the missionaries, and I will shoot the first person who sets foot on my property."

One of the missionaries came out the front door and asked to speak to the mob. Clem agreed if the Elder would not get within reaching distance of the mob.

Whether it was fear of Clem and his son, Jim, or whether the hearts of the mob were softened by the message from the missionary—we do not know; perhaps it was a combination. The mob disbursed.

The missionaries offered to leave our uncle's home, but were told to stay. While the Elders remained in the home, it was decided to have a "cottage meeting" and invite some of the neighbors. They were not certain anyone would dare to come.

One neighbor, a good-hearted man, but not of a religious nature, said, "Well, I don't care what people think about me, I'll come." When others saw him walking into the meeting that evening, they decided to satisfy their own curiosity. Soon the rooms were filled, and then the porch, and then the front yard.

Persecution continued to rage through the town, but many considered the message given by the Elders. Clem and his family continued to study the teachings of the gospel. After some time they were baptized by an Elder Francom, who whispered to Clem at the baptism, "Brother Nickle, you are taking a step you will never regret."

As the years passed, Clem was able to preach the gospel to his widowed mother, and his brothers and sisters. They all joined the church. Clem and his family moved from Arkansas. But he returned many times as a missionary himself. He converted and baptized several hundred people.

He arranged for a Mormon missionary to officiate at the marriage of Dan, his youngest brother, and his bride Lena, who were not members. This couple would later become our parents.

Many hundreds of members of our family have since accepted the gospel; as well as many others whom the family came in contact with. A large number of missionaries came from these family members, as well as temple workers, teachers, and speakers who helped build the Kingdom of God, not only in Arkansas and Missouri, (where our parents lived) but also in Utah, and other states and countries.

The Rest of the Story

Some fifty years passed. One day in the Manti Temple, Clem's oldest son, Jim, a temple worker there, met an elderly man who looked at his name plate and asked, "Do you know an F. C. Nickle who lived in Arkansas about fifty years ago?" Jim replied that F. C. was his father. The man said he was on a mission in Eureka Springs fifty years ago, and he had a story to tell him.

They found a room where they could talk. The man said he had come to Clem's home as a missionary, and because of illness, he was sent home early. Jim told him of the many members of our family who came into the Church because of the early missionaries.

The man said, "And all these years I thought, because I had to come home early, that I did not teach or convert one soul."

They stood in the temple, embraced and wept.

Nearly forty years after that incident in the temple, Jim's daughter, Billie Sue Nickle Coffin, was substituting in her ward Primary in Sandy, Utah, when one of her neighbors, a fellow ward member, gave a presentation to the children.

As she spoke about difficulties her grandmother suffered while raising her children, and helping to support her missionary husband who served in Arkansas and Missouri, she mentioned her grandfather's name. It was Francom. Our cousin recognized this as being the name of the man who had baptized her grandfather, and his family, into the Church. As she listened tears streamed from her eyes.

When the meeting was over, my cousin embraced her neighbor. She told her that her grandfather was the missionary who brought our family into the Church. They both wept.

The neighbor was able, through her family, to verify all the events Billie Sue had heard about our family's conversion and has received copies of letters exchanged between Elder Francom and F. C. Nickel and Nellie.

We mentioned earlier that Clem arranged for a missionary to officiate at our parents' wedding. This was most displeasing to my mother's family.

As a gift to the newlywed couple, the missionary presented them with a copy of the Book of Mormon. They accepted it but placed it on a shelf. One day mother showed it to her Protestant minister. He told her the book should be burned. Accordingly, she threw it into the fire. But when the book started to burn, she could not let it burn. She scraped it out of the fire with a stick, and brushed the ashes from it.

Later, she had a dream about this book. She began to study it. The story was told to us many times. We now have that book in our possession, with all her notes along the borders of the pages.

She and our father were baptized into the Church in a large pond close by where they lived. There was a deep hole in this pond, suitable for baptisms. On this day, a thin sheet of ice covered the pond. As they walked into the water the ice broke around them. They were baptized by Clem, the brother of our father.

Because of all these faithful people, there are hundreds of members of our family in the Church.

Submitted by Nadyne and JoAnn Nickle

The Norwich Miracles

In March 1996, Ben and I decided to take a third genealogical trip to England. We needed to obtain 60 carly wills, plus several other documents unavailable in the Salt Lake City Family History Library.

A few weeks prior to departure, Ben received a prompting during his morning prayer that we should also pursue family research on the Burrell lines during our week-long stay in Norwich. There was no time for me to make a study of Burrell records. So, I went as did Nephi, "And I was led by the Spirit, not knowing beforehand the things which I should do." I had faith that if there was information needed to extend our family lines, I would be led to find it. I remembered Uncle Burt giving me a brief pedigree of the Burrell family some time ago. I hurriedly located it and tucked it into our briefcase.

We arranged for our bishop, Jacob DeJager, to give us each a priesthood blessing prior to our departure. In the blessings he set us apart as missionaries! Doors would be opened to us, our every need would be taken care of, we would have our health and strength, hearts would be softened, we would be speaking before people we had never seen, a promise of protection and peace of mind, angels would attend us, the Holy Spirit would be with us, and the Lord himself would go before us!

We had been to Norway and Germany. Now, in Shakespeare's description, as spoken by John of Gaunt in *Richard III*, we flew from Frankfurt to Heathrow Airport and were now on:

This royal throne of Kings, this sceptered isle;
This earth of majesty, this seat of Mars;
This other Eden—demi paradise,
This blessed plot, this earth, this realm, This England!

We exchanged German marks for British pounds, and took a cab to Liverpool Street Station. On the way, we talked to the cabby about the Church, and the Gospel of Jesus Christ.

The cab ride took all the cash we had. Fortunately, we had our railway tickets to Norwich. There was one problem. It was Sunday. We could not cash our travelers checks. How would we get to my cousin Barbara's house? We couldn't even use the telephone to let her know we were there. Still, we both felt at ease. Something would happen. We would be all right. The train left. There were half a dozen stops along the way. A woman and her grandson boarded and took seats opposite us. Just minutes before we had moved from seats across the aisle.

The woman turned out to be an inactive member of the Church. She still had a testimony of the gospel and clung to her Book of

Mormon, even though her husband was very negative. We told her about our problem with the travelers checks, and that it had cost all the cash we had for cab fare.

"Don't worry," she assured us. "I'll have a word with a cab driver when we reach Norwich." True to her word, she flagged several cab drivers until one pulled over. She talked with him about the fare.

"It will not be more than 10 pounds," she said. Her daughter and son-in-law, who had been on holiday in Ireland, arrived. She borrowed a ten-pound note from them, handed it to us, and we were on our way. We soon reached our destination of Sprowston, a suburb of Norwich.

After breakfast the next day, I spoke to my cousin Barbara about a longing to visit Yarmouth. My grandparents, Alfred and Emma Burrell, had lived with their family in Yarmouth for a few years. I wanted to see this old coastal city. Barbara told us that a bus ran out and back each day. After breakfast we caught the city bus into downtown Norwich. The bus driver directed us to the bus station where we could purchase tickets to Yarmouth on the following day.

To make sure we were headed in the right direction, we frequently stopped passersby. At an intersection, we stopped a middle-aged, dark-haired man. Recognizing our American accents, he asked why we wanted to go to Yarmouth.

I explained that my father was born in Norwich, but the family had lived in Yarmouth for a time when he was young.

"What was your father's name," he asked.

"Alfred Bur-rell," I replied.

"You mean Burrell. That's the way we pronounce it here. Do you know that the Burrells and Colmans are related?"

"Yes," I said. "My great-grandmother was Louisa Colman."

"Would you believe it? My name is Barry Forster, and I'm a Colman. My mother's family are the Colmans of Norwich: the mustard people. I have a fifteen-foot long pedigree chart, all proven on the Colman family. Come with me. I'll take you to a woman who knows more about genealogical research than anyone else in Norwich: Jennifer Edmonds. She's a Mormon. It's only a ten-minute walk from here. She has information on your Burrell family. She's a professional researcher. I'm not a professional. I do it for a hobby. I work with Jennifer."

We were nearly in shock. Of all the thousands of people on the streets of Norwich, how did we meet this one man who could help us with our research? Barry was not a member of the Church, but he had corresponded with two Colman brothers who moved from Norwich to Edmonton, Canada. The two of them have made a life-long study of the Colman family. They had resolved a serious error on the line, and had positively identified two main branches of the family. Barry worked with these brothers. He had in his possession copies of all documents relating to the Colman family, including pedigrees, wills, and marriage bonds. He was happy to share what he had, and to give us photocopies! We made an appointment for Thursday morning. This is the kind of experience you only read about. We were in tears. We thanked God for answering months of prayers; our blessing by Bishop DeJager; and the great influence of the Holy Spirit, for opening doors and raising up friends, and assistance.

Jennifer Edmonds lived in a small flat on Hornes Lane. She was in the process of moving her shop to a more suitable location. She greeted us warmly and asked if we had a pedigree showing the various Burrell family lines. I brought out the papers I had hurriedly gathered before leaving home. She immediately recognized a number of our surnames. If we could give her until Friday morning, she would have time to search her files. Her charges were $15 an hour. I asked her to go ahead.

We were amazed at all the information Barry Foster had to show us when we met on Thursday. Sometime back, he had received an impression that he should go to the Norwich Public Library on a particular Friday and photocopy all information on the Colman family. The following Sunday, a fire completely destroyed the building, and all library materials. He alone had these precious Colman records which he was so willing to share with us.

In our final meeting with Barry on Friday morning, September 27th, he gave us photocopies of all his records, which were pertinent to our early Colman family, and would not accept pay for his services. We insisted that he accept a ten-pound note, to at least pay for the cost of photocopies.

Jennifer Edmonds spent an hour and a half with us in the afternoon. She had two pages ready for us on the Burrell and Brett families. We were impressed with her ability, knowledge, her keen mind, and cooperative spirit.

Jennifer met me in the Relief Society room on Sunday, at the Norwich Ward, with information to extend the Read family back two generations.

We went to Yarmouth on Tuesday. It was no longer the quiet

fishing village my father had described. There were arcades, mid-ways, gambling casinos, and many other places of entertainment—the Las Vegas of England.

We were looking for members of the Brett family. We found a Brett Furniture store. We tracked down every lead and finally found an 85-year-old gentleman who told us that his nephew had all the Brett family information. We were told there was a Charles Burrell Museum in the town of Thetford. We went there and made some interesting discoveries.

Charles Burrell was founder of the Burrell Ironworks. The museum was filled with huge pieces of machinery, from threshing machines to steam engines; each piece of equipment was stamped with the logo of the Burrell Ironworks. I saw three large burlap bags fastened to a railing. Each bag was stamped in huge bold black lettering with the wording *London and Northeastern Railway*. Grandfather Alfred Burrell had been an engineer for this very company. I was nearly overcome to find yet another lead to extend the Burrell family line.

About this time Ben came running down the stairs. "You had better come upstairs with me. There is a large printed pedigree chart on the Charles Burrell family." It took me some time to copy it all down in my notebook. The line went back to 1486.

Thetford, Norfolk, is the birthplace of Thomas Paine, noted American statesman. He was a prolific writer before and during the American Revolution—author of *Rights of Man, Common Sense, The Age of Reason*, and *The American Crisis*. He became known among his peers as the The Morning Star of The Revolution.

On Wednesday, we had a singular experience while dining in an ancient Norfolk church, now converted into a restaurant. A gentleman named John Scott asked if he might join us. He was a patent attorney from Old Chiswell Hall in Edenbridge, Kent. Upon learning of our backgrounds, he said, "There is a temple 15 minutes from our home. Come and see us. It must be on a weekend when I am home, then you can meet my wife. We will take you to the temple."

He was a fine impressive gentleman, probably in his fifties. He scarcely took his eyes off Ben, savoring every word spoken about the gospel. At the end of our meal we shook hands and said goodbye. We realized there was only a remote possibility that we could accept his kind invitation.

As it turned out, we met relatives in Brentwood who were willing to take us anywhere we wanted to go on the following Sunday. We chose Edenbridge, Kent. We made arrangements to meet them right after our Church meeting. We phoned John Scott on Saturday. They had dinner guests coming on Sunday, but invited us to come around two o'clock. Traffic on the Queen Bridge spanning the Thames river was lighter than usual. We were nearly an hour early. We called the Scotts' for directions to Old Chiswell Hall. The Scotts' were still involved with their guests. They suggested that we drive over to the London Temple at Lingfield, Surrey. By the time we returned they should be free to visit with us.

As the temple came into view, we could feel the presence of heavenly beings. At the visitors center, a missionary couple came forward to greet us. John Thomas, the husband of our relative who had offered to drive us there, was touched by the Spirit, as the teachings of the Church were unfolded. He accepted a Book of Mormon, other tracts, and a picture of the temple. My cousin whom we had gone to Brentwood to visit, had her guard up. She stayed at a distance, and kept her daughter with her.

We returned to Edenbridge. We phone again for directions to Old Chiswell Halls. We were to locate a particular street, drive over three speed bumps, and we should be there. John and Penny Scott were outside, in spite of the rain, watching for us. Our relatives went to a restaurant for dinner while we visited with the Scotts. We spent the most inspirational 90 minutes of our lives answering questions and teaching the gospel. Penny Scott commented on their negligence in not investigating the Church over the years they had spent driving back and forth past our beautiful temple, and the visitors center.

Upon reading several verses from the Book of Mormon, she exclaimed, "Why, it amplifies the Bible!" There was such an outpouring of the Spirit. The Scotts willingly accepted the Book of Mormon, and the challenge to read it, study it, and pray about the truthfulness of it.

While tearful good-byes were being exchanged, Ben quickly went upstairs. He knelt down and left a priesthood blessing upon their home. We thank the Lord and praise His name for the blessed privilege of being instruments in his hands on that memorable afternoon.

Submitted by Dorene B. Booth

The Old Black Pasteboard Suitcase

Mable McGoon Stemple was a tiny lady, well under five feet in height. The death of her husband in 1914 left her the sole support of two children; Merle, a six-year-old boy, and Evelyn, who was four. Having only a fourth grade education, there were few jobs open to her.

Mable moved into the home of her father and earned a living by taking in laundry. The following year, she heard the message from Elders of The Church of Jesus Christ of Latter-day Saints, and was baptized.

There was no formal Church organization in the area. She and her family welcomed the missionaries traveling through Aurora, Illinois, into their home. It was to the Elders that she paid her tithing, often in pennies she had saved in a Mason jar.

Mable later took jobs in a restaurant and a bakery to support her family. Merle left school and got a job so he could help with the family income. Evelyn graduated the 8th grade. She then went to work also. It was a hard life, but during that era life was hard for many people.

A branch of the Church was not opened until 1928. Mable became one of the stalwarts. She continued to welcome the Elders into her home, and encouraged her children to remain faithful to the gospel teachings.

Evelyn married and began raising a family. She had four boys. Mable enjoyed being a grandmother. She was the kind of woman who was called "grandma" by many people. Declining health required her to give up her home. Her few possessions went to the home of her grandson, William, who was called Bill.

Bill, and his wife Marlene, lived in a large old farmhouse at the edge of town. A carriage house was part of the property. The second story of the carriage house was dry, and well-floored. Grandma Mable's belongings went into the carriage house attic.

After Mable's death, three years later, Evelyn, and Bill's wife, Marlene, began the task of sorting through her possessions. Decisions were made about dividing her small estate. Evelyn recalled a black pasteboard suitcase and inquired about it. A search was made. It was not found, but since nothing had been thrown away, it was sure to turn up.

In sorting through papers, Mable's patriarchal blessing was found. Evelyn carefully read it. She noted that her mother had been told she would become a Savior on Mt. Zion, but this had not happened.

"Ma didn't really understand about genealogy, and she never did any temple work."

When the sorting was finished, the black suitcase had not been found. But Evelyn said not to worry, there was nothing of value in the case, just some old newspaper clippings, and maybe a few letters.

The Rest of The Story

I, Marlene, am a historian. For many years I researched the history of the Church in Illinois. I was visiting the school one day close to Thanksgiving and the teacher said to me, "I just realized we don't have a program for Thanksgiving. Do you have any suggestions?" We went through a few ideas, which she did not feel good about. Then I asked if she thought the children would like to hear from a woman in the Netherlands who missed going on one of the ships headed for America with the Mayflower? She loved the idea. I went home and designed a costume, got the material and put it together. Then I wrote a story in the first person, of Grace Rogers, who was left behind because there was not enough room on the Mayflower. I told her story and stayed in character as I answered the children's questions afterwards. It was a hit. From there I began doing other historical characters. Margaret Seyler, one of the early settlers in Illinois was a favorite of everyone. I made her a costume, and also wrote her story in a first person narrative. Margaret went to many Historical Society meetings in Illinois.

And there were others, all of whom I made different costumes for. I kept their dresses on a pipeline hanger in the carriage house. Also hanging in the carriage house were dozens of costumes from Stake plays.

We had done *The City of Joseph, Aurelia* (the story of Aurelia Spencer Rogers, who founded the first Primary, in Farmington, Utah), *Hello Dolly, The Music Man,* and many others. I was the only one who had space enough for keeping all those costumes; I became the unofficial wardrobe mistress. The attic also held various things in cardboard boxes, which were labeled and stacked against the walls. Two cats did a perfect job of keeping the carriage house free of mice, making it a safe storage place.

One day, I was going through the women's costumes looking for a certain one. I parted, and re-parted, the clothing. As I took out the costume I wanted, I saw behind it the little black pasteboard suitcase. Found! At last! My heart was happy.

I called Mom (Evelyn) immediately and asked permission to open it. "Oh, yes," was the reply.

Another kind of sorting began. The old black pasteboard suitcase was filled with newspaper clippings of births, deaths, and marriages; some glued to sheets of paper, others pinned together in small groups. There were also notes in Mable's handwriting.

I spent hours going through the papers. Bill came home from a late meeting and asked if I was ready to go to bed.

"I'll be up in a few minutes," I said.

An hour went by. Bill called down, "Are you coming?"

"In a few minutes," I answered.

Finally, he gave up, and I went merrily on, reading notes and matching family groups. I had the definite feeling that these people were watching me go through the contents of Grandma's careful collection.

"Oh, here," one would say. Another would say, "Oh, yes, here—and here." "Oh, here is one you need to see." Finally, when my eyes would not stay open, I had to tell the people in the room, "I must go to bed. But, I promise you, in the morning I will carry on."

I slept about two hours, waking refreshed and ready for the day. I went downstairs and back to the suitcase, stopping only long enough to get my family off to work and school. All day long I read notes and newspaper clippings. After dinner I called Bill's mother.

"Mom," I said, "I have sorted everything out. I have filled out family group sheets. I'd like to read them to you. You tell me if you know whether they are correct."

Mable knew she was intended to be a Savior on Mt. Zion, but with her 4th grade education, she did not know how to go about doing this. It seemed such a daunting task to her. But she wanted the family to be together forever. She began the only way she knew. Each time there was a birth, marriage, or a death, related to her family published in the newspaper, she carefully cut it out, writing the date on an edge of the clipping. The black pasteboard suitcase became her repository for everything she collected.

Now, the information was recorded on family group sheets. I found information for Mable's parents and grandparents, her siblings, their families, and their descendants. From the small black suitcase, sixteen family group sheets were completed, with information about the current generation noted on the back.

Mable Stemple had done all she knew how to do in order to fulfill her charge to be a Savior on Mt. Zion. I can testify that she was delighted when her years of clipping, writing, and saving bore fruit.

I kept Grandma's suitcase. It has become my own repository for genealogy records.

Submitted by Marlene C. Kettley

The Healing Of Elizabeth

Elizabeth Horne, the daughter of Richard S. and Elizabeth Price Horne, was born 27 August 1872. From infancy she was a delicate child. As she grew into womanhood her physical frailties increased until almost every organ in her body was afflicted.

On the evening of July 9th, when Elizabeth was twenty-three years old, she became very despondent. She wept bitterly and expressed the wish to die. She did not want to live and be such a burden to her family.

Her fourteen-year-old brother, Arthur, had a strong feeling that Elizabeth would live. All the next day, words of the Savior kept going through his mind. "In my name shall they cast out devils, and nothing shall be impossible unto them." That evening, obeying the prompting of the Holy Spirit, he told Elizabeth that she would be healed on the following day. Surprised, yet impressed by the strong faith of her brother, she sought her own assurance by earnest petition to the Lord.

The following morning, 10 July 1895, she received the promise that she would be healed if she and other members of her family would unite in fasting and prayer. Almost immediately, her brother entered her bedroom, his face transfigured. He related to her several visions which had been opened to him during the night.

"I saw a great battle fought between our family and thousands of wicked enemies in the form of humans. They were of a dark red color. They had no hair. Their Captain was more than six feet tall, much taller than the others. He wore a pointed cap, and was girded about with a red cloth.

"Our family was fighting for you, to bring you into glory; the enemy fought to take you away as a slave. A light from above shown down on us in a circle just large enough to cover us if we kept together. If anyone stepped outside the light, the enemy grabbed that person and we had a real fight to bring them back into the circle. While we were touched by the light the enemy could not reach us.

"Another light, which seemed to come from the first one, rested on your head. Through this light a dove flew and rested on your shoulder.

"The battle lasted for some time. No weapons were used. The enemy surrounded us and exerted one last struggle, trying to pull us away from the light. We withstood this attack and they faded from sight.

"I awoke and received an interpretation of the dream. The enemy was Satan and his followers. The light was Faith. As long as we exercised faith we were safe. But when we permitted doubt to enter our minds, Satan and his followers were waiting to slip in and lead us away.

"I fell into another sleep. I was carried back to the battlefield where we had stood before. An angelic person dressed in a white robe stood beside me. I was given to know that he was your guardian angel. A bright fire surrounded him, but there was no blaze and no heat.

"He said to me, 'This is the hardest battle your family will have to fight with Satan. If you remain faithful, you will win and your sister will be healed. The dove you saw flying toward her signifies the blessings of the Lord that will be showered on her in the future. She will receive her endowments and become a mother in Israel. She must not lament her past suffering but rejoice in having overcome them. Your family must give the glory to God. If you take any honor unto yourselves for her healing, the Lord will surely punish you.

'Your family must hold the anniversary of this day, 10 July, as a day of fasting and prayer every year, in gratitude to God for this blessing. Elizabeth must bear testimony to God's goodness all her life.'

"At the conclusion of the angel's words, I came to myself, pondered what I had seen and heard, and was carried away in another vision.

"I saw my father and brother returning from their work in the canyon. I ran to meet them and asked my father if a deacon had the power to rebuke disease. He replied, 'Yes, if it is necessary.' I then ran back into the house. Satan was in the dining room. He took me by the shoulders and shook me. I tried to pull away but was powerless in his grip.

"Finally, I broke away. I ran into Elizabeth's bedroom and took her by the hand. I said to her, 'Elizabeth Horne, I command you in the name of Jesus Christ to be made whole. Every member of your body will again receive its natural strength.'

"I saw her arise from her bed and begin performing household duties which she had not been able to do for some time. I saw her acting as organist at a church meeting, and I saw her standing before people testifying to her healing.

"I then awoke and am as you see me now.

"On the day of 10 July, all occurred as I had seen in my dream. I took Elizabeth by the hand and blessed her with the same blessing I had been instructed to use by an angel. As a result Elizabeth has been made whole.

Written by Arthur Pratt Horne
Submitted by Dorothy Price Robinson

The Rest of the Story

On the evening of 13 July, three days after my healing had taken place, I knelt to offer my devotions to God before retiring. Suddenly a power of darkness came over me. I could see that the room was filled with evil spirits. Satan was there. He was head and shoulders above the others, and dressed as Arthur had described him. Though they surrounded me, none of them seemed to have the power to touch me, yet they began tormenting me. Each devil had a pointed stick in his hand. As they danced around me, they thrust their sticks at me. I trembled with chilling cold. I was filled with dreadful nausea, and at times my body burned with feverish heat.

I remained on my knees in prayer for about two hours. My sister Isabel, who slept in the same room, awoke. She came to my side. Seeing my condition, she wanted to help me. She tried to persuade me to get in the bed. But I was impressed that I should not go to sleep, the enemy would then have power over me.

The Lord made known to me that this was the "last hard struggle of the evil one," and that they would leave at daylight. I must stay on my knees until then, and all would be well with me. Having informed Isabel of this, she knelt beside me. How we longed for daylight. Satan continually whispered to me that I had not been healed; God had forsaken me, and I would not receive the blessing of health I had been promised.

What a terrible night. How tired I became kneeling hour after hour. Many times I felt that I could endure the agony no longer. Satan danced around me in fiendish delight at my suffering.

Daylight came and I was freed from bondage. I could barely move. I needed help to get on my bed where I rested for a few hours.

I believe this experience was given to me that I might fully understand the difference between good and evil. The vast difference between the Power of God and the terrible power of darkness. This is incomprehensible to all who have not themselves been confronted with it. That one night was so terrifying, what must be the effect on those compelled to endure it for ages?

I received every blessing promised me. I married Wm. R. Durrant. We had four children who grew to maturity. They have been active, contributing members of the Savior's Church all their lives. And we have done as commanded. Every year on the 10th of July our entire family has held that as a day of fasting and prayer, in gratitude for the "healing of Elizabeth."

Elizabeth Horne Durrant
Written at the age of sixty-three
Submitted by Dorothy Price Robinson

My Illness and The Healing

The following inspirational account was written by my mother, Ethel Margaret Rawlings Peterson. It was taken from her personal history. The year was 1926. The place was Ephraim, in Sanpete County.

We were all saddened when my daughter Kathryn was only five weeks old, for me to contract pneumonia. Mama came right down to help us. Teed, (daughter Dorothy) at eighteen years of age was a good worker and manager, even though she went to school. The other children gave what help they could, and Pete (husband) was good to do many things to help.

Weeks went by and instead of my getting well, I developed complications. By the first part of December, it was decided that I should be taken to the LDS Hospital in Salt Lake City. I shall always be grateful to Uncle Aaron for coming from Salt Lake to get me, because his car was large enough for a bed to be made for me in the back seat, so I could lie down.

When we got to Salt Lake an emergency case had come into the hospital, and they had filled my room, which was the last private room due to the flu epidemic at the time. I was too ill to be placed in a ward, so they phoned the Holy Cross Hospital. Their rooms were filled also, but they offered to let me have the Sisters' room.

My parents had taken baby Kathryn and her belongings in their car to their home. Grandpa took Bill (son William) up with him to Grandma's too. How hard it all must have been for grandma. (She had been on crutches for several years because of knee problems.) She had not had the care of a baby for 22 years. Then she had Bill to look after much of the time, since Pete came to the hospital often. To complicate matters, Bill had the measles while there. I felt heartsick when I had to wean the baby, and, of course, the artificial feedings made much more work for Mama, and she was in her early sixties.

Teed took over at home, and with the other children's help, somehow they managed. Ethelyn was good to wash the dishes. Of course, the boys had a lot of chores, with cows to milk, wood to chop, sheep to feed, etc. Teed had the responsibility of it all.

I felt so sorrowful to have to go to the hospital in the first place, because it was so near Christmas, and I felt that I must be home and prepare for the children. Dr. Nielsen assured me that there wasn't a question of my going home by that time.

A few days after arriving at the hospital, Dr. Lund was aspirating with the large needle. It broke and was quickly drawn into my pleural cavity. This necessitated immediate surgery.

An operation was performed by Dr. Root, an imminent surgeon. Pete and Cal (Calvin Rawlings, her only sibling) were with me. Dr. Root secured the needle and removed it, but I developed the dreaded streptococcus infection. This worsened my condition. I had to have a special nurse day and night. There were no wonder drugs such as penicillin to fight the infection.

Pete made trips home and back to see how the children and the animals were. He was with them on Christmas day. Grandma and Grandpa brought our sweet baby up to see me that day, which helped a lot. She was doing so well. Grandma (with Grandpa's help) was taking good care of her.

I had the Elders who visited the hospital often administer to me, but none of them promised me that I would live.

It was a busy time with the sheep in the spring, so Pete was busy at home. Each week, the doctor would tell me that maybe next week-end I could go home. On May 20th, 1927, (the day Charles Lindberg made his successful non-stop flight across the Atlantic) I came home. What a happy day after more than five months in the hospital.

Although I was still bedfast, it was so good to be home where the children were. They had all grown so much. Sometimes it sounded like a stranger was in the kitchen when Nute (Peter Knute) was speaking, because his voice was changing. During the spring of 1928 Nute broke his arm on the school playground.

Teed had been elected vice-president of the student body at Snow college, which made us all happy.

We were lucky to get Blenda Dahl, who had experience in nursing care, and could also help in the house, to come and stay each day. This helped lift the burden from others in the family. The baby was still with Grandma and Grandpa. They were good to bring her down often to see us during the summer. She was a very pretty baby. Grandma made such cute dresses for her, and kept her looking like a doll.

Through that winter I didn't seem to improve as I should. I shall never be able to express my gratitude to the people of Ephraim for their many kindnesses; and especially to members of the West Ward who were so loyal. The Brethren administered to me many times; none promised that I would live.

In the spring of 1928 it was decided that I'd have to be taken back to Salt Lake City to be seen by a specialist. The members of the West Ward held a special fast and prayer meeting on my behalf. This gave me great courage.

Pete took Blenda and me to Grandma and Grandpa's. Grandma had been forced to give up the work she loved as a member of the Primary Stake Board, and also a trip they had planned to the Northwest, to take care of Kathryn for us.

They went to Wildwood for the summer so it would be quiet at the house for me. Neal (Cornelius Rawlings, another son) went with them to help take care of Kathryn, for she was now old enough to run around, and quite a task to watch in the canyon.

Before they left, Grandpa asked his old schoolmate and friend, Elder James E. Talmadge of the Council of the Twelve, to come and administer to me. When he put his hands upon my head, I felt a great power, (come over me) and he promised me that I would live!

The specialist who saw me seemed to know just what needed to be done to clear the infection. I began to improve immediately. My greatest hope had been that I could become well enough to be in a wheelchair, to be able to take charge of my home, and help plan for the children until they were grown. If that could happen, I would be satisfied.

But now I knew I would become well, because I had been promised by a special servant of the Lord. I promised the Lord if he made me well so I could have the joy of rearing my six children, I would never refuse a request of my services in His cause so long as I was well enough. I kept this promise for He did make me well, and I served in many positions for the Church.

Submitted by Ethelyn P. Taylor

Fulfillment of Prophesy

Apostle Mathew W. Cowley interviewed me for my mission in September 1950. He also gave approval for me to marry first. Two weeks after getting married I entered the mission home in Salt Lake City.

I was set apart by Antone R. Ivans; part of the blessing stated that I "would have many experiences that would stay with me until my dying days." I did have many wonderful experiences, especially during the extra month I was asked to stay.

I had four months at home and then came two years in the Marine Corps. Fourteen of those months were served in Korea. I didn't want to leave my wife after such a short time. I didn't want to go to Korea, but the Lord made it plain to me that I should go.

One afternoon I was running an obstacle course where we would climb a twenty-foot ladder to the top. There were poles about three feet apart that we had to jump for. Then, at the end, we had to jump for one of the dangling ropes and return to the ground. Two lines of men were formed and when I reached the front, ready to climb, the Marine behind me asked to trade places so that he could go with his buddy in the other line. When he jumped for the rope, it broke, letting him fall over twenty feet to the ground. He had picked the rope I planned to take. Had we not traded places, I would have been the one hauled away in the ambulance, too crippled to go to the military conflict in Korea.

I felt that the Lord wanted me in Korea. Now, over 50 years later, I can look back and enjoy remembering the good part of the experiences there.

I was in the Marine Corps but spent twelve months TDY (temporary duty) with the Eighth Army Honor Guard in Seoul.

A treasured experience from that time was teaching a Sunday School class with Dr. Kim, Ho-Jik. I would take the first half period in English, Dr. Kim would interpret and add his own thoughts. I had to create my own lessons geared to the Korean members and investigators (there were no lesson manuals) who were mostly college students with much more schooling that I had.

One student looked up the word "Mormon" in a Chinese dictionary. All it said was, "A man with many wives." We had to teach the class better. It was thrilling to find out years later that at least two of that original group have served as mission presidents.

When the first missionaries entered Korea in 1959, there were approximately sixty members to greet them. Dr. Kim being a government official as well as a member of the President's Cabinet--he was Minister of Health and Education--was able to obtain permission for our missionaries to enter the country. Without his help it could have taken another ten years.

I enjoyed cottage meetings in Dr. Kim's home where we would sit on the floor in a circle. Sister Kim would bring in a pan of hot coals and set it in the middle to keep us warm. Dr. Kim has been dead many years, but I have been told that every time President Hinckley goes to Korea, he pays a visit to Sister Kim, and that he has left instructions with Church officials to see that she always has a home, and plenty of food to eat.

Leaving a lot unsaid, I mention one experience with Harold B. Lee, who was an Apostle at the time. He visited Korea in the fall of 1954 bringing Mission President Hilton Robertson from Japan. They were given the accommodations of a one-star general and a change of army clothes. A meeting was held in Seoul for all Latter-day Saints who could get there. They then spent a week or more participating in other L.D.S. meetings throughout Korea.

President David O. McKay had instructed them to meet with as many commanding officers as possible. Near the end of their stay I was able to meet them again when they came to visit the 8th Army commander, General Maxwell D. Taylor. I was one of the General's personal body guards at the time, so I knew in advance of their coming. When they came out of the meeting, I told Brother Lee, "Most VIPs get about fifteen minutes with the General, but you have had forty-five minutes with him."

Brother Lee stated, "We tried to excuse ourselves but he said to sit down, that these things are important." Then Brother Lee made a prophesy that was fulfilled very quickly. He stated that of all the forty or so officers he had visited, he was more impressed by General Taylor than any of the others. He felt that General Taylor was going right to the top. President Robertson, Chaplin Woods, (non L.D.S.) and myself were the only ones present at the time.

In approximately two months, President Eisenhower relieved General Taylor of the 8th Army Command and made him Far East Commander, moving him to Japan. And then in about six months, General Taylor was moved to the Pentagon as Army Chief of Staff. A prophesy fulfilled right to the top in less than a year. After retirement he was sent to Viet Nam as the U.S. Ambassador.

A few years later I met Brother Lee at a stake conference in Ogden, Utah, and presented him with a colored slide taken of him. He said, "You are the one I met there." Then he asked, "Did you see how fast General Taylor went to the top?"

My response was, "Yes, I did."

His further comment was, "You boys planted some good seeds over there. We now have about five thousand converts."

It has been exciting to me to see how a country, new to the Church, has taken the gospel into their hearts and continued to flourish.

As for my wife back home, we've been married more than fifty years.

Submitted by Isaac Fenn

I Need You to Come Home

My wife and I had been called to work one week of each month in the Portland Temple. On 18 December 1989, we had finished our commitment and returned home to Medford. I had some Christmas shopping left to do. I dropped my wife off at home and drove into town.

Normally, I would not call home without a reason, but as I went about my business, I kept getting a strong feeling that I should call my wife. I found a telephone. When my wife answered, she wanted to know where I was. This was not a usual response from her, and her voice sounded strange.

I asked her if anything was wrong. She said, "I need you to come home."

I went to my car, making it onto the freeway as fast as I could. I drove with a prayer in my heart that whatever was wrong we would have the strength to bear it. I knew in my heart that something bad had happened.

When I walked in the front door, my wife was waiting. "You will need to sit down," she said. The tragic news was that Laura, our seventeen-month old granddaughter, had drowned in the bathtub.

My son was the Elders Quorum President. People who knew CPR had tried to resuscitate the child. But a doctor pronounced her dead. A counselor to my son then asked if he could be alone in the room with the child. The parents gave permission.

This was a man who had great faith, who lived an exemplary life, and he had great spiritual power. His intent was to call upon the Powers of Heaven to restore life to our little girl.

As he knelt at her bedside, it was revealed to him that Laura had completed her earthly mission. She had already been called to serve a mission on the other side of the veil. She would prepare the way for her maternal grandfather, who would soon die.

She would teach the gospel to him, and other members of the extended family who had died without accepting it, or without hearing it This good brother made no attempt then to recall her spirit.

Six months later, on July 5th, my daughter-in-law's father became very ill. That night, Laura appeared to Becky, her mother, as an adult. A large crowd of people stood with her. Becky saw a great gulf between her and Laura, and the other people. The gulf separated them so they could not come together.

Laura let her mother know, "Now it is up to you." Becky knew at once that Laura had come for her grandfather, and that she was also referring to genealogy work that needed to be done for him, and all the people who stood with Laura. Becky recognized some of her relatives who had passed on, but most were strangers to her.

On the 7th of July, Becky's father died. .

Working in the temple helped us to feel closer to Laura. We felt that we were helping with her heavenly mission.

Submitted by Jack Mills

And The Blind Shall Hear

In August of 1998, I had such a strong feeling that I should go to the Handi Ham camp. I do not always go, but a voice kept telling me I needed to go. The time drew nearer. I didn't want to go because Northwest air lines went on strike, which made it very difficult to transfer your plain ticket. I decided to stay home. The Spirit said I needed to go. I listened because I have found through the years that I am sorry if I don't pay attention to that voice. It took the entire day to get there. I had to go to Texas and then transfer to another plane before I could get to Minnesota. We then rode a special bus to the camp.

It is about a five hour drive from Minneapolis to the Handi Ham camp in Lake George, Minnesota. When I finally arrived there was a co-counselor from Australia. When she heard that I was from Salt Lake City, Utah, she asked me if I knew where she could get a copy of the Book of Mormon. I had one in my back pack, which I gave to her. I didn't hear if she ever joined the church, but that must have been the reason why I was supposed to go through what I did to get that book to her.

I would also like to share this story with you. I was trying so hard to get my general ham license. The first time that I went to the camp in Minnesota was in 1988. I was struggling to learn the Morse code. I did not think I could ever pass the test. I asked my home teacher to give me a blessing. In that blessing he said I would pass the test. The test day came. You are given five tries to pass the Morse code test. It took all five tries before I finally got it. After the fourth failure, the people giving the test asked if I didn't want to wait and try it again when I got home. But the words of my home teacher were in my mind, saying that I would pass. I took that one last test and passed it.

Submitted by Linda Reeder

An Unexpected Cross To Bear

I grew up as an Army dependent. My father's thirty-two year career in the U.S. Army gave my family the opportunity to travel, and live in a number of places within the United States, and Western Europe.

Because of my father's position, I was expected to 'toe the line' when in the presence of family, friends, and military acquaintances. However, little did my parents know that I wasn't so obedient when I was off with my friends gallivanting around the U.S. and Europe. My language was not as proper, and my actions were not as socially, or age appropriate, as my parents would have liked. When I was a child, as a family, we attended a Protestant Church on Sundays. At that time in my life, I didn't have any solid feelings about religion. In the late 1950s, when I was about 9 years old, I remember sitting through the hour-long service, just waiting to go down stairs for the coffee, donuts, and cookies; and then heading outside to play.

About that time, missionaries from The Church of Jesus Christ of Latter-day Saints started coming to the house. At that time I learned that my mother was born in the Church, with ancestors going back to the early Mormon pioneers. I don't know if she called the missionaries or not, but I believe she asked them to come and teach our family the gospel. It took my father three years before he would join the Church. My father and I were baptized together in 1963, in Arlington, Virginia.

I tried hard to take my baptism seriously, but I was confused. My memories of those days attending the ward were not happy. As the only military family in an affluent ward, I felt left out and hurt. I had no friends in the ward. My real friends were not in the Church. Shortly after that, my father was assigned to a series of posts in Europe. That is when my behavior began to follow the ways of the world, instead of following the teachings of the Church, and the disciplined expectations of my parents.

The Stroke

We were back in the U.S. by October of 1970. My parents were settled in Norman, Oklahoma. My Father was the ROTC Commandant at the University of Oklahoma. At that time, I had graduated high school, had two years of college in North Carolina, was living in an apartment in Arlington, Virginia, and working as a clerk in an insurance company in Washington, D.C. I am sorry to admit that I was still following the lifestyle of my nonmember friends. I was drinking, smoking, and enjoying that lifestyle.

In October of 1970, I moved into a furnished basement apartment. The food and garbage from prior tenants had been left in the apartment and attracted large cockroaches. The first night I slept in my clothes. The next day I attacked the two dresser drawers with bug spray. I immediately felt dizzy and staggered up a flight of stairs to another apartment. I asked them to call my sister who lived only ten blocks away.

An 'angel' of a man, took me outside for fresh air. Someone called an ambulance. I was taken to a local Arlington hospital. The last thing I remembered seeing were the curtains in the emergency room. I was later told that on admittance I complained of severe headaches. I had a stroke in the hospital.

I woke up months later in Walter Reed Hospital. The stroke left me paralyzed on my right side, took away my speech, and the ability to walk. I had a vocabulary of about 10 words. At Walter Reed, I was taught to crawl. I was taught to feed myself. I laugh now, but they were mean people. No one was allowed to help with the things I was being taught. I had to feed myself. I wore as much food as I got in my mouth. I drooled. I was embarrassed. It was a horrible time.

In January 1971, I returned to live with my parents in Norman. I was little more than a grown woman in a baby's body. My mother did everything for me, including taking care of my personal hygiene needs.

Arrangements were made for me to take speech and physical therapy at the University, twice a day for a year. It was then reduced to once a week. We lived within a mile of the campus. My mother drove me back and forth each day. It took ten years for me to learn to walk, speak, drive, and live on my own.

Lessons Learned

My stroke gave me the time and opportunity to share with others what has been given to me. Before the stroke I was often cocky, sometimes unkind. Because of the help I was given, because of the care that I received, I have become a better person. I try each day to be better, to be kinder, to be loving, to be humble and to give service to other people.

My ability to drive is a gift and blessing. It affords me the opportunity to drive the older residents in my building to Sunday services, and to temples that are wheelchair friendly and have facilities for those who are hearing impaired. I pick up supplies for quilting service projects, and can take care of my own needs as well.

My cockiness gave way to opening my home for dinner and ice cream most Sundays. I give hugs and kisses freely, with true feelings of friendship and love. I laugh more. I feel the Spirit often. I reflect on my patriarchal blessing weekly for direction and guidance.

My love has turned to my Father in Heaven, and my Savior. I owe everything to them. I've told a good friend, "During those years of misbehavior, the Lord wanted me to slow down and listen. I didn't. So He made me."

I don't believe that the stroke was anything more than an accident, but it had a purpose. Fourteen years after my stroke I was called on a genealogical mission for the Church. The surprise was that the mission call was to Salt Lake City, at the now Family History Library. It was the first of two missions. I am now permanently settled in Salt Lake City. I do family genealogy at the library. I have a Church calling that involves greeting new members of the ward and taking their pictures. I was active in an older singles ward that had members with varying types of needs. I have friends that are near and dear to my heart.

I find that I still need help with things because of the stroke. But in a small circle of friends, we all have needs and we all have strengths. Where one of us is lacking, another fills in. Where one of us is strong, they boost the others.

I know my Father lives. I know that Jesus is the Christ. I know that they love me. I will live the remainder of my days, doing for others as they would wish me to do, as others did for me. I say these things and bear witness of the truthfulness of my words. In the name of Jesus Christ. Amen.

Submitted by Susan Land
Assisted by her 'Aaron' and good friend Judith Locke

(Authors note: My husband and I met Susan when she was a member of the singles ward that he was bishop of. She took out her endowments during that time. She is a joy in the lives of many people. We have always thought of her as an Earth Angel.)

Escape To Freedom

December 26, 1950 was a legal holiday in East Germany. Passenger express trains were packed with holiday travelers on that day, minimizing police security. It was an ideal time to put into effect a plan conceived months earlier: to escape to the West in an effort to avoid the ever-increasing encroachment upon basic human rights under Communist rule.

Our mother was serving a mission for the Church in West Berlin, in accordance with a religious tolerance law still on the books in East Germany. She was called on this mission partially with the intent of paving the way for us to emigrate to the United States.

Mother had purchased one-way tickets for me and Rudy, my younger brother. I was fourteen; Rudy was twelve years old. The tickets were for Werdau, our alleged destination in Rostock, a city near the Baltic Sea to the north.

After singing "God Be With You 'til We Meet Again" with our grandparents, who stayed behind, we boarded a passenger express train. That evening the train made a scheduled stop in East Berlin.

Even though our tickets did not allow us to get off the train there, we stepped off under the pretense of wanting to visit with our mother. Under the law we were allowed to visit her, but not if she resided in West Germany. West Berlin, where she lived, was part of West Germany. The most crucial moments of our escape plan had arrived. The next hour or so would determine our fate for the rest of our lives. At this point, we risked our lives if we proceeded with our plans to cross the border illegally.

President Walter Stover of the East German Mission had driven his big American car across the border into West Berlin to meet us at the train station. He parked the car in a dark nearby street. As an American citizen it was legal for him to do this. But it was impossible for him to justify transporting citizens of East Germany into West Berlin. He too risked his life.

Upon disembarking from the train, our mother met us. She put me on the bicycle we had brought along. She pointed west on the main east-west artery of Berlin, and told me to start pedaling. She gave me instructions to act as stupid as I possibly could when I reached the tightly policed military border at the Brandenburg Gate (Brandenburger Tor); meaning that I should not give details to anyone, such as my name, where I came from, and where I wanted to go.

The risks were high and involved anything from being allowed to pedal through the Gate, to being turned back, being deported, or killed. In the meantime, Mother and Rudy quickly disappeared in the direction of President Stover's car. They would try to cross the border illegally at another checkpoint.

I remember reaching the Brandenburg Gate in the dark of night. That was the single most critical moment of my attempt to escape from East Germany. I have no recollection of what happened from the time I left my family until I reached the Gate. Border guards searched me thoroughly. They found nothing. I do not remember their questioning me. My mind is strangely blank from the time I left my family until the guards decided to let me through the Gate. I only recall the relief I felt when I was allowed to proceed into the haven of West Berlin.

Two hours later, tired and emotionally exhausted, I arrived at the Mission Home, our rendezvous point. Mother, President Stover, and Rudy were anxiously awaiting me. They were beginning to think that I had been detained by the police, since it had taken me such a long time to travel the six or seven miles through Berlin.

We were reunited as a family. Neither of us had encountered any life-threatening problems at the two different border check points.

My mother and President Stover had passports for going in and out of West Berlin, but Rudy did not. A policeman swept the car interior with his flashlight, but for some reason, he did not see my brother who was sitting alone, and motionless in the back seat.

The plan of our escape to a land of freedom and democracy had worked perfectly. The Lord protected and guided us once again in our righteous endeavors to serve him.

Submitted by W. Herbert Klopfer

A Special Trip on Easter Morning

Between Mom and Dad, Mom was always the health conscious one, making sure they ate a good diet. She worked daily in her beautiful yard, getting good exercise, and eating her nutritious home-grown vegetables.

Dad, on the other hand, loved his sugary desserts, and fatty red meat. He always assumed that Mom would outlive him. It came as a great shock to us all when in 1996, at the young age of seventy, my mother was diagnosed with liver cancer. She went to the doctor, originally for another problem, and during the medical testing, it was discovered that she had several medium-sized tumors in and around her liver.

We were told that liver cancer was almost always fatal, and very painful toward the end. Mom decided to take the chemotherapy treatments to prolong what time she had left, but the cure seemed to take a greater toll on her health than the cancer had.

It affected her already weak heart and she quickly began to fail. She no longer could work in the yard, or do much of anything. That was very frustrating to her as she had always been a "doer."

Within nine months, it was apparent that she wouldn't be with us much longer. However, she never complained of pain associated with the cancer. She was just tired and weak. A few days before Easter, I was pondering and contemplating my life. In my mind's eye, I saw masses of people, all standing in the northeast foothills of the Wasatch Mountains, a short distance from my house. It seemed to me that it was a vision of all the spirits—and there were so many—on the other side of the veil that had come to meet Mom, and take her home.

I called my sisters who were out of town and told them that they needed to come now or it might be too late. I felt great comfort, yet urgency.

Very early Easter morning, Mom passed away. My oldest sister, who slept by her bedside at night, reported that she had asked Mom the last time she awoke, if she was in any pain. Mom said no and went back to sleep.

It was such a blessing that she was able to go so peacefully. We felt that Mom had a hand in choosing the time of her passing, so as to leave us with the very important message of the resurrection of Jesus Christ, and a lasting testimony of her belief in that message.

Mom's brother, Jerold Ottley, was at that time still conducting the Tabernacle Choir. Before the broadcast that morning, he related to the choir members that his only sister had died during the night. He wanted to dedicate that morning's Easter program to her.

Of course, they had a beautiful presentation about the Resurrection already prepared; but to us, there was an extra element of comfort and love, as the choir's music and the spoken word was not only about Christ, but about our mother as well.

Submitted by Janet Yamamoto

Faith to Be A Simple Mother

In 1994, while traveling on a small cruise ship down the Volga River in Russia, I was introduced to a pretty young sister by the name of Irena. She and her husband had become members of The Church of Jesus Christ of Latter-day Saints only a few months before. Irena was currently serving as Primary President and her husband was the Branch President. The light of the newfound gospel radiated in their eyes.

We became closer day by day, even though each of us only knew a few words of the other's language. At the end of our journey we exchanged small gifts and addresses along with hugs and tears.

One of her letters that I received a few months later touched me deeply.

She wrote, "I became a simple mother who doesn't go to work. It was a very serious step, and it wasn't easy for me to do. I don't even know whether I regret it. Now in our country it is very difficult for the father alone to support the family. But, I hope that God will help us, as the children's relationship to me is just as important as food and clothing."

To me, the key thing of importance in her statement was that she knew they may not have food or clothing without the extra paycheck. Family relationships were more important to her. Her faith was strong. She had learned from Church leaders that, if at all possible, her major role as a mother was to be there for her children. To be home when they were home.

A few months later I noticed in our local paper that a missionary had just returned from Donetsk, Ukraine, where Irena and her family lived. I called to ask if he knew Irena and he told me that he knew the family well. I asked if things had gone well since she had decided to stay at home with her children. He excitedly told me that just a few weeks after she quit her job, her husband was offered a second job which worked in well with his current employment. He told me of her joy in the realization that if we have enough faith to follow the teachings of the gospel, our Heavenly Father will help us in many ways. A parent, a mother, was now able to spend more time with her children and be the very best Primary President she could possibly be.

Submitted by Sherry Bratsman

The Upper Road

In her journal, Martha Thomas wrote of the trials faced by her husband, Daniel, and their family of five children (ages 13 to 3) after leaving their home in Missouri. Martha also wrote of her husband's brother, Henry Thomas. The Prophet had sent word from Liberty jail for the Saints to travel the "upper road and cross at Quincy."

But Henry, being a man who liked choosing his own road in life, reasoned:

"The lower road was in good repair with plenty of provisions to sell (buy)."

Daniel and Martha followed the Prophet's counsel and traveled the upper road. Henry took the lower one. Along the "upper road" they found way stations with provisions for those with money, and also for those who had none. Martha wrote:

"We were much surprised as this was the first station we ever saw. We acknowledged the hand of God. We went on to the next, until we reached Quincy in safety."

And what of Henry and his family? The Missourians along the lower road would not sell anything to them. The family suffered for want of food. Martha noted:

"He traveled the lower road until the day of his death. He never gathered with the Church again. I speak of these things that the young and rising generation may take warning, and obey counsel."

Traveling across the State of Missouri in winter was hard even in the best of circumstances. Martha wrote of leaving their home, and of their journey:

"We now bid farewell to Zions we anticipated building in Missouri. I said to Mr. Thomas, 'All I want now is a horse, or wheels, so we can turn and travel in any direction the Lord may direct.'

On the 14th of February, 1839, we started across the prairie to

Tenny's Grove, about twenty miles. The snow was about six inches deep. The children were all barefoot, except the oldest boy. To hear them crying at night with their feet cracked and bleeding was a grievous sight for a mother to bear. I would often grease them and put on clean stockings instead of making them wash them when going to bed.

We could not cross for the ice, several hundred families were camped on the river bank. Brother Brunson came over the river, and called the brethren together. After a few minutes Mr. Thomas came back in a hurry saying,

"Mother, what do you think of our team going back to Far West? The Brethren and Sisters (for there were many widows and children) are all to be shot if they are not out by such a day."

"Well, dump the things out by that log."

"What will you do if you are taken sick?" he said.

"I will do what Sister Wight did in Daviess County, when confined by a log in a snow storm."

"According to your faith so shall it be," (he said to me).

And so it was done. Their wagon was emptied of personal belongings and was soon on the way to save Saints at Far West, driven by one of the brethren of their company. That night, it appeared that Martha would give birth to their baby. Quickly a bed was made by driving poles into the ground, a frame constructed and then "roped with the bed cord, making a nice bed." Other poles were driven into the ground, quilts hung from the poles except at the foot of the bed, where the heat and light from their fire would be admitted to the rude shelter. Martha recorded:

"I have often thought a queen never enjoyed such a bedroom. It was a comfortable place but I got better, had one good night's rest in it."

The next morning, Martha recorded:

"The ice was leaving the river now. The boats made one trip today. It fell our lot to cross, having no wagon we could not put our goods all in the same boat. The little children and I sat under the wagons under some bedding. Mr. Thomas and (son) Morgan stayed back to get the cow across next trip."

Assured that her husband and son would follow, both boats started out; but the river was soon covered with large pieces, and chunks of floating ice. Martha and her children reached the shore and Quincy, but the other boat was surrounded by ice and taken out of sight, below the town. Imagine the fear that filled her mind and heart; left alone on the shore; alone with her four small children. The sun sliding behind the horizon made it impossible to see across the Mississippi River. She did the best she could to keep the children warm, wrapping them in the bed clothes. Martha continued:

"It was very cold. I sat down on the bed to watch for the boat. I began to look at my situation, not knowing what moment I might be taken sick (labor would begin). For the first time tears stole down my face, on my own account. One of the little ones said, "Mother, are you sick?" "No," said I, "the wind is so cold."

As if in answer to an unspoken prayer, a brother Wiswanger rode up and inquired about her husband. Being a family man, he recognized her situation, and stayed with them until they heard the boat coming. This good man then traveled 12 miles in the dark to reach his destination, but not before promising to send a wagon and team in the morning. He invited them into his home, offering them half of it. He added:

"It is twelve foot square, we have five children, you have five, four grown persons, plenty of standing room. We will fix a bed for you."

Before long, Martha's family was reunited. Other friends joined them, as they camped by the river for the night. When the wagon came for the Thomas family, they made their way to the home of Brother and Sister Wiswanger.

In a few days (March 17, 1839) Martha gave birth to their sixth child, named Joseph Alma. This family, like so many, felt themselves blessed. With the other faithful, the Daniel S. Thomas family resided in Nauvoo, and migrated west with the Saints.

Autobiography of Martha Jones Thomas
Submitted by Marlene C. Kettley

As Moses Parted the Red Sea

My husband, Alma, came home to Arizona for a few days, but then had to return to Oregon where he was building a shopping center for my parents. He came on his birthday, 8 October, and stayed with us two weeks before flying back to Portland. While he was there he and his cousin tolled and planted a garden. During that year we enjoyed having the fresh green food.

We had neighbors who gave us a feeling of danger, so we were always careful to stay together. On my daughter Karen's tenth birthday, the kids and I decided we would drive to Oregon. We got their homework assignments, and prepared to leave. Alma called and gave me a blessing over the phone.

His blessing was that we would be protected, and I was told I could call upon the Lord, using the priesthood that Alma held, if the need arose. He said that the Lord would make a pathway for me, even as Moses had parted the Red Sea, and the children of Israel walked on dry ground. I was also told that these things should be taught to the children and kept in remembrance for future generations, that they may know what things are done by faith and the power of the priesthood.

At three in the morning while it was still dark, so our neighbors wouldn't know we were gone, (my son) Rob and I loaded the car as quietly as possible with sleeping bags, pillows, dishes, food, clothes, and toys. We then carried the little ones out and got Ric and Karen in the car. Ric sat in front with me to navigate. We left quietly and quickly. For several hours we drove in the dark. Off to the west there were huge dark clouds, and lightning; showing a fierce desert storm. We were driving directly into it. As it became daylight we could see that we were on the main highway headed for California. The storm was directly ahead of us. Remembering the promise, I held out my hand and asked that the storm be parted for us by the power of the priesthood that Alma held. As I watched, the storm parted on both sides of the road, one part going south, the other part going north. It separated like a hot knife going through butter. The lightning continued on both sides of us.

Then a beautiful rainbow came before us. It stayed ahead of us for miles, later a lighter colored second one joined with it. We arrived in Blithe, California around noon and took a secondary road heading north to Las Vegas. All the while we were skirting the main storm. The road went up and down. In all the down places there were rocks and mud across the road and pools of water. It was a narrow road. One car coming toward us passed another car and missed us by inches.

The storm was so bad it stretched from Los Angeles to San Francisco. In Los Angeles three lanes of the main freeway were covered with mud. When we stopped for gas the attendant told us that a woman just behind us had been killed when she was hit by a four foot wall of water in one of the lower areas. It was a violent storm which created a lot of damage. But we believed that we were divinely protected by my husband's blessing. The seas did part, and we were on dry land most of the time. We arrived safely at our destination.

Submitted by Jan Johnstun

Faith in The Power of The Priesthood

I was serving in the Presidency of the Mesa Temple when this event occurred.

On December 13th, 1979, a call came to my desk. I was told that a young man was there who wanted to see me. I inquired about his standing in the Church. Was he a recommend holder? The person calling said, "yes." I said, "send him in."

Minutes later, a tall well-built young man wearing sun glasses appeared in my doorway. He had no hair on the right side of his head and face. His face was scarred. His nose had the appearance of having been rebuilt.

"President Garn," he said, "I am Larry Henderson. I know that you know my story. It has been told to me that you have repeated it many times in talks you have given."

Words cannot adequately express my pleasure in meeting Larry Henderson. I took his hand and asked him to be seated. I asked him to tell me first-hand the story of his accident. This is his story:

"I am a pilot. One day several years ago, I was crop-dusting a cotton field near Queen Creek. At the fore end of the field there were high-powered electrical lines. After passing over the field, I miscalculated in the pull out. Instead of going up over the lines, I hit them. My plane crashed to the earth and burst into flames. Two men who were out in their fields working, ran and pulled me out of this fiery inferno.

"At the same time a man in a pick-up truck drove up and he ran to see what he could do for assistance. He asked the two men if they were Mormons, and if they held the priesthood. One man answered in the affirmative to both questions.

"'Just a minute,' the man said. He ran to his pick-up and brought back a bottle of consecrated oil. The two men anointed me, and gave me a blessing.

"My hands were scorched, as were my feet. My face was on fire. But this blessing gave me peace and a feeling of calm.

"They put me in the pick-up and rushed me to Williams Air Force base. 'We cannot handle him here,' the doctors said. 'Get him to the hospital in Mesa as quickly as possible.'

"On removing the garment of the Holy Priesthood, it was found that I suffered no burns under the garment. But where the sleeve ended on my right arm, the doctor pressed his finger into a large indentation and found that the tissue was burned almost to the bone.

"In my semi-private room there was another brother who was burned in a similar kind of accident. He died. Yet still I claimed my blessing which said I would live. My nose has been rebuilt. I have had 32 operations on my face. I know that the priesthood of God, and the honoring the garment of the Holy Priesthood saved my life. I wanted to meet you, President Garn, and bear testimony that I know the Church is true."

I admired Larry Henderson for his strong testimony honoring the priesthood, and his love for the church. He now lives in Utah.

As I think of Larry Henderson, I ponder about miracles. If miracles have ceased, it is because faith has ceased. Brother Henderson had faith, and he claimed his blessing. We must not forget the two men who anointed and blessed him. They are heroes as well. The outcome may well have been different without the exercise of their own faith and belief.

In Ether 12:12, we are told, "For if there be no faith among the children, God can do no miracles among them. Wherefore, he showed not himself until after their faith."

Submitted by Stacy D. Garn

My Child Was Blessed to Live

Bill, our baby, was terribly ill. Twice we took him to the doctor. He told us Bill had a flu virus that was going around. His temperature hovered around 106-107 degrees. We were told to bathe him in alcohol to help bring the fever down. Bill had nothing in his stomach to throw up, because he could not even keep a drop of water down. But he kept heaving and retching.

We did not believe that Bill had the simple virus that other children had. His symptoms were so different. Again we took him to the doctor. He told us to seek another doctor.

When we walked into the new doctor's office, carrying Bill, he said, "We need to do a spinal tap; he may have meningitis." Then he told us, "Only two hospitals will take people with contagious diseases, the General Hospital (which did not have a good reputation) and the Children's Hospital. We took him to the Children's Hospital.

The doctors there said there was little chance Bill would pull through; he was very ill, and had been for so long. His fever had been too high. He was already "frozen" with his little back arched backwards. If he did live he would be crippled. He would have brain damage because his fever had been over 107 degrees.

My husband and I were frantic. Jack began calling men who could come and give Bill a blessing. It was Friday night. No one was home. After calling for more than a half hour, Jack thought of our daughter Nancy's Seminary teacher, Brother Weston. He was not at home; but his wife, sensing our urgency, said she thought she could find him.

She would send him to us.

Brother Weston came to the hospital. We dressed in white gowns and masks to enter Billy's room. Brother Weston took a diaper and wiped Billy's perspiring face. He talked to him as you would to an adult. He then blessed Billy that, "Angels will attend you. You will get well, and have no ill effects from this illness."

In ten days Bill was completely well. He recovered so fast the doctors were spellbound. We knew he had been saved by Brother Weston's faith, our prayers, and the power of the priesthood.

This was one of the most awful two weeks I ever lived through. It seemed like years. I prayed constantly, and ate so little I lost nine pounds. The miracle of his healing was amazing and hard to believe. When you see your baby so sick he does not move or cry; and breathing is so hard for him, he gasps for breath, and your doctor says there is no hope, and if he does live he will surely have brain damage from the fever, and he may be paralyzed; no one can know the agony.

Then, confused by the results of the priesthood blessing, the doctor changes his diagnosis, and says he must have had an infected pancreas; and after two more days, he throws up his hands and says, "Go home. Billy is cured." We took him home and rejoiced in the miracle God had given us.

Submitted by Violet Seaver Mill

Listen to the Voice

Yea, thus saith the still small voice, which
whispereth through and pierceth all things,
and often times it maketh my bones to quake
(D &C 85:6)

"And it came to pass when they heard this
voice—it was a still voice of perfect mildness,
as if it had been a whisper, and it did pierce
even to the to the very soul—"
(Helaman 5:30)

"David! Don't Go!"

It was May 1, 1981. My son, David Apelinario Pacheco, attended school that day at the Pahoa High and Elementary. It was a special day for the Pahoa School because it's a tradition at this school to celebrate May Day. All the students would participate in Hula Hoolaulea, a day of dances, songs, and celebration. It was David's duty to set up the P.A. system for the school program. There were about five of his friends helping to do this and they wanted to leave the school and do something together after the work was done. One of the friends came to David, and said, "Come on, boys, let's go for a ride."

All of the other boys got into the truck, but as David started to get into the truck a voice said to him, "David! Don't Go!" It was a soft voice and David looked around to see who was calling him.

"David! Don't Go!" The voice said a second time. David turned and listened.

"David! Don't Go!" The voice said louder. It had repeated three times, from soft to louder. David got out of the truck and went back toward the gym. The boys started to yell at him while he was listening for the voice, and trying to learn where it was coming from. He felt he should listen.

David called back to his friends. "Go on," he said. "I forgot something I need to do."

The boys drove off without him.

About an hour later, David heard a siren coming from the Hilo side of the school, up toward the rubbish dump. The truck his friends had been in, the truck in which he was supposed to go for a ride, had been in a bad accident. Three of the boys jumped out of the truck before it turned over, but his best friend was hurt so badly that the rescuers got a helicopter to fly him from Big Island to Queen's Hospital in Honolulu. His friend had a broken leg and injuries so serious that he would never be able to father children. He would need to take medications for the rest of his life.

David is thankful to this day that he was obedient to the voice that came out of nowhere, and saved him from being in the accident. The Holy Ghost helped David to realize that Heavenly Father and Jesus Christ had other plans for him. He was not meant to be injured then. He was meant to begin preparing for a mission.

David served his mission in San Diego, California.

I love this gospel of Jesus Christ. My husband, David K. Pacheco, Jr., and our ohana (family) are an eternal family. We love Heavenly Father, Jesus Christ, and our special Pahoa Ward.

Submitted by Linda Pacheco
Pahoa, Hawaii

The Genesis of C.U.D.D.L.E

Sometimes when I am praying, my heart is so overwhelmed by the Holy Spirit that I pledge myself to be a vessel for Him, to do whatever He would have me do. I've learned that you must be careful when you do that; because He is listening, and takes our pledges seriously.

In the year 1999 God placed upon my heart His desire to reach children who have been abused and abandoned. He told me that there are many children in the world who have only heard His name used in a profane way. He wanted them to know that He loves them; in fact, that their names are written on His hands. (Is. 49:16)

For the next few months, I tried to reason with Him, I told Him I lived in an obscure town in the middle of nowhere; I ran a business that took all my time, (like He didn't know that.)

I had at that time owned and run a flower shop for about nineteen years. I thought I knew everyone in town. I was not aware of any children like He had told me about. And anyway, what could I do to teach those children? How could I reach them?

I'm sure you are thinking that it was presumptuous of me to argue with the Lord. You would be right. But really I didn't know where or how to begin; He wasn't forthcoming with that part of it either. He kept repeating what He wanted; not a word about how I was to go about doing it.

Then one day a light came on in my mind. I knew what I could do. "If I find a way to do this, how will I reach all the children who need to know that you truly are a real and loving God?"

I should have asked in the first place, instead of arguing and trying to convince Him there was no way I could do what he was asking. His answer was so sweet and simple: "Give them a quilt of their own with My Name on it telling them I Love them. How hard is that?" I agreed to make five of these quilts, but I assured Him that no one would take the quilts. And so it began.

I called women from my church and asked them if they would help me tie five quilts, which would be given to abused children. It then dawned on me I didn't know how I was going to get the message on the quilt. If I wrote it on, washing would fade the letters away. I like to do cross-stitch so I decided to do that on the back of each one. We agreed to tie the quilts in two weeks. I came up with the size of letters that seemed appropriate, and began. By the end of the fourth night I had picked the lettering of the first word, "JESUS," out five times; it was crooked every time I did it. How was I going to do this? Frustration was setting in. This was not simple—the message was—but the work was not going to be.

I realized it would take forever to do this by hand. I complained to a friend who promptly told me I was going about it all wrong. The quilts should be embroidered on a machine, then they would all be the same, and done so much faster. Why hadn't I thought of that?

The problem was, I didn't have one of these machines, and I didn't know a person who did. Where could I get one real quick? She had an answer for that also. One of the ladies at our church happened to have an "embroidery machine." My friend was sure that all I had to do was ask. I did. The "embroidery lady" had twenty questions that I had no answers for. This was getting harder and harder, but I had promised to do five quilts. I would persevere.

There was the question of color, the size of letters, and then what about a picture to match the front material. As we sorted through patterns, JoAnn became satisfied about what she felt I expected and away she went. Two days later she brought the finished pieces to my shop. They were beautiful. She had placed "JESUS LOVES YOU" in the upper left hand corner of each quilt, with a little picture that matched the front of the material. I cried.

On the appointed date the ladies came to my store and we tied five quilts with matching yarn. They were so pretty. One of the ladies asked if I had considered a Bible to go with the quilts. I hadn't, but said I would pray about that part. And then another lady said we ought to put in toiletries for the children because they are usually taken out of their homes with only the clothes they are wearing. I felt good about the quilts and now there were all these other ideas; and they were good ideas.

The quilts were done, but I didn't know who should receive them. I called a friend who works for the Police department. I asked if she knew of any foster children in our town. She laughed like I had asked a really dumb question.

Then she said "Yes, of course I do, Linda." I told her what I was doing, that I had five quilts made, and asked if she thought she could take the quilts to five children who needed them.

She got real excited. Then I told her what was on the back of them, and asked if that would be a problem. She said she didn't think so, and that I should bring them over the next day. I went to the book store and found Children Bibles that were perfect. One was a Toddler Bible with illustrated stories. The other was a Bible with cartoon pictures for the older kids, which would work with the quilts that had an older pattern on them. Then I picked up toiletries. A woman made wash cloth bags for the toiletries. I then decided we needed to put everything in a bag. I bought large bags for each set. They looked so cute and I felt really good about what we had done. I was euphoric.

All that evening, as I thought about the wording on the quilts, and the Bibles, I began worrying about what was really going to happen when I took them to the Police department the next day. I was sure there would be a problem with the 'church and state' thing, because of His name and the Bibles. When I arrived the next afternoon, Chotta wasn't there. I was told just to leave them and they would get them to her. All day long my heart thumped each time the phone rang; since I had a floral shop that was pretty often.

I would just know it was Chotta calling to say, "Linda, they are so cute, but there is a problem because of the "JESUS LOVES YOU," and the Bibles. She didn't call even by the next day. I got excited then and promptly thanked God for this wonderful opportunity to help some of His children. I told Him how repentant I was for doubting what He had wanted and promised to do more.

In my excitement, I ran out and bought more material, delivered it to JoAnn to be embroidered, and set a date for everyone to tie more quilts. The evening arrived. No one came to help. I thought up excuses for everyone and set another date, put it in the church bulletin, and waited for the day to arrive. No one came. This happened four times.

Now I began to question if I had really heard from God. Did I just think He had spoken to me? I became depressed and started adding up how much money I had spent and rationalized that I didn't have the funds to do this, and I didn't have the time. Maybe God hadn't really asked me to do this after all, because if He had it would have worked. All the excuses came back.

One Saturday evening, after closing the store, I sat on the floor behind one of the trees in the shop. I told the Lord how sorry I was that it hadn't worked. I gave Him all the excuses again. I felt so bad that it had failed. After my initial arguing, I truly had wanted the project to work. I wanted what He wanted—to reach the children and show them His love. I sobbed heart-felt tears for a long time.

Sunday morning I sat alone at church, feeling like I had let God down. I was desolate. During the announcements, a high school girl came forward. She told about a concert that was being given at the high school by 30 students. The year before they had raised $500 for the Breast Cancer Walk. They were hoping to raise $750 at this concert. And they had unanimously decided to give the donations to Linda's Quilts for Kids. I couldn't talk; tears streamed down my face. It was His work. He had heard my prayers.

The concert was to be in three days. There were no quilts made. I called the same women again. This time they came. The next day our pastor's wife called. She wondered if I had a name for what I was doing. I didn't. She said if I could think of one, a small poster could be made to go with the quilts, and I should have a mission statement.

All day I prayed. I asked, and begged Him to give me a name. The word I kept hearing was "cuddle." I continued asking for a name. Around 9:00 P.M. I finally said, "Father, this is your project, you have to give me a name for it." Once again I heard "cuddle." I said "That's great, that's what they will do with them, but I need a name." "Cuddle." I said "Ok! What does it mean?"

Very clearly I heard, "Children Under Duress Divinely Loved Everywhere!" I am learning to be humble, just not as fast as I need to. The poster was made, C.U.D.D.L.E. Outreach was done in crayon colors. We have a mission statement which He also gave us. The concert took place, but not many people knew about it; the attendance was poor. I left feeling sorrowful for the young people who had worked so hard to make it a success.

In fact, I felt so badly about it that I didn't open the shop that day. There was a knock on my door at home. When I opened it, there stood the young girl who had planned the concert. I took her hand and brought her into my house, telling her how sorry I was that it hadn't been a success, and how I appreciated her heart and help. She gave me a surprised look and handed me an envelope.

"Linda," she said, "this contains the money we raised last night: $800. People are calling for the CD. We will give you that money as well."

Remember Trust, Faith and Humility? I'm trying.

The very next day, I received requests for more quilts from Child Protective Services, the Highway Patrol, and the Police Dept. That was nearly three years ago. Since that time we have made and distributed 1,600 "Wellness Kits" to children who have been abused and abandoned.

We have three centers making the Kits, and are opening up three more this year. A friend who is an attorney set up the Foundation for us pro bono. We have a board of directors which meets once a month to review what we have done, and establish new goals. We have set a goal to cover the State of Arizona by the year 2006, with monthly distribution to each Child Protective Service and group home. That is what we aim for, however, I am listening to God, and waiting for His direction at every turn.

It doesn't always work, I get ahead of myself, but I am trying to slow down, watch, listen, and wait. We have wonderful stories from agents, foster parents, and from the kids themselves.

One fifteen-year-old girl buried her face in her quilt and wept. She asked the social worker if it really was hers to keep. When told that it was, she said, "I've never had a quilt for my very own."

A tiny four-year old would not let go of her quilt to take a bath. She was afraid the quilt would disappear. The foster mother folded it neatly, put it where the child could see, and reach it, then the girl got in the tub. She sleeps with it under her so no one can take it away while she is asleep.

One eight year-old boy was being taken 250 miles away to his foster parent home. He rode in the back seat of the social worker's car, holding his quilt, and reading his Bible all the way.

The work of God is done through us. He searches out those who will hear His message, and then follow through. I feel totally humble that He chose me to carry out one part of His important work. I love being a VESSEL for Him.

Submitted by Linda D. Dodds

Nothing Too Unusual About This Day

Nothing too unusual about this day . . . or so it seemed. I was a junior attending BYU during the mid-1970s. My last class for the day had just ended. It was fall. The air felt cold as I walked briskly, wanting to make it home before the sun set. In my rush, I made a quick decision to take a shortcut down a less traveled path. Ahead was a narrow street I needed to cross to continue this unfamiliar way home.

As I came closer to this narrow street, I noticed a light-colored Volkswagen drive slowly by. There was nothing unusual about this car, but a voice undeniably whispered to turn and walk away from the vehicle as quickly as I could. I immediately slowed my pace, but I did not stop. The car I was watching did stop. The car was now traveling in reverse. The window was being rolled down, exposing a young man with brown hair. It was obvious that he was about to say something to me.

Once more, I heard this familiar voice, "Leave now." This time I listened, and obeyed. My heart was racing. I purposely avoided eye contact with the stranger. I turned and walked as fast as the beating of my heart. I saw several students off in the distance. I pretended to know them and gave a big wave. I felt calmer now. I turned my head enough to see the light-colored car quickly leave the narrow street.

Later that night I shared the experience with my fiancé. He reassured me. Listening to that still, small, but powerful voice was the right thing to have done. We both tucked the experience away, and life moved on.

Not long after this, and for several years, a number of girls in that area were found slain or missing. Years passed, with murdered girls being found in other areas of the country. Finally, one day in another state, the man responsible for these crimes was caught, charged, and found guilty. He finally admitted to the murders. His name was Ted Bundy.

As my husband and I watched the story unfold, it was discovered that he drove a light colored Volkswagen, and seemed to be drawn to girls with long dark hair (which I had at that time.) My husband and I looked at each other in shock. I began to tremble inside. That very instant, the reality we both knew struck us; on that cold, brisk late afternoon, my life had been spared because I listened to the whisperings and promptings of the Spirit.

Submitted by Tanya D. Robinson

Get off the Train!

In September 2000 I escorted a group of students to the Edinburgh Festival of Arts in Scotland. At the end of the Festival, I took some time for myself, hosteling alone through Britain.

The trip to Edinburgh had been more hectic than I'd imagined. I was suffering with increasing chest pain. It was getting harder to breathe, and I found myself more frequently suffering spells of disorientation, and profound fatigue. These symptoms had been going on for some time. Medical tests from the previous year showed no organic cause for my health problems.

I have had a weak heart since birth. I thought my problems were perhaps due to this, and a combination of age, stress, and depression. While traveling with the students, and during the Festival I tried to cover up my condition to spare the students any concern. The stress was enormous. Now, it was over and they were safely on their way home.

I traveled to Exeter where I spent three days in that picturesque village. I intended to go on to Penzance but I had the impression that I should return to London. I really wanted to visit Penzance, but there were also things I wanted to see in London. I heeded the vague "feeling" and boarded an afternoon train for London. .

There was a lovely hostel there, near an area of the city known as King's Cross. It had excellent security. I could get a private room with a full English breakfast. I could relax, and hopefully my health would improve. I looked forward to staying there.

I enjoyed the train trip from Exeter through the British countryside, past the small towns and into the suburbs. Soon I was on the "underground" system of the city. Rush hour was just beginning, but luckily I had a seat. It was necessary to hold my luggage on my lap. At the "tube" stops I became increasingly uneasy. I had the feeling that I should get off the train. This seemed ridiculous. In an hour I would be resting at my hostel in King's Cross.

Still, with each stop, my unease grew. We were nearing an area of the city known as Earl's Court. There was a hostel there that I was familiar with, but it had little security, the rooms were cramped, and the sanitary conditions less than desirable. Still, the closer I came to Earl's Court, the stronger the feeling I should get off the train.

I wondered if my health had affected my brain. More and more people were boarding the rush hour train. The aisles were packed with standing-room-only commuters. The voice kept repeating, "Get off the train." I argued. King's Cross and the nice hostel were waiting just a bit beyond, only another half hour.

The Earl's Court stop was coming. The voice was now shouting, "Get Off The Train," but still I argued, "I don't want to get off here!"

The train was slowing. It was the Earl's Court stop. A crush of commuters waited to board. The inner voice continued, "Get off the train!" With great difficulty I grasped my suitcase, left my seat, and struggled through the crowded aisles to the exit.

Soon I was standing on the platform watching the train to King's Cross pull away and wondering, "What have I done?"

Toting my suitcase, I proceeded to the less desirable hostel. Chest pains stifled my breathing again. At the hostel, people at the front desk greeted me warmly. They said I was most fortunate, a single room had just become available.

In my room, I collapsed on the bed with a sense of overwhelming fatigue. The room had a television that I flipped on. In one of those moments that send chills up your spine, I learned that a massive power failure had just shut down much of the "underground," including trains to King's Cross. I would not have made it.

I spent the next three days in bed. At times the chest pains and fatigue became so overwhelming that I could barely rouse myself to get something to eat. The hostel staff were most helpful, allowing me to use the office refrigerator to store groceries from a nearby shop, so I wouldn't have to leave my room.

The breakdown of the "underground" system had thrown off their bookings. From the staff, and from the television news I learned that the system had been shut down for hours, some sections into the next day. Rescue workers had to remove people from the trains. A number of people, overcome by the crowded conditions, and lack of ventilated air, had to be taken to hospitals. Had I stayed on the train, I would have been one of those people.

I stayed at the hostel for a week, seeing only some museums and plays, spending most of my time in bed, before flying back to the United States. In the following year I was able to find doctors who discovered what was wrong with my body. I underwent major surgery that saved my life.

I do not claim to be a particularly spiritual person. I am not prone to inexplicable experiences. But, once in awhile, it seems to me that there are unseen spirits around, and I know Heavenly Father is looking after me. I will always be grateful that I heeded the warning to get off the train. I have a continuing testimony that He cares about me. I feel the warmth of His love.

Submitted by Joan Oviatt

Promises To Keep

"Before you make a promise, consider well its importance; once made, engrave it on your heart.

My family had come from Switzerland and settled in Star Valley, Wyoming, in 1885. They loved Star Valley; it seemed almost like home to them. They came because of the gospel. They had sorrows and joys. But they always felt blessed.

The incident I want to share concerns my father, Lawrence Weber. It was late October, just beginning to get a sharp nip in the air as the sun went down. My father had been out all day rounding up stray cattle and herding them towards the home fields. He was close to a creek in the ravine he had been following. The air got colder. He turned around to untie his jacket from the back of the saddle. This sudden movement startled a yearling calf which bolted from the willows.

The alert Indian pony Lawrence was riding sprang forward, almost unseating him. Rider and pony headed after the calf with a burst of speed. Unknown to the horse and rider, a barbed wire fence had been strung tightly along the creek, to act as a drift fence, heading off stray cattle.

In the gathering dusk the wire was invisible. The spirited pony plowed into it at an angle, ripping hide and flesh. The movement carried them forward, throwing Lawrence to the ground where he lay dazed.

The horse hobbled a few feet away from the fence and stood there quivering and bleeding. Lawrence never knew how long he lay sprawled unconscious on the ground. He finally opened his eyes and tried to sit up. A sharp pain shot through his right foot. Looking down, he saw blood spurting into his shoe, and there was a large blotch on the ground. Up to this point he had only felt numbness and surprise. But fear gripped him now as he realized his helplessness. He called out, "Help, help." But there was only the echo of his own voice in the hills. A wave of nausea swept over him, and he wanted to cry. He called out again for help. And then he blacked out.

From somewhere he heard his mother's voice saying, "You are not alone, son. The Lord is always near. Put your trust in him."

When he regained consciousness he was on his knees praying aloud; "Heavenly Father, if you will bless me at this time, so that I will not die, I will serve you all my life."

After the prayer, all fear and panic vanished. A wonderful faith was wrapped snugly about him. He looked at his ankle again, and to his surprise the blood had stopped spurting. He pulled himself up and began hopping toward his horse. In the remaining light he could see a gaping wound in his pony's shoulder and neck.

His new-found faith gave him the strength needed to pull himself across the saddle, onto his stomach. Using his elbows, and his voice, he urged the pony forward. The faithful animal stumbled on toward the ranch. They traveled at a snail's pace, choosing the easiest way, but always inching toward the ranch house.

About three hours later, the dogs set up a commotion in the yard. Uncle Fred had been uneasy about his brother's long absence. He hurried to the door and called out; "Who's there?" Then he heard Lawrence's voice; "Fred, I've been hurt!"

Fred ran out to the yard. He helped his brother off the horse, and carried him into the house. Fred's wife, Hazel, got hot water and began tending to Lawrence's wounds.

Fred led the pony into the barn, gave him water and made a bed of straw for him. Then he hitched his team to the surrey, and was off to Bedford to get Dr. Fink, who was a hardened old-timer, with little faith in that which he could not see, touch, or feel.

At the ranch house, Dr. Fink bent to his work. His examination showed that a large artery had been severed, but it was not spurting blood. Instead a thin watery substance mixed with air was being pumped out.

The doctor shouted out several profane words, stating that in all his career, he had never seen anything like it.

"That artery is supposed to have blood in it. What happened?"

Lawrence looked up at the doctor and said, "The Lord stopped the blood flow when I asked for help."

Dr. Fink mumbled something about 'perfect nonsense' as he fumbled in his bag for anesthesia. Lawrence told him that he did not want anesthesia because it might take away the wonderful feeling that had come over him when he prayed, and it was still with him.

"Please," he said, "just go ahead and sew it up." The doctor shook his head as if to say, "I will never understand you Mormons."

He proceeded to do the repair work while Lawrence lay in a euphoric state, conversing with his brother, and the doctor.

The pony was attended to, but she did not recover.

After the doctor had gone, Lawrence shared the experience of his mother coming to him; assuring him that he was not alone. "Have courage and trust in the Lord."

Fred said, "That sounds like Mother. She repeated those words to us so often when she was alive."

The Rest of the Story

In a few years, Leone Barrus came into Lawrence's life. They married in the Logan, Temple. They began having children two years apart. Then one day a letter arrived for Lawrence from Salt Lake City. It was a call to fill a mission in California.

There was sadness and joy in the Weber family that night. Joy because of Lawrence being called to serve as a missionary, and sadness because this meant two years away from his family.

Lawrence told Leone, "I can't say no, because of the promise I made to the Lord when he saved my life."

"Of course you cannot say no," his wife agreed. "I will manage somehow."

This was the first real test to see if Lawrence would keep his promise. It would have been so much easier to serve a mission before he was married. But this was evidently not part of the Lord's plan.

On a cold day, 16 January 1927, Lawrence kissed his wife, and three children; Sterling, six; Rex, four; and Nola, who was two, good-bye. Arriving in his mission area he plunged in with all his heart to do the work.

At home, Leone, did all that was possible to support her husband, and care for her little family.

"We must have been really poor; I don't remember. I only remember that mother loved us, and that we prayed morning and night for our father, who was doing the Lord's work in a far away place.

Submitted by Nola Weber Sears

The Story Of A Tie Clip

One day in 1994 while serving at the temple, I learned that I would have the opportunity to officiate at a session with a group who were coming directly from Siberia. I was not told whether anyone in the group spoke English. The witness couple was part of the Siberian group.

A couple knelt at the altar. The spirit whispered to me, "Give this good brother your tie clip."

"What? My tie clip?"

I thought this a very strange request or suggestion or whatever it was. But the prompting was clear. Each time this couple came to the altar, the prompting was repeated.

After the session was over and my duties fulfilled, I hurried to the Celestial Room to see if the couple was there. I had in mind the idea that if the prompting truly came from the Spirit, the couple would be there.

Sure enough they were. I went to the brother, removed my tie clasp, and offered it to him. He did not understand English, but his wife did. I explained to her that I wanted him to have this gift. The man beamed. He nodded his head with a smile. He stood up and shook my hand. I was perplexed about the incident, but felt that I had done the right thing.

The Rest Of The Story

About six months later a brother in the temple started a conversation by admiring my tie clip (which I had replaced with a similar one).

He then told me that one day he was assigned to welcome people in the foyer; a group of people came in who were from Siberia. A man in the group saw a tie clip like mine and wanted to purchase one. There was no time to go to the gift shop before the session began. It would be closed by the time they finished. He was disappointed but left to attend his temple assignment.

Why was it so important for this man to receive my tie clip? I doubt that I shall ever know. I have fantasized that somewhere in Russia there is a man wearing it. People admire it and say to him, "What a nice tie clip. Tell me about it."

The man replies, "Thank you. It represents a sacred building in the United States of America. It is called a temple. A temple is a place where people can go and be sealed as husband and wife; and children to parents, for time and all eternity; and where we can be baptized by proxy for our kindred dead."

Perhaps my little tie clip has become a great missionary tool.

Submitted by Jack Mills

Get Up! Get Out of Bed!

The story begins when I was returning from a trip to Hawaii. I worked for United Airlines, and was traveling first class. I met Gail Anderson, who worked in the office at United, and her husband, who was a doctor. I had not met him before. They were not members of the Church. I gave him a Book of Mormon and told him the Joseph Smith story. Gail only worked part time so I did not often see her. I talked to both of them about the Church. They seemed quite interested in what I told them.

My husband, Bill, and I were living in Portland, Oregon. Shortly after this encounter with the Andersons, United Airlines transferred me to Seattle. We decided to keep our larger home in Portland, and buy a small Condo for me in Seattle. This meant that my husband and I would be separated during the week.

However, we kept a car at both airports, and when our jobs permitted, we flew back and forth to be with each other. We always managed to spend Sundays together. I worked the late shift on Saturday nights, and was tired Sunday mornings. We usually attended church services at 1:00 PM, which allowed me to sleep later.

On this particular Sunday, Bill arrived at 7:30 AM. He came into the bedroom and said, "Nola, For some reason, I feel like we should go to the early morning services."

I was annoyed because he had awakened me, and especially annoyed that he wanted to attend the 9:00 AM services. I said "No way. Forget it. I worked late. I'm tired. I'm going back to sleep." I buried my head in my pillow, and closed my eyes.

As soon as he left the room my conscience began setting up a clamor. I was wide awake. Usually, I can go right back to sleep. I tried, but my mind was too alert.

Get up, the Spirit said. *Get out of bed.* I had the thought that my husband came all the way from Portland to be with me. All he asked was for me to attend an earlier service. There must be a reason.

I got out of bed, but I was still cranky. "All right," I called to him, "I'll get ready."

It was testimony meeting in Relief Society that day. We did not attend that ward very often, so I did not know many people. A young woman I had never seen stood up to bear her testimony. She had barely started when she burst into tears. She and her husband had been married several years. They wanted a family, but had been unable to start one.

During the previous week she had been to the doctor. After a number of tests it was determined that she could not bear children. She said that was the worst news she could have ever had. I wept with her. Other women were also crying.

After the meeting I went up to her and put my arms around her. "It may not be possible for you to bear children naturally, but have you and your husband considered adoption?"

"Oh, yes," she said. "We have looked into it. But the process is so long. And it is very costly."

I encouraged her to pray about it. "If you are willing, and you want a family, the Lord will bless you with a child," I said.

She hugged me and we parted. On Tuesday, I went to work. Gail Anderson, the woman I had met on the plane, came over to me.

"Nola," she said. "You are the only Mormon my husband knows, besides a nurse who works at the hospital. Last week, a patient of his who is only fifteen, came with her mother to see him. The girl is pregnant. She has decided that she is too young to handle the responsibility of being a mother. She will not have an abortion. But she and her mother have decided that the only people they will consider as adoptive parents are "card carrying" Mormons. I don't know what that means. Maybe you do."

I smiled and said that I did know what it meant. "Look no further," I said. "I know where that baby is supposed to go." I then told her about the young woman I had met on Sunday.

"Oh," she said. "It is not that simple. According to law, my husband must have the resumes of three couples. The young woman will decide from the resumes who shall have the baby. Her one firm criteria is that the couple must be 'card carrying' Mormons who will give the baby a good home. My husband knows this nurse who has one child but cannot have any others. Do you know another good Mormon couple who want to adopt a baby?"

"Well, I know a wonderful couple in Seattle who have two children. She has had to have a hysterectomy. They want very much to have other children, but the adoption agencies won't take an application because they already have children. I can call and tell them of this child and ask them to send a resume"

"Would you do that? My husband must have three."

I answered that I could do it, and I would. "But I don't want to. I know that child is supposed to go to the young woman I told you about." I couldn't tell her, but the second I heard abut the baby, the Spirit spoke to me and said, "Now you know why you were supposed to go to the earlier church meeting."

"Do you know anything about this young woman?" Gail asked.

"No," I said. "But I will find out, and have her get a resume to your husband."

I called the bishop's wife as soon as I got home. I told her why I was calling and asked if she knew the woman who had borne her testimony the Sunday before.

"Do I know her! Those two people are probably the choicest young couple in our entire ward. They are both returned missionaries. They come from wonderful families. He is one of thirteen siblings. She has five or six siblings. I can highly recommend them."

I got the name of the young woman, and her telephone number. I called and told her who I was and related the situation.

She was so excited she could hardly talk.

I told her not to get her hopes up because the doctor needed three resumes and the young mother would choose between them. She was thrilled to even have a chance to do this. "We will get it done and send it right in," she said.

Every day that Gail was there, I would go see her and ask how the adoption process was going. She did not give me any encouragement.

"We have two in, and are waiting for the third," she said.

Three weeks went by before the morning that Gail came to my desk. She looked so sad.

"All the resumes are in. I am sorry to tell you this because you seemed so sure you were right . . ." My heart fell right into my shoes and nearly stopped beating. Then Gail smiled, "You were right. As soon as the young woman read that resume, she said, "This is the couple. I know they will be good parents for my child."

The Rest of the Story

About two months later we went to the testimony meeting where the baby was going to blessed. The entire family, all the siblings and their families, had come from Othello, Washington, to be there when the baby was blessed. There was hardly room on the stand for all the priesthood members.

During testimony meeting the maternal grandmother stood up. Tears streamed down her face as she said how much all of them loved, and appreciated the young mother who had given up her child so that she could be raised in a good Mormon home. We will give thanks to her all our lives for this wonderful blessing. She also thanked me. Which I wish she had not done. I was only following directions from the Spirit.

Submitted by Nola Sears

Help That Woman!

I was feeling pretty sorry for myself, caught up in my work-day world and wondering if I was doing anybody any good. Maybe a lot of us have these feelings from time to time.

I was in a hurry to get to work that morning. I lived in the Avenues district of Salt Lake City, about a mile from my work place downtown, so I generally walked to work. Walking at a brisk pace gave me exercise and helped build up energy for the day. That particular day was bright with springtime sunshine.

I turned off South Temple onto State Street; there were two more blocks to go. The street was busy with morning traffic, pedestrians, and tourists. I went past the old Alta Club, and was going past the Hansen Planetarium when I noticed an elderly woman standing in front, looking up at the building. There was nothing especially remarkable about her, nothing to attract my attention, just a strange feeling when I passed her. I slowed my pace but kept going. The feeling persisted. I walked a bit farther, stopped, and looked back.

The woman was still standing there, only now she was facing the other way, looking toward the ZCMI Center building. I continued on and got almost to the end of the block when I stopped again and looked back. I felt there was something wrong. An instinct, an impression, and an inner voice saying, "Go back and help that woman."

I argued with myself. There were lots of people about, why should I notice her? If the woman needed help, she'd ask somebody. She didn't look like she needed help. If I approached and asked if I could help, she'd surely think I was crazy. Plus, I was only a block from my work place. I didn't want to lose time by going all the way back up the street.

The woman began walking slowly in my direction.

"Help that woman," was repeated in my mind.

I decided that if she thought I was crazy, too bad; at least I wouldn't be wondering all day about some silly impression.

I turned and walked back up the block. When I got to the woman she had again stopped and was looking toward the ZCMI Center.

"Can I help you?" I asked.

She turned to me and, and with eyes glazing over said, "Do you think if I go stand on the corner a policeman will find me?"

A strange feeling washed over me. "Where did you come from?" I asked.

She said she was from Salt Lake City, but couldn't remember how she got where she was.

"Do you know where you are?"

She looked back at the Planetarium and said that it was the City Library on State Street, then she looked back across the street and said those buildings didn't look right.

As a historian, I knew that the Planetarium had once been the City Library--decades before. I wondered if the woman had lost her short-term memory, if she had Alzheimer's Disease.

She said she was scared and began to cry. I put my arm around her and told her we'd find her home. We walked back up to a phone booth in front of the Planetarium where I telephoned the police. They asked me to stay there with the woman. They suspected she was the patient they had been looking for, an Alzheimer's patient who'd walked away from her care facility. They asked me to stay by the phone while they contacted the facility. A woman called me back on the pay phone. Together we were able to establish the patient's identity. She had been missing for hours, and had walked several miles.

I stayed with her until a cab arrived for her. She was afraid to get in a car with a strange man, but I assured her it would be all right. The man was going to take her home.

I do not know if the lost woman had family praying for her to find her way back, or if I had people praying for me to find my way in life.

I continued on to work with the thought that stays with me today; Heavenly Father guides our feet on life's pathways, for the good of others, as well as ourselves; if we pay attention, and allow him.

Submitted by Joan Oviatt

The Spider

Though I was born of goodly parents, and raised in the Church, It was not until I was in my forties that I experienced that "mighty change of heart" spoken of by Alma. It was through constant and daily teaching by the Spirit that I gained a firm testimony of the Savior and his love for me.

I would like to share one of those special teachings. I recorded this in the fall of 1978, in Kansas City, Kansas.

We lived in a house in the woods. It was a crisp and cool autumn day. The sky was a vivid blue that one sees only during that time of the year. There was the barest hint of a chill breeze coming off the lake across the road.

The dogwood, maple, and redbud trees had given up most of their beautiful foliage. Leaves lay almost knee-deep on the ground. Squirrel shadows ran silently over the carpet of leaves as they frolicked along the nearly bare branches of trees. My little white dog bounded happily through the leaves in hot pursuit of phantom squirrels on the ground.

It was a beautiful world. Feelings so tender they were almost painful filled my being. My heart was warm with appreciation for all nature; it's majesty and miracles. Love for the Creator of it all warmed my soul.

There on my hillside acres, raking leaves was a joy. Mostly the mechanics were simple; pushing them down to the bottom of the slope where they would evolve into compost and become nourishment another year for the same trees.

As the rake swept away a swath of leaves, my eyes caught the iridescent gleam of a beautiful little spider. It was scurrying away in panic because of the catastrophe that had destroyed its small world.

I do not normally enjoy things that creep and crawl, but feelings of love and empathy welled up from deep inside of me. My bones seemed to be melting with the intensity of my feelings.

As I watched, the spider stopped abruptly, paused for a second or two, and then turned and started directly toward me. I waited, mesmerized, until the spider came right up to my shoe. I had no doubt that his intent was to climb on my shoe.

Courage to wait and see what might happen next failed me. At the last moment, I stepped over and behind him. He stopped, turned, and again came toward me.

The little spider and I played this scenario over and over. Each time the spider seemed determined to climb onto my shoe. But what then? I did not have the courage to find out. I hadn't a clue whether the spider was poisonous or harmless.

I contemplated the situation. I wondered why such a thing was taking place.

It happened then that a still small voice whispered, "You are feeling charity, or the pure love of Christ. All nature responds to it."

I was left with the distinct impression that this is part of the power by which "worlds, and all things that in them are" was created.

I am deeply grateful for that experience. I now have deep and tender feelings of appreciation for all of God's creations, and the Power that brought them into being.

Submitted by Marilyn Williams McBride

"You Shall Greatly Rejoice"

One of our favorite family scriptures is found in Alma 37:37; which begins with the admonition to "Counsel with the Lord in all thy doings, and he will direct thee for good."

In the Bible Dictionary under *revelation* we read: "Continuous revelation from God to his saints, through the Holy Ghost or other means; such as visions, dreams, or visitations; makes possible daily guidance along true paths, and leads the faithful soul to complete and eternal salvation in the celestial kingdom."

Because I hold dear this privilege of seeking daily help through the Spirit, I take a few minutes each morning to "check in" with my Father in Heaven and listen to see if he has some specific instruction for me. One morning I simply heard the words in my mind say, "You shall greatly rejoice in the events which will follow this day." The sentiment was repeated a second time with slightly different wording. "You shall joy in that which shall follow." Curious about what I had just heard, I simply wrote these thoughts down in my journal.

The first event that fulfilled these impressions came when I received a letter from the University of Utah. My son was a freshman and, though a great student, had not initially qualified for a scholarship. It was now time to register for Winter quarter.

Following his graduation from High School I had received an impression to ask him if he would like to begin his studies that summer instead of waiting until Fall Quarter. After discussing the matter with my husband and our son, we each had a confirmation by the Spirit that he should begin his university studies that Summer rather than work full time, though funds were tight.

The letter from the University of Utah offered my son a four-year scholarship, tuition free. They had a few unclaimed scholarships that they offered to freshman students who had attended Summer quarter and did well in their courses. The scholarship not only covered the next quarter's tuition and every quarter through graduation but included reimbursement for Fall's tuition. Had my son decided to work full-time during the summer to save more money for tuition, he would not have qualified for the scholarship.

This was not the only joyful event of the day. My oldest daughter, who had recently married, called to announce she was expecting.

She met her husband during her second semester at BYU. I recalled the day they met. She had asked me to come and bring her home for the weekend. We lived only forty miles to the North. I was about to leave to make the trip when I had a sudden feeling that I should not go. I questioned the impression, wondering if I was just weary, so I asked my son to make the drive. He willingly agreed.

The strong feeling not to bring her home intensified. I called my daughter and told her that I had received several strong impressions that she should not come home that weekend. I joked saying, "Perhaps you are going to have a social experience that you need to remain there for." She was obedient to my request.

That evening a young woman in her dorm asked my daughter to accompany her to an open house in one of the young men's dorms. She had never approached my daughter before to do something on a social basis. She knew a young man in the dorms from her home town in California who had just returned from his mission. She hoped to rekindle the relationship.

When my daughter walked into the room, she had a strong impression that she would certainly get to know this young man better. Seven months later they were married in the Jordan River Temple.

Her husband had returned one month early from his mission because he had developed testicular cancer and the surgery could not wait. His hair was just growing back from the effects of chemotherapy when they met. When he asked her to marry him, he shared the fact that he likely could not be a father by natural means. The Spirit whispered to her that this was not to be a concern and then she recalled an interesting phrase in her Patriarchal blessing which stated, "You will be led to a young man who will feel it an honor to become a partner with you in the greatest creation that is available here upon the earth."

She had a quiet assurance that the sweet promise could and would be fulfilled with this young man. Her phone call came only three months after their marriage. They now have three beautiful children.

What made that day so joyful was not just receiving financial blessings, and news of an expected grandchild; but these events confirmed earlier impressions that we had been guided by the Spirit when my son attended summer school, and when my daughter stayed at school instead of coming home for the weekend. I am so grateful for the blessing of seeking and receiving guidance from the Lord in my day to day affairs.

Submitted by Vicki Jo Robinson

Visions and Dreams

The initial text of Mormonism was precisely that which formed the basis of Peter's colossal sermon on the day of Pentecost.

"And it shall come to pass in the last days, saith God, I will pour out my spirit upon all flesh; And your sons and daughters shall prophesy, And your young men shall dream dreams, and on my servants and on my handmaidens I will pour out in those days of my spirit; and they shall prophesy."

The Gospel of a new dispensation came to America by the administration of angels. But let it not be thought that Joseph Smith alone saw angels. Multitudes received angelic visits in the early days of the Church. Thousands spoke in tongues, and prophesied. Visions, dreams and miracles were manifested daily among the disciples. The sisters were as familiar with angelic visitors as the Apostles. Their individual Pentecost of spiritual gifts were of frequent occurrence.

(Women of Mormondom, pages 21 & 22, published in 1877)

On A Scale of One to Ten?

A dream that taught me an important perspective occurred during the time I was serving as a counselor in the Stake Relief Society. In the dream, I was preparing for an upcoming Stake gathering and my portion in it. I was working hard trying to prepare a fancy border for my poster. Everything I tried failed. I worked even harder to make something beautiful, but the border only got more messy looking. Finally, in frustration, I tore off the border. I concentrated instead on three essential gospel points written on the poster. I was flooded with the spirit. The dream ended.

During the Stake presentation, my greater focus was upon the points of doctrine I would teach, not on the fancy borders. Since that time, I have taught many classes and courses. While serving as president of an auxiliary organization, I knew some attention must be given to decorations and mementos; but recalling my dream, I tried to place greater emphasis upon seeking to know what it was the Lord wanted taught and emphasized.

Teaching the gospel has been a large part of my service in the Lord's kingdom—one of the great joys of my life. It has never felt like a burden. Truly his yoke is easy and his burden is light. The Lord doesn't over-program me, but I can over-program myself by a desire to be impressive. The Spirit will not only tell us what to do, but can also whisper to us what is not expedient.

One of the most important dreams I recall taught me the importance of perspective in relation to the efforts I would expend in rearing my children. In this dream I had gathered my little ones and taken them to a beach. When we arrived we could see a mother with her children on the shore. She was making them a most exquisite sand castle.

The woman was first forming a wall around this castle. She formed each brick with such skill, I was amazed. She even had wonderful tools to accomplish this. I felt inadequate as a mother, as I watched this talented woman create her masterpiece.

But then, my attention was diverted to the water. I noticed that the tide was coming in. It was not an ordinary tide, it was more like a tidal wave. I quickly took my children to a safe place.

I looked around to watch the efforts of the other mother wash away.

She had never reached a point where she was actually constructing the castle itself. I awoke with a strong feeling that there are many things we can do with our children. We can take hours to make sure our children have the most impressive birthday parties, holiday experiences, etc., and record them in impressive scrapbooks.

But if we never get the time to teach them vital principles of the gospel, the Signs of the Times, what it feels like to have the Spirit, and what principles of the gospel bring us that great privilege, we are expending efforts solely upon the outer fences. If we never get to the actual castle and make it of a more enduring substance—which is to teach them of Christ, our Rock and our Redeemer—all these efforts will leave us with nothing as the tide washes away our sand castles.

Our children have very simple scrapbooks. We have not had many fancy vacations. But there isn't a day we don't gather and discuss the gospel.

Submitted by Vicki Jo Robinson

Listen and Follow Through

I was married to my first wife, Gladys Clark, when she was eighteen years old. We had three boys, two and three years apart. We were happily married. When Gladys was twenty-six years old she was struck with a sudden illness which doctors could not diagnose, or cure.

As she grew weaker and it seemed that I would lose my beloved sweetheart, I clung to her. I fasted and prayed. I called upon members of the priesthood to help in anointing and blessing her, that she might rally and live, for her family loved and needed her.

After several days some of my priesthood brethren talked with me about the blessings. They seemed to feel that she wanted to go, and it might be her time. Perhaps she had fulfilled all that she was required to do on earth. If God was calling her home, then my fasting and prayers, and the anointings were holding her back. Perhaps I was interfering with God's eternal purpose. They suggested that I should let the Holy Spirit work through me. If it was the Lord's wish, then I must release her to Him.

This I did after more fasting and prayers. Finally, I was able to lay my hands upon her dear head, and release her if this was God's will.

She smiled up at me, closed her eyes, and on a perfect April day her spirit abandoned her young body.

Six months later, I married Florence Gorringe.

In February 1921 my youngest son, Clark, became very sick. The doctor diagnosed his illness as Brights disease, and said he could not get well. Clark spent most of his days in bed. On Sunday June 19th, I had just come home from Sunday School, and Clark was lying on the couch in the living room. He looked so thin, so tired and sad. I knelt down beside him and asked what I could do for him.

"Please, pray for me," were his words. I began the prayer. As I did so I thought of my recent experience, of having been told by the brethren that I was holding the child's mother back when she seemed to be wanted on the other side. I did not want to repeat this error.

I told the Lord that if Clark's mission was complete I did not want to hold him. But if it was His will that Clark could be spared, we desired to raise him to manhood.

When the prayer was finished Clark asked if he could be taken to his bedroom. He wanted to lie in his bed. This I did, propping him up with pillows in a semi-sitting position. I sat down beside him.

Suddenly, his eyes brightened and a smile came over his face. He held his hands up, pointing over my head, "Mama. Oh, Mama," he said.

I called Florence, although I was sure it was not she he was calling. She came into the room. I said to her, "He is calling for you, mother."

He turned his head, looked at her, and said, "No, not you." Then he looked in the same direction as before; smiled, and called "mama" again.

"Where is mama, son?" I asked. "She's out on the porch, now," he replied.

Then he relaxed and lay back against the pillows. "I've got to go," he said.

He closed his eyes, sighed several times, and joined his mother in the spirit world. It was a lovely June day. He had just passed his third birthday. I could not be sad that the dear sick child was now with his mother. She had known his spirit was leaving its earthly home. She was there to take his hand and show him the way to Paradise.

In November of that same year, my mother went to Sunday School as usual to teach her class. The building was cold, and she became chilled. Four days later she was dead of pneumonia. She had been a wonderful mother. Being without her presence caused all members of her family to realize what a good woman she had truly been.

Six months later my brother Royal came to me and said that our mother had visited him during the night. She told him that his mission in life was finished. He must make preparations for he would soon be called to leave. He said he recalled her saying the number five.

He did not know if he would be taken in five weeks, months, or years. He hoped it would be years as he had a young family, and could not bear the thought of leaving them alone. He also expressed to me that Julia and the children had no way to get on in life without him.

When the crops matured and were sold that year, he said he would buy as much life insurance as he could afford for the protection of his family.

Royal was different after that. Usually he went about his work whistling and singing. He became quieter and more introspective. He did not tell his wife, Julia, about Mother's visit. He did not want to lay the burden of knowing about this dream on her.

On the exact day of his dream, five months later, Royal died. He had gone up the canyon to bring down wood which would be cut for the winter fires. The wagon was loaded and he climbed on. As they went down the hill, the wagon brake slipped off the wheel, allowing the wagon to push against the horses. They began to run. Royal tried to get the brake back into position, but by then it was too late. He saw disaster coming and jumped from the wagon. As he fell, he was thrown against the brake lever and it pierced his side. Many bones were broken when he was thrown to the ground by the speeding wagon.

We ran to him and saw that he was in a pitiful condition. We sent a man on a fast horse for the doctor. Royal was chilling from loss of blood. We covered him with our coats. When the doctor arrived he gave no hope. We put him in the doctor's carriage. I sat with his head in my lap. He died before we reached Oakley.

When we arrived at my home, we found many neighbors gathered there who had heard of the accident. The Stake President was there. We called Frank Lynch's farm.

He lived only one and a half miles from Royal's home. I asked him to go and tell Julia that her husband had been injured and we were bringing him home.

The morning we left to get the wood, Julia had pleaded with her husband not to go. She had not been told of the dream, but she had a strong premonition that something adverse would happen that day.

Mr. Linley went to Julia's home and knocked on the door. She opened the door. Before he could say a word she burst into tears.

"Oh, Mr. Lynch, its just horrible. I can't stand it." She had heard nothing, but her premonition was so strong that she knew what had happened.

The Rest of the Story

Julia was thirty-five years old when her husband died. She never went back to the farm after his death. Royal had not bought the life insurance that would have helped provide for his family. Julia had no schooling or training. She was ill-prepared to support a six-year-old boy, and a four-year-old girl. She returned to Salt Lake City where some members of her family lived. She got a job clerking at ZCMI. She worked six days a week, for very little money, until she retired.

Her son, Burton Horne Price, graduated from the LDS Business College. He has held many authoritative positions in the Church. Dorothy Price graduated from the LDS Secretarial School. She received her practical training as secretary working for several prestigious law firms. She was paid $1.25 week. This was enough for her trolley fare and a 5 cent sandwich for lunch. She also worked many years for Dr. Homer Warner at the LDS Hospital. She has been called to serve in many different capacities in the Church, including that of ward Relief Society president twice.

When Julia retired she went to live with her daughter, Dorothy, and her son-in-law, Byron Baker Robinson, until her death twenty-five years later.

Submitted by Dorothy Price Robinson

Inspiration From The Other Side

Loved ones we have lost through death have not forgotten us, just as we never forget them. I am sharing one of many experiences I have had since the passing of first my mother, who lived with me and my husband, Clarence, for more than six years before her death; and then my husband, who died in January of 1993.

We were close in life, and now we are close in death.

Barbara, my husband's sister, had supplemented her family income by doing dried flower arrangements at home while her children were in school. By profession she was an Interior Designer. In 1975, when the children were older, she went back to work as a decorator. This meant that she no longer had time to work with dried flowers. She asked my husband and me if we wanted to take her inventory and work up a part-time business for ourselves.

I was only an amateur flower arranger. I also worked full-time, but we decided to try it. We had to rent a garage close to where we lived for storing the merchandise. I then began trying to make more professional arrangements. I made some perfect 'lemons' to start with.

As I gained more expertise, I began finding markets for my work. I sold some in grocery stores, and to friends who requested certain colors which matched the decor of their homes. I rented a booth in a boutique, and began selling things there. This went on for nearly twenty years. Clarence also helped with the business; painting and antiquing containers, doing the marketing, and keeping the books.

I had added to the inventory that Barbara gave us until we had two storage rooms full, besides the garage. It was never a lucrative endeavor. It was mainly an expensive, and exhausting hobby.

Clarence was a retired geologist. During the 1950s, and into the 1970s, he worked as a consulting geologist for different companies. Wearing his black head-light he went down into various caves in Southern Utah, searching for veins of ore.

In late 1992, he began to have worrisome health symptoms. He went to the University of Utah where he was diagnosed with uranium poisoning. His liver was almost completely destroyed by the time he went there.

He lived only a few months after the diagnosis, dying at home in January 1993.

A few months after Clarence's funeral, I sat down and began working on small tea cup flower arrangements. I was tired and very discouraged. I said to myself, "Why am I doing this? I'll never sell them."

Immediately I heard Clarence say, "Yes, you will. Don't give up."

The sound of his voice gave me heart. I kept trying. Many unusual breaks came my way. One morning, just before I woke, I heard beautiful piano music. The composition was 'Families Can Be Together Forever.' Clarence's grandchildren had sung this at his funeral. The music continued to play. I had never heard anything so exquisite.

I saw as in a dream, my husband leaning over me at the edge of the bed. I immediately awoke. I looked at the clock. I had overslept ten minutes.

On the way to work, rushing to make up lost minutes, I saw my lawyer. I had not seen her since the death of my husband ten months before. She asked if I still did flower arranging. I said yes. She ordered one of the large fireplace baskets that she had seen in my home. I then knew why Clarence had stood over me that morning: to wake me in time to meet this future customer.

To my delight she wanted the arrangement in the same colors I had recently bought, which meant I needn't add to my inventory. What I wanted to do was get rid of everything, not buy more. Through her I was able to sell 25 large fireplace baskets. These orders allowed me to clean out the garage we had rented; one more monthly expense that I need not worry about.

Now, what I had left were two large storage rooms filled with dried flowers, baskets, vases, styrofoam, paint, etc.

'Liquidate' was a word that continually came into my mind.

I was bothered that I had all that 'stuff,' and no time for doing anything profitable with it. One morning, just before I woke, I was dreaming of my dilemma. I repeated over and over, "It is too much. I can't get anything done." My mother, who had died nine years before, appeared to me.

"Don't worry. I'll help you," she said in her sweet voice. I awoke with the dream fresh in my mind as I got ready for work.

I didn't usually talk to people at work about my personal problems; but that morning I told Joyce, a co-worker, about the pressure I was under, wondering out loud what I could do to get out from under it.

She said that she was going to take some things to the "swap-meet" on Saturday. She offered to take my things along and try to sell them. She brought a large van and packed it with everything I had. The storage rooms were empty.

Joyce did not sell everything. What was left she stored in her basement and said she would try to sell it at other 'swap-meets." I was profoundly relieved. I was free of the burden that had weighed me down for months.

I told Joyce that whatever she sold, I wanted her to keep the money. She had recently been involved in a car accident which left her unable to do computer work.

I know it was not my imagination when I heard that heavenly

music; what a wondrous "wake up" call the piano music was. How my husband managed it, I may one day know. It worked.

I know I heard my husband's voice whisper, "Yes, you will!" in answer to my doubtful thoughts.

I can still hear my mother reassuring me that she would help.

I believe our departed loved ones look in on us from time to time. They are aware of our problems. They are angels who help us get through this earth life, which is filled with problems, and is seldom an easy ride.

Submitted by Marlene Felix

Get The Book! Get The Book."

Elder Lynn from Wyoming had worked in the Gallup, New Mexico area several years before. He gave a Book of Mormon to Pearl Davis who was a full-blooded Indian woman. She read the book and believed its contents. She had two sons who lived with her in a small two-room cabin. She owned a ranch about two miles outside the town.

One day when she was working on the ranch, her home caught fire. The neighbors went out to notify her. When she came home the fire was still smoldering. The Gallup fire department responded, but they were too late. All was gone.

Everyone gathered around her and expressed their sympathy. But she heard only one voice.

"Get the book. Get the book."

She broke away and walked down into the water, and the burned remnants of her home. She reached into the black water. From beneath a large timber she pulled out the Book of Mormon. It was scorched, but the title was still there, and the reading material was as good as ever it had been.

Shortly after this she had a dream of the Prophet Joseph Smith. He told her that the book was a true history of God's dealing with her ancestors. This added to the testimony she already had. She applied for baptism for herself, and her two sons.

The only place we could find for a baptismal service in that area was a pond at the site of a coal mine four miles outside Gallup. We contacted the owner and obtained permission to use the pond for our baptisms.

Along with Sister Davis and her sons, there were children of the Saints in the Branch, and a few new converts who needed baptism. In all there were about fifteen people.

About 60 persons from the Branch came to see the baptisms. We had a nice service. We had a song and prayer. Then Elder Bybee spoke to the congregation. I followed him with a few words. It was agreed that I would baptize the first group. Sister Davis and her family were going to be first. I went down into the water. Never in my life had I felt such cold water; it was like ice.

Then Sister Davis asked, "Elder Garn, may I bear my testimony before mankind?" I said yes, even though my legs were beginning to lose all feeling.

She related her experience of receiving the Book of Mormon several years before from Elder Lynn. She told of the dream she had when Joseph Smith appeared and testified himself of the truthfulness of the book. She then pulled her own book from under her dress, and held it up so all could see.

"This book has gone through fire for me. Now I feel that I can go through fire for it, and The Church of Jesus Christ of Latter-day Saints." She handed the book to her son and submitted to the baptism.

She became very active in the Church. She was 54 years old at the time.

Submitted by Stacy D. Garn

You Know This Guy

On Sunday, April 22, 2001, the (then) Deseret News, published a profile of Larry H. Miller, written by Doug Robinson. The story made a profound impact on me. Mr. Miller was so perfectly candid about his life; about his failures with relationships, about his work ethic, about his religion, about his enterprises. He is a larger than life person. Utah has been blessed because (I seriously believe) God brought him back from Colorado to the place of his original roots.

As I read the piece written by Mr. Robinson, I could clearly see where God was having a hand in dealing with one of His special sons. For this reason, I asked permission from Mr. Miller, and subsequently Mr. Rick Hall, of the (now) Deseret Morning News, to reprint some parts of Mr. Robinson's story for inclusion in this book.

(I should state that Doug Robinson and I are not related. I read everything he writes, and we exchange e-mails occasionally. The author)

In (Mr.) Miller's mind, any discussion of his meteoric rise in the business world must include his religious faith. Early in his married life he strayed from his Mormon roots. His re-conversion to the Church was a seven-year process, culminated by a late-night meeting in which he told his local church leaders there were three sticking points: a weakness for swearing, playing softball on Sunday, and paying tithing (donating ten percent of his earnings to the church). He vowed to change.

The next day he told Gail (his wife) "Starting with the next paycheck, pay ten percent tithing on my gross earnings, and I don't want you to ever talk to me about it again."

Six weeks later, Miller was summoned to a meeting with the owner of the dealership. (He was working for a car dealership in Denver, Colorado). (The owner) wanted to reassign Miller elsewhere so the owner could take over the car dealership operation, and work with his eight sons.

This was what he got for paying his tithing?

Miller decided to leave the company. He moved back to Salt Lake City and bought his first car dealership, drawing up the contract on a place mat in a restaurant. That day he came home and told Gail, "I just spent a million dollars." He had spent their entire savings, $88,000, as a down payment.

"I don't think anything scared me as much as that first dealership." says Gail.

Miller, whose dealerships sell 60,000 cars a year now, tells the tithing story for a reason.

"That was the beginning, absolutely," he says. "When I had that meeting (with his boss in Denver), it forced me out of a situation where I thought I would be indefinitely. There were forces at work that sent me back to Utah."

A few years later, Miller had a dream that he says was remarkable in its clarity. He was in a high-ceiling room with open skylights, and there was a knock at the door. He took a white package wrapped with white ribbon that lay on a table, and gave it to someone at the door.

Moments later, there was another knock. This time there were more white packages on the table. He took them to the person at the door. The scene repeated itself over and over. Each time he gave away a box he discovered it had been replaced by many more boxes on the table until eventually they filled the entire room.

"Where are they coming from?" he asked Gail. "The only thing I can figure is they're coming through the skylights."

Finished with this story, Miller lets it settle on his listener before concluding, "I have been so fortunate in my life, not just in material ways. So much so that I wonder, why me?"

The Gifts

(Perhaps the answer to Mr. Miller's dream lies in what he gives back from what he has been given.)

Over the years, his motivation for work beyond the car business is rooted in religion, philanthropy, and his interest in art, history, and community.

He spotted an old turn-of-the century fire station while out for a drive one day and embarked on a project to rebuild it at This Is The Place Heritage Park. He supervised the construction of Franklin Covey Field. He funded the building of BYU's new baseball field. He is funding and overseeing the construction of three buildings for Salt Lake Community College that will comprise the Larry H. Miller Entrepreneurship Center. He is working with artists on painting and sculpting projects. He donated funds to expand Rice-Eccles Stadium. He provides scholarships to the children of employees who graduate from high school with at least a C-average. He teaches a three-hour entrepreneurial course one night a week at BYU.

Then there is Larry H. Miller Charities, which has received as many as 30,000 requests in a single year for financial help for individuals and organizations. He is besieged with personal requests. He went to a dinner recently and was approached by more than 30 people who wanted something—("It's hard to know where to draw the line," Miller says. "You can't be all things to all people . . . I think of myself as a bridge builder. You have someone on this side and someone on the other side. Our job is to build that bridge and hope once we get them there, they will be able to establish themselves.")

"There are a lot of other things done that people don't know about, and neither do I," says Mr. Allred, who is president of Larry H. Miller Charities. "What we see is the tip of the iceberg. He doesn't like to talk about it."

Written by Doug Robinson
Senior Editor Deseret Morning News

The Missing Sheets

Mina Jensen Olsen Olds was born in 1894, the daughter of Danish converts to the Church.

In 1922 she was living in Ephraim, Utah, an active wife, and the mother of young children. Her parents, Hans and Annie Jensen, lived nearby. Mina recorded in her diary and autobiography: "In 1922, my mother had a hard time gathering her genealogy. The records had been burned. Mother (Annie) had worked so hard to get the names of her own mother's family. At last she had gotten four sheets back from Denmark and we were to do the temple work. It was so cold that winter; it had snowed where we lived so badly that we could not travel anywhere until Spring.

"Then the Asiatic Flu hit the town of Ephraim, and we all took it. In my family we were all very ill. We could not get any help. We had to care for each other the best we could."

Homes were quarantined. Public meetings, including funerals, were discouraged, and sometimes banned, to reduce the spread of the epidemic. Mina's children were ill. Her home was quarantined. .Her mother, living nearby, contracted the disease.

"Mother and I were always very close. She had been ill for many years and was not able to do her work, so I cared for her. I saw her every day until I was stricken ill, and then I did not see her again. I had promised my mother that I'd be with her when she died. She kept calling for me but I was too ill to go to her."

It was a dismal March day. Mina, ill and quarantined, could only watch from her front window as the hearse with her mother's body went slowly by. Only two of Mina's siblings were at the small graveside service.

Spring came, the epidemic passed, and roads cleared. The family prepared to go to the temple. But the four sheets needed to get the temple work done could not be found.

The family searched the Jensen home from top to bottom, but it was no use. As Mina recorded; "We could not find my mother's records. I prayed and prayed that I might know where mother had laid those precious sheets with the names of people whose work needed to be done.

"One night late, I had just gone to bed (about midnight) when I heard a voice call my name twice. I said, 'Here I am. What is it?' I looked up and mother was standing right above my bed. She was dressed in white. She had her temple clothes in her arms. She put one hand on each corner of them at the top and shook them. The genealogy sheets rolled down to my bed. I knew exactly where mother had put those sheets. Then she disappeared. She hadn't said a word.

"I could not sleep during the night. I got up early in the morning in my room, and tried my best to wait for the children to wake up. I couldn't wait. I got their breakfast before my husband and I left to go to my father's.

"As soon as I got to my father's house, I told him, 'Father, I know where mother's sheets are now.'"

"Where are they?"

"'They are in the folds of her temple clothes in her drawer.'"

"He said, 'I've gone all through those clothes and they are not there.'

"Then I told him how mother came to me and showed me where they were. We went immediately to their room, picked up her temple clothes, unfolded them and there they were, all four of them. I was thrilled. I think you could say that we were all amazed.

"Later, we went to the temple and did the work for those whose names were on the sheets."

Mina Jensen Olsen Olds lived to raise four children, serve three full-time missions, and serve in numerous capacities in the Church before passing away in 1980 at age 85. Her life demonstrated these words written in her autobiography: "I have really and truly a testimony of the gospel. Nobody, yet nobody can tell me there is not a God. He's here. He hears, and answers our prayers.

Written by Mina Jensen Olsen Olds
Submitted by Joan Oviatt

Dream Of Mother

On Saturday September 24, 1988, I called my father in Bountiful, Utah. This was a weekly practice since my mother had become quite ill with cancer. (I lived in South Carolina with my wife and three children). We talked for a while. Then Father told me that mother had been feeling worse the past few days.

I went to bed with a heavy heart that night, and had the following dream: I saw my father's sister Nelda. She was in my Uncle William's back yard. My father and mother lived next door to William. My father and his brother always had a big garden,

Aunt Nelda walked up to Thelma, William's wife, who was standing between the house and the patio. Thelma held an ear of corn that was golden yellow and fully ripe. The kernels were large, and seemed ready to fall from the cob.

Nelda said the corn looked beautiful. Aunt Thelma responded by saying the corn was indeed beautiful, and that it was ready for immediate harvest.

Nelda asked, "How is Thelda (my mother) doing?"

"Not very well," Thelma said.

"How long does she have? Ten, or twelve?"

Thelma shook her head, and said, "She only has five."

I immediately awoke and looked at the clock. It was almost 5:00 A.M. on Sunday, the twenty-fifth of September. I was unable to go back to sleep. The dream troubled me.

I decided not to wake Tanya (my wife). I thought I would just lie there for a while and see if the dream would fade, or if it would continue to be as vivid as before.

We got up, and I went to church. (I was the ward bishop). There was no time in the flurry of Sunday morning activities to talk with my wife. For the next several hours I continued to feel troubled as I reflected on the dream.

I was in the hall during Sunday School. My sister-in-law, Karen Petersen, inquired how my mother was doing. I related the dream to her. While telling about it I became quite emotional. I told her I was leaving for a business meeting in Chicago that afternoon. Tanya was leaving Thursday to drive to Washington, D.C. where we would meet on Friday to witness the sealing of some friends. We would not be back until Saturday.

I was concerned that mother would die on Friday before we could get back, and no one in my family would be able to contact us. It was decided that we should give my brother Bryan, Karen's telephone number. If my family in Utah needed me, Karen would know how to contact us.

Karen found Tanya and told her of the dream, and my concern. Tanya asked my counselors, and my brother-in-law, Mike Petersen, the executive assistant, to give me a priesthood blessing. They did this. In the blessing I was promised that my mother would be all right until I returned from Washington, D.C.

I attended my business meeting, and the Temple sealing. Tanya and I arrived home October 1st at 12:30 P.M.

On Sunday the 2nd, my father called to let us know of my mother's passing.

I understood the dream to mean that my mother's life, like the ear of corn, was beautiful, and fully ripe, ready for the harvest. I also feel that because of the priesthood blessing I received, mother was not called home until I was available, and my father could talk to me personally. This was very important, and a great help to both of us

Submitted by Kent C Robinson

The Importance of Dreams

I have always felt it important to pay attention to my dreams. I recall the words of Wilford Woodruff, "There are a great many things taught us in dreams that are true, and if a man has the spirit of God he can tell the difference between what is from the Lord and what is not. And I want to say to my brethren and sisters, that whenever you have a dream that you feel is from the Lord, pay attention to it . . . the Lord does communicate some things of importance to the children of men by means of visions and dreams, as well as by the records of divine truth. And what is it all for? It is to teach us a principle. We may never see anything take place exactly as we see it in a dream or a vision, yet it is intended to teach us a principle."

The importance of dreams was reinforced to me as a young woman. I had a roommate in college who always recorded her dreams.

One night, she dreamed I married the young man I was dating.

She said that a large circle of children hovered above us as we wed in the temple. I had received my own witnesses and dreams that I was to marry my husband, but this seemed a sweet double witness.

Ten years later, we had just moved to our new South Jordan home. As we walked into the bathroom in our master bedroom, our two-year-old daughter was suddenly awestruck. The room had a double set of mirrors that faced each other, one above the sinks, the other on the closet doors.

She looked at me and simply stated: "Mommy, this is just like when you were married."

"Were you there?" I asked her. She looked at me matter-of-factly, and said, "Of course, Mommy!" She was the fifth of our ten children.

I had adopted the practice of recording my dreams since my marriage, many of which were introduced with the phrase: "I am not sure this dream is inspired, but I dreamed the following dream . . ." Through the years I have been utterly amazed at how much the Lord has reinforced, foreshadowed, and taught me through dreams. I don't do something solely as a result of a dream, but it gives me something special to pray about. It is only the validation of the Spirit that moves me to action.

Some of the things that I most appreciate are the simple gospel principles I have learned and how the Lord has helped me establish priorities through dreams. In one dream, I was on top of a mountain and saw the Savior approaching me. I feared he would ask me to jump. As he approached me, he inquired if I would do anything he asked.

I answered, "Yes." He then asked me to jump. With some trepidation, I jumped. In the next scene I was in a room with a young mother who had recently moved into our ward. I had been assigned to be her Visiting Teacher. I was on the floor playing with her young children as we visited.

As I prayed about the dream, I came to know that though I would have many callings, none would transcend in importance that of being a Visiting Teacher. Through the years I have had varied callings, including being the gospel doctrine teacher in three different wards; but that precious perspective has never left me.

Visiting one on one with others is often where the greatest work of the Lord is accomplished. I didn't know until years later that this young woman was not active prior to moving into our ward.

She said there was something in our first visit that made her want to become active. She wanted to feel what we felt and know what we knew. She determined after out initial visit that she would start coming to church, though her husband was not a member. I had not known she was not active prior to that time. I got to know her children well since I had two children that matched the age and gender of her children. They became good friends.

That dream occurred almost twenty years ago. I have received more than I have given in these relationships. It has produced friendships and insights that I treasure.

I truly believe, "For where two or three are gathered in my name, there am I in the midst of them" (Matt 18:20).

Submitted by Vicki Jo Robinson

Other Spiritual Blessings

I exhort you my brethren, that ye deny not the gifts of
God, for they are many . . . For behold, to one is
given by the Spirit of God, that he may teach the
Word of Wisdom; . . . and to another, exceeding
great faith; and to another the gifts of healing by the
same Spirit; . . . and to another that he may work
mighty miracles; and again to another that he may
prophesy concerning all things; and again to another,
the beholding of angels and ministering spirits, . . . to
another, all kinds of tongues; and to another the
interpretation of languages . . . and all these gifts
come by the Spirit of Christ, and they come to every
man severally, according as he will.

(Moroni, 10:8-17)

Fear of People Who Are Different

In the early 1970s, I was living in California and attending college when I heard about a church-sponsored young single adults dance being held in another region of the state. I traveled with friends several hundred miles to attend.

I'd always been a shy child; fearful in social settings. In my teens, like most girls my age, I'd been obsessively worried over whether people liked me. I was a good Latter-day Saint. I'd graduated from four years of Seminary with a top attendance record. I'd read the Bible and Book of Mormon before most students in my Seminary class. I went to church. I did volunteer work.

Shy as I was, I stood up for my religion several times. I shared scriptures with my friends. I tried to live a good, Christian life and to be an example to others. With the egocentric vanity of youth, I was quite proud of my spirituality!

At the dance we attended, I was in a new situation. The only familiar faces were those of my friends, and a few kids from another college that I had previously met. One fellow I'd met before was named Gary. He was cute. He was confidant. He was friendly. He remembered me. He might ask me to dance.

Mingling about, I saw on the sidelines, a fellow who obviously had cerebral palsy. Being proud of my friendliness toward disadvantaged people, and perhaps wanting to impress Gary with my spirituality (should he glance my way), I walked over to the young man with cerebral palsy, and said hello. With much effort he spoke to me, slowly and carefully forming the words. I strained to understand him but understood only a portion of his words. A girl who was lingering closely approached. The fellow's name was Brian. The girl was his sister. His sister seemed a bit wary of me as she interpreted Brian's words. After polite chit chat, and feeling I'd done my good deed for the day, I returned to join the crowd surrounding the dance floor.

I was asked for only a couple dances and spent most of my time watching the other dancers and enjoying the music. I was especially watching for Gary, hoping he would look my way, see that I was available, and come over for a chat.

After one dance, I caught movement in the corner of my eye. I turned to see Brian. He had left his chair on the sidelines, and was struggling to walk. He was coming, one painful step at a time, in my direction. Sudden horror came over me. In my mind I said over and over, "Please don't ask me to dance. Please don't ask me to dance."

I couldn't explain the feeling. Before the dance I'd been practicing all my dance moves hoping to impress people. I envisioned lots of people dancing with me then. Now I envisioned dancing with Brian and all the other kids watching us, and feeling sorry that Brian was the only one who would dance with me.

To make matters worse, I looked toward the dance floor to see that Gary was looking in my direction. Then he began walking my way! My mind was screaming, "Ask me, Gary! Ask me."

But Brian was nearer to me and closing in. What would I do? Then Brian was beside me, forming words with great difficulty.

"I'm sorry, I don't understand you," was my polite reply. Brian persisted. "I'm sorry," I repeated, "but I don't understand." I knew full well what he was asking. Visions of Peter denying Christ came to mind. Brian persisted till I could no longer deny that I understood. "I . . . I'm sorry . . ." I finally stammered; while praying in my heart, "Please don't let Gary think I'm with him."

But Gary, without a glance at me, had passed by and asked a girl behind me to dance.

Brian staggered away. He later found another girl to dance with him. I watched, mesmerized, as the other girl struggled to hold him up in order to help him dance. Even so, Brian fell onto the dance floor. The girl and several other dancers helped him get up. I was glad it was not me on the dance floor, trying to help him, with everybody looking at us, staring in embarrassment. While I was thinking those thoughts, I also realized that the other girl on the dance floor with Brian was a much better person than I was. Gary never did ask me to dance.

It was a long ride home that night; a ride filled with reflection. At home I looked in the mirror. Before the dance I'd done my hair up nice, and spent a lot of time on my make-up. I felt I was passably pretty. But now, home from the dance, I looked in the mirror and felt ugly. I couldn't stand to look at myself.

I was a hypocrite. I tried to look spiritual on the outside, to tell myself that I was not a prejudiced person, to tell myself that I accepted God's children no matter their age, color, religion or disability. But when it came down to the test, I had failed miserably. I sobbed myself to sleep.

Over the days, weeks, and months that followed, I thought about the dance. Brian was a human being with feelings. He'd had the courage, and made the incredible effort to ask me to dance. What must it have been like for him? I'd probably encouraged his invitation with my seeming friendliness, but I didn't have the courage to say yes. I tried to analyze why I'd behaved in this way. I came to realize it was fear. Fear of being embarrassed, fear of shame, fear of not being socially accepted, fear of people who were 'different.'

As irrational and ridiculous as it was, I was afraid of . . . what? . . . catching what he had, as if it was a disease? I prayed time and time again for forgiveness. I knew that Heavenly Father would forgive me; that was His job, but I couldn't forgive myself. "Help me," I prayed. Help me to overcome my fear. Help me to see people for themselves, and not for the outward appearance. I want to love people for what's inside, but why is it so hard to get past the outside?"

Several years passed. Brian's face and voice continued to haunt me. I continued to pray to Heavenly Father for a second chance. I needed to repent somehow, I needed to make it up to Brian somehow, but all I knew of him was his name.

In the scriptures I read, "Love casts out fear." "Okay," I told myself, "If disabilities are what I'm afraid of, then I've got to learn about them, and learn to love the people who are tried by them."

I transferred to Brigham Young University in my junior year and lived in May Hall at Helaman Halls. A sign on a bulletin board said a blind girl needed help with her homework. I was nervous around blind people, not knowing what to say or how to act, so I signed up for time slots to read textbooks to her. I became comfortable with the people I got to know who were challenged with blindness. The girl I was tutoring told me that the Utah State Training School in American Fork needed volunteer help with swimming therapy.

I signed up. The patients had physical disabilities that at first over-whelmed me; bodies, limbs, and minds deformed to an extent I'd never seen. I prayed for the strength to face it. Over the weeks and months that followed, my own vision of the world began to change. The joy, the strength, the courage my new friends showed during their therapy sessions, their laughter and joy at having me join them, began to change my heart. These were beautiful people!

As I felt the Spirit changing my heart and vision, I felt more forgive-ness for myself. However, in the back of my mind, I still remembered

Brian. Time and again I would find myself asking for a chance to make it up to him.

One day as I was walking into the lobby of May Hall, I heard a familiar voice. Brian was in the lobby talking with a friend. It had been two years and a thousand miles since I'd seen him at a dance in an unfamiliar city in California. Our meeting had been brief, but it had made an indelible impression on me.

I took the miracle for what it was; and it was a miracle to me. I walked toward him, all the while saying a silent prayer of thanks to Heavenly Father. I struck up a conversation with Brian and listened intently while he formed his replies. I reminded Brian of our meeting a couple of years before, but he did not remember me Brian's friend left, but Brian and I continued to talk. The more I listened, the easier it was to understand him.

Over the following months and years, Brian and I became friends.

He was working on his master's degree, typing his thesis, one finger at a time, on a special keyboard. He had difficulty feeding himself, so I often showed up at the Cougareat around lunchtime, to help him out, and catch up on news. I lost the feeling of embarrassment when food dribbled down his chin, or fell on the table. Brian wasn't, so I wasn't either. We went to devotionals and other events together. He taught me not to care what anybody thought, if you were doing the right thing.

I lost track of Brian after college. But I will never forget the lessons he taught me, and how Heavenly Father helped me to forgive myself.

I'm in my fifties now. I suppose it would be great to say I never judge people by appearances, but the opposite is true, and for that awareness I am grateful. I still catch myself judging people by how they're dressed, their age, or what they look like. I also find myself trying to overcome sneaky little stereotypes about religions and backgrounds. I often wish that Heavenly Father would instantly allow me to see people for the heart and soul they possess on the inside, not by the outward appearance.

But I suppose that's part of our test here on earth, to work and learn for ourselves how to see people for who they really are. One thing I have learned: it's an adventure, and a blessing, to know about people who are different from me. I may have a few million of these adventures left to go.

So be it. Each one is a lesson in love.

Submitted by Joan Oviatt

A Fish To Feed My Family

My name is Brother G. A. Tolentino. I have a story to tell you. One day I went fishing. I packed my sleeping bag and all the things I needed for fishing. I packed them all in the car. At about 6 AM. I got in my car. I prayed to our Father in Heaven to guide me safely to my fishing spot, and to watch over my family, in the name of Jesus Christ, Amen.

Then I started my car and went. While driving I started singing "I Am A Child of God." I sang it, and whistled it all the way to South Point.

It took me two hours of driving to get to my fishing spot. I prayed again to our Father in Heaven for safety and thanked Him for the beautiful day of fishing.

I found a place up on the high rocks looking over the ocean. I began fixing my fishing rod. I took a plastic bag and filled it with air, tied it with a fishing line, and threw it out to the ocean, connected it to my fishing rod and let go. There were four hooks with bait, eighty feet in between, and two plastic gallon jugs for floaters. I let it way, way out.

I put my fishing rod in the crack of a stone next to where I was sitting down. All of a sudden the reel rang and the rod bent down. I grabbed my fishing rod. Oh boy, it was a big one! I prayed to our Father in Heaven and thanked him for the catch and asked Him for strength to bring it in. I fought for it one half-hour or more. My arm was hurting.

Suddenly a guy bent over my shoulder and said, "Can I hold your fishing rod for you?"

I looked at him and said, "Did you fight a fish like this before?"

"Yes," he said, "but in a boat."

"Okay." I backed up and gave him the pole. He tried to pull it in, but he could not. I grabbed the line and helped to pull for him. We did that together for half an hour to get the fish close to the beach. It was a big yellow fin tuna.

I asked the man if I could hold the rod. I got it and it took me quite a while to get the fish to a good place to bring it up. As soon as I got it to the place, I prayed again. I asked Father in Heaven to help me bring it up to feed my family and friends.

Not a minute after my prayer, three guys came along. One of them had swimming goggles and the other two had big hooks. The guy who had swimming goggles and fins came by me and looked down in the ocean.

I asked him if he was going down, could he hook the fish for me.

"Yes," he said, "but you can not pull up a fish like that, so hang on to it and I will go down to the other side."

He went down but as he came around the bend, the fish saw him and ran outward.

He almost pulled me over the cliff. The other guy grabbed me and said, "I got you. You hang onto the fish."

The other man put down his big hook for the guys who were all in the water now, and they hooked the fish. He told the guys to pull it up. They got the fish up on land.

"Wow," I said, "It's a big one." Then I prayed to our Father in Heaven to thank Him for the fish, and all those who helped me. As soon as I opened my eyes, I saw the guys were all walking away. I called them and said, "Friend, give me your phone number and I will give all of you some fish."

"No, thank you," they said. "Bring it home for your family and friends."

I said, "Thank you guys. God bless you and your family." I prayed for them.

I called my family and told them, "I am coming home now. I catch a big yellow fin tuna."

The fish fed my family and several other families and friends.

Submitted by Guillermo A. Tolentino

An Empty Life Is Now Full

The gospel changed my life from black to white. Twenty years ago I led a party life. I believed the philosophy that a person had to be stoned, or drunk to be happy. That made my life real empty pretty fast. I had an unhappy marriage that would lead to divorce. We argued about everything. Missionaries from the Church came and talked to me.

There were many things I could not understand, like tithing. I had many questions.

I was invited to hear a talk given at the Stake Center in Hilo, Hawaii, near where I lived. I didn't want to go listen to a speech but the speaker was a man named Elder Kikuchi, a General Authority of the Church. I am third generation American Japanese and grew up on the Big Island of Hawaii. Since Elder Kikuchi was also Japanese, I thought he might understand some things.

I went to the Stake Center. Elder Kikuchi was in the front of the building, greeting people. I started to ask him questions. I wanted to know what was true. Elder Kikuchi did not have much time to answer my questions. I stayed and listened to his talk. He told about how the missionaries found him, and how he wanted to know why American bombs had killed his parents in Japan during World War II. The missionaries told him how a fourteen-year-old boy once wanted to know what was true, and Heavenly Father answered him.

After telling his own story, Elder Kikuchi said with much conviction, "I know this Church is true!" He looked right at me from the pulpit and said, "Brother Yamamoto, I know it's true! I know!"

The spirit hit me hard. I couldn't talk. I began crying and couldn't help it. From that minute I knew it was true.

I kept crying and could not stop. After the meeting I went to see Elder Kikuchi. I wanted to talk to him but he had to leave. "We will see each other again," he told me.

The next day I was in Hilo, I forget why, and went to the stake center. Elder Kikuchi was there and he talked to me awhile. A couple of days later I had to go to the airport. Elder Kikuchi was there too. We talked for more than an hour in the terminal. One week later I was baptized. I was forty-five years old.

Six months later I was ordained to the priesthood. I told my bishop, Don Heinzen, "I have only been in the Church six months." He said I was ready and I was ordained.

My life is now rich and filled with meaning.

A few years ago I met my wife Jan, and we were married. She is the blessing of my life. I did not know it was possible to have such a rich relationship. She came from divorce also. Neither of us knew that the gospel would give us such fulfilling relationships. In our Pahoa ward Jan and I teach a class on "Marriage and Family Relationships." We have learned a lot. We still have challenges but we know we are doing what we should be doing.

Like Elder Kikuchi, I also know the Church is true.

Submitted by Rodney Yamamoto

My First Solo Flight

I graduated high school and enrolled at the University of Southern California when I was but 16 years old. When I was nineteen the war in Vietnam was imminent. The United States Navy was starting a new sixteen-week long class of Pre-Flight students once a week.

About 14 months after completing Pre-Flight, successful student pilots will have finished the entire course, and earned the much-coveted Navy "Wings of Gold."

I was now eligible and recognized the opportunity for what it was. I signed up immediately.

The 16 weeks of Pre-Flight training serve as the Officer Candidate School (OCS) for Naval Aviators. It is a rigorous program. All of us who graduated were delighted to move on to actually flying the aircraft that we had seen and heard daily as they zoomed around overhead.

My family went to church every Sunday. It was a basic Christian church that used the King James' version of the Holy Bible and baptized by total immersion. I found it to be an easy step from that church and that faith to the restored gospel, modern day prophets, and the exquisite Joseph Smith story.

My conversion was classic in its simplicity and spirituality. I studied the missionary lessons and the Book of Mormon, prayed to Heavenly Father for the truth, and precisely as promised by the scriptures. The truth was made manifest to me through the Holy Spirit.

On June 29, 1963, I was baptized and confirmed a member of The Church of Jesus Christ of Latter-day Saints.

One year later, on the 21st of June, 1964, I was ordained an elder. I now held the Melchizedek Priesthood, with all its rights and privileges, with all of its responsibilities, and with all of its protective armor.

One year later, that same June of 1964, my schedule consisted of half a day of ground school and half a day actually flying. I was in a classroom four hours a day and spent a second four hours flying one syllabus "hop" a day. A "hop" consisted of a one-hour oral examination, and briefing on the procedures and maneuvers that I was to learn on that flight, a thirty-minute preflight inspection of the aircraft, one and a half hours actually flying, and a one-hour debriefing after the flight.

June 26th, 1964 was a perfect day. Five days after being ordained an elder, I was scheduled for my first solo flight. I'd had all twelve of the primary syllabi-required flights and was now cleared to fly solo. After that flight, my flight instructor would, in full view of a camera and all of the other student pilots, cut off the lower half of my necktie and present me with a single, small, gold bar to wear over my left breast pocket. About six months later, when I carrier-qualified, I'd get a small, double gold bar to replace the "solo" bar.

The solo flight was only half over and I'd successfully completed all the requirements. I knew basic aerobatics; barrel rolls, half-Cuban eights, loops, spins, and spin recovery. I'd never heard about a "Split S," let alone knew what it was, or how to do it. But when I overheard the advanced student pilots talking about it, I knew I had to try one. I knew I was going to do one the first chance I had.

The "Split S" maneuver is dangerous, at best, and virtual suicide if you don't know how to do it. It is critical to start the maneuver at a relatively high altitude so as to have sufficient room to recover to level flight. It is also important to correctly set the throttle and the pitch of the propeller blades. And it is important to be at the correct air speed when the maneuver is started. I knew none of these things; not even one of them. I didn't even know I was supposed to know those things! All I really knew is what a "Split S" looked like.

In level flight, just roll over inverted and let the nose of the aircraft "fall through." It resembles the second half of a simple loop. But there is a critical distinction, of which I, of course, was blissfully unaware. The second half of a loop finds the aircraft at a relatively low air speed as the nose of the aircraft begins to "fall through." The air speed had "bled off" during the first half of the loop, the climbing portion.

There I was on my first solo with my first chance to break the rules. I entered MY "Split S" at normal air speed and from level, powered flight. I simply rolled over and let the nose drop.

I soon realized that the nose was not falling through very quickly. Essentially, I was now nose down, heading straight for the ground at an ever-increasing air speed, and at an awesome, ever-increasing rate of descent. I pulled the throttle all the way off. I was now frightened.

Suddenly, I could tell it wasn't going to work. I knew I had neither the time nor the altitude to pull the nose through. I panicked and immediately rolled back over to be right side up. But now my nose was too far down to recover level flight. So I immediately rolled back over and pulled the stick back as far as I could. I was severely limited in this attempt. Because of my relatively high air speed the control surfaces on the horizontal stabilizer couldn't be coaxed to move very much.

I started to black out because of the tremendous G-forces I was inducing. I didn't know what to do. I knew I wasn't going to make it. There were no more options available to me. I felt so incredibly stupid. I'd had the bravado of youth; the ignorance of youth, and it was going to kill me here and now.

I continued on with the only thing I knew to do; keep full back-stick pressure and try to pull it through and regain level flight. Then, I was no longer frightened. I experienced an eerie, icy calm. I kept the back pressure on the stick, as much as possible, and rode the tunnel vision gray-out that precedes the black-out. I knew if I blacked out completely I'd release the stick, crash, and die for sure.

Finally, the nose of the aircraft crept up to the horizon and I did regain level flight. I was no more than 50 feet above the tops of the trees. I was trembling and felt the post-adrenaline shock as I cruised back home to Saufley Field.

I had intended to start my "Split S" at three or four thousand feet, where loops are started, but for some reason I changed my mind and went on up to five thousand feet. I then continued on up to six thousand feet. Then, most oddly, I consciously decided to go on up to nine thousand feet; though at the time I didn't know why. I just felt impressed to do it. I knew the Navy required supplemental oxygen at and above ten thousand feet during daylight operations, so I decided to go to nine thousand feet.

As it turned out, that's what saved my life. I had recovered level flight only fifty feet above the tops of the trees.

The silver lining is that since then I have always been a most conservative, follow-all-the-rules pilot. There are no old and bold pilots. Certainly I was never bold again.

Even at the beginning of my new life as a Latter-day Saint I had a miraculous, life-changing experience. Perhaps my life was spared because Heavenly Father knew that I, in turn, would be needed in the future to save the lives of a few other people. I may one day know the answer to that.

Clearly my work here on earth, in this life, was not yet completed.

Submitted by Russell Jobst

Sacrifice For Temple Blessings

In the fall of 1956, when I first arrived in the mission field, and once more, in the spring of 1957, I received especially rewarding assignments as a young missionary in Switzerland. My duty both times, was that of a guide on the grounds of the newly dedicated Swiss Temple, and as a worker inside the temple.

My assignments inside the temple were varied; such as greeting members of the Church, giving them official instructions before sessions, providing organ music in the chapel, serving as ordinance worker throughout the temple, officiating at, and performing baptisms for the dead, and working in the kitchen. In these capacities, I came in close contact with hundreds of the most faithful saints living in Europe; from Austria, Germany, Norway, Sweden, and Finland. They came to the temple as often as they could to receive their blessings.

A wonderful highlight of these experiences was during the week-long presence of one hundred Saints from East Germany in May 1957. They came to the temple in two separate trains. They came illegally, so far as the East German government was concerned, who had only given permission for travel into West Germany "to visit their brothers and sisters." They brought with them the lame, the blind, and other handicapped saints. They sacrificed all their savings to make this trip. The demonstration of their strong faith was overwhelming. I felt the greatest love for them as I took charge of the group, welcoming them and giving instructions pertaining to accommodations, food, and money.

We served them breakfast each morning. Simple food was most appreciated. These Saints were not accustomed to other kinds of food. We served them lunch free of charge in the temple dining room. I washed dishes alongside Samuel E. Bringhurst, the Temple President. I averaged only four hours of sleep each night during this wonderful week because of the need for constant service.

The most choice moments of this inspirational week happened when I was able to be reunited with my three living grandparents. They were part of the group who had come to receive their temple blessings. I had not known they were coming until I read their names on the sleeping accommodations list, only a few weeks before the Saints from East Germany would arrive.

As a temple worker at some times, and as a family proxy at other times, I witnessed their endowments, and subsequent sealings to deceased relatives. I served as proxy for my own father as he was sealed to his parents.

When departure time came, this group of Saints assembled in the cultural hall for final instructions. Before leaving, they sang, *How Firm a Foundation* with all their hearts. At the train station, they bid us farewell by singing, *God Be With You 'til We Meet Again.*

My heart was touched. Chills ran up and down my spine. My testimony was strengthened by daily association with those wonderful Saints. As the train pulled away, I realized that their personal freedom would soon be curtailed when they arrived behind the Iron Curtain. They would probably never again have the opportunity to return to a temple during their mortal lives. But they took with them treasured memories of one week's freedom on earth, in a hallowed and Holy place.

Submitted by W. Herbert Klopfer

The Joy of Sisterhood

I am a member of the Salt Lake Eagle Gate Eighth Ward, which is a singles ward. I have been blind from birth.

In 1987 a group of sisters in our ward decided to go on a river trip over the Labor Day weekend. We went to Jackson Hole, Wyoming. On the way home disaster struck. I developed a splitting headache. I thought it was a migraine. We stopped in Star Valley, Wyoming to get something to eat. The sisters hoped that if I ate something I would feel better, but instead, the headache intensified. My visiting teaching companion had me lie down in the back seat of her car. The next thing I remember was being pulled out of the car.

We were in Montpelier, Idaho. I was vomiting and saying things that didn't make sense. Fortunately, one of the sisters with us was a nurse at Primary Children's Hospital. If she had not been there, I'm sure I would not be here today.

Marcia knew there was something seriously wrong. The doctor in Montpelier told her that it was probably a migraine headache. Marcia became very firm with him.

She said, "Listen! This woman needs a neurosurgeon, and I want one here, Pronto."

I was sent by ambulance to McKay Dee Hospital in Ogden. The neurosurgeon told my parents that I had an aneurysm on the left side of my brain. Somehow the blood vessels came apart and put themselves back together again, forming a blood clot. He told my parents that if it couldn't be dissolved with heavy medication, they would have to operate, and I would have a fifty-fifty chance of making it through the surgery. Fortunately, the doctors were able to dissolve the clot with the medication.

I spent three weeks in the hospital, and another three weeks at my parents' home in Roy, being slowly withdrawn from the medication.

The sisters in the Relief Society came often to visit with me. My visiting teachers came all the way from Salt Lake to see me. They recorded sacrament meeting so I could hear the ward choir sing. They informed me that the sisters who were on the river trip told them that when they had pulled me out of the car in Montpelier, a bishop saw us and gave me a blessing. In that blessing he said that I would fully recover and be able to lead a normal life.

During this time I had been praying diligently for Heavenly Father to take me. I did not want to be a burden to my parents. This message from the visiting teachers gave me great comfort. They also encouraged me to re-read my patriarchal blessing. In the blessing there is a passage that had never held so much meaning as it did then.

It said, "You shall be strengthened both in your body, and in your mind, and in your spirit, which will enable you to carry on and keep the commandments of your Heavenly Father."

Because of my being an amateur radio operator, my visiting teachers, along with my mother, encouraged me to get on the radio and talk with ham friends whom I used to talk with every day. I said I was afraid I would offend them because I couldn't remember their names and call letters.

A few days later, Otto, one of my ham friends called long distance and said, "Linda, I'm on the 62 repeater. Please get on and talk to me." I did, and it wasn't as fearful as I had anticipated.

My roommates, Jean and Pauline, were also a great comfort to me. Jean made important phone calls for me while I was in the hospital. She called the Salt Lake City County Health Department where I am employed full time, and KSL which was my part time job, explaining what had happened to me. She also called KRCL, a community radio

..ion where I had my own radio program. It was on the air once a week, and they needed to be informed.

My Relief Society sisters were a tremendous support to me during those two months when I was very ill. They were also there for me when I came back to Salt Lake, and began putting my life back together.

The Lord has truly blessed me. I have fully recovered. I am not taking any medication. Most people who have the kind of aneurysm that I did, rarely live to tell the story.

The Salt Lake City County Health Department held my job open for me. I am still in the singles ward. I am the temple coordinator, and a visiting teacher.

Submitted by Linda Reeder

Saved Through the Influence of a Wife

He was ordained a Deacon at age twelve. At fourteen he became a Teacher. In the years between fourteen and sixteen, he fell in with boys who did not keep the Word of Wisdom. He began some bad habits. When he was sixteen a member of the bishopric called on him.

"The bishop would like to ordain you a Priest," he was told.

"Doesn't the bishop know I smoke?" the young man asked.

"He knows that you know you shouldn't," the counselor replied.

The young man did not want to quit smoking. He did not become a Priest.

He married a young woman who was active in a Protestant church. Every Sunday she took the children and went off to church. Every Sunday he stayed home, read the paper, drank coffee and smoked.

They had been married sixteen years when his wife began to be dissatisfied with her church. She came home one Sunday at the end of her meetings and said, "Next Sunday, we are going to your church."

Next Sunday came. The man was then forty years old. He got dressed in his suit and took his family to the ward that was closest to where they lived. He soon threw away his cigarettes, and began keeping the Word of Wisdom. He was ordained a Priest at age forty. He baptized his wife.

The Rest of the Story

The man and his wife became active in the Church. They have been called as temple workers in four temples. She has served twice as a Relief Society President. She is now the Family History Director in their Stake. He has served in two bishoprics, and been a High Counselor.

While their daughter was on a mission in Las Vegas she served as Assistant to the President.

One of their great joys now is a granddaughter's delight in attending BYU after coming from a large high school where she was the only member.

Submitted by Morris Mower

Angels Can Play Football

I believe I was the first Samoan girl who wanted to play High School football. But I wasn't entitled to. My coach told me it was too dangerous for a girl.

One day I went over to the football field to watch the boys practice. Some of the boys needed work on their defense and offense lines. When practice was over the coach had the football players sit down. He said he wanted the football boys to know about the Church. He wanted to tell them about gospel principles, how working together, looking out for each other, and having a good plan was good for life as well as for football. Some of the football players were members of the Church. They tried helping out but they just kept being pushed away.

That's when I felt inspired to help! I asked the coach to give me a chance.

"Let me just help with practice," I pleaded with him.

He said, "Okay, after school tomorrow."

The next day, when school was over, I was ready! I was nervous, but ready. I suited up and went to the field. All the boys were kind of laughing at me.

I said, "You can laugh but you'll never know what hit you."

The coach tried to get the boys to listen, to cooperate so everyone could win. I already had a plan and dared them to run that plan on the field. It was time to practice so we all huddled in. They let me do the first play. We took our positions and we started. I told the boys, "This is how we're gonna do it. Okay? Everybody has a partner. We're trying to get to Jesus Christ, but we need to use the right path. So I'll be the shield protecting you from temptation."

We played, and I tackled all the guys down, so I could let the guy with the ball score. It worked! Then they began to understand. I knew that my work with the team was over. The coach got some missionaries to help the boys train. Before the season was finished, half of the boys that weren't members, became members of The Church Of Jesus Christ of Latter-day Saints.

I didn't do this alone. I have a testimony that I had help from an angel.

Submitted by Angel Pahoa

When The Prophet Dies

When the Prophet of the Church dies, his casket lies in state in the foyer of the old Church Administration Building; so it was when President Kimball died in November of 1985. I went down to pay my last respects, and had a most interesting, and inspiring experience.

The line forms and goes up the steps, through the first doors, past the elevators and the stairs, then continues through another set of doors into the foyer area. The casket stood in this large foyer. The line of people passed on the right of the casket. Straight ahead and to the right is the hall leading to the outside of the building.

As I approached the casket, a young girl in front of me spoke softly to her mother, "Do you see them over there?" Her mother looked around, apparently seeing no one, she said, "No, who?" The little girl said, "All the Presidents of the Church are standing over there together." She then named them off, and told how they were all wearing white, and standing just a little above the floor.

"What are they doing?" the mother asked. "They are watching the people in the line," the little girl replied.

I had seen where the child pointed. I strained my eyes to try and see what she saw, but I could not. Oh, how I wanted to be a part of that experience. I lingered as long as I could, but because there were others behind me, I had to go on down the hall.

As I opened the door to exit the building, I felt the cold outside in stark contrast to the peace and warmth inside. I turned to re-enter but could not, there were so many behind me pushing to go out. I was thrust back into this world.

I realized that I had had a profound experience. I stood in the presence of the Prophets, and angels; and felt the power of the Holy Spirit. My testimony had been strengthened with the confirmation of life after death, and the truthfulness of the gospel of Jesus Christ.

Submitted by Jan Johnstun

Miracles Do Happen

This experience began many years ago when my husband Paul was laboring as a missionary in the city of Hamilton in the Eastern Canadian Mission. Paul and his companion taught and baptized the Buckingham family; father Albert, mother Alice, and son Bruce. This experience is mostly about Bruce, and his wife JoAnne.

Years later, Bruce retired as a principal from what we in America call high school. JoAnne is a nurse and still works in this capacity. The Buckinghams were always stalwarts in the gospel of Jesus Christ. They have been an influence for good in the lives of many people.

Bruce and JoAnne planned early in their marriage to serve a mission together when they were older and retired. They have three daughters who are married now, and raising their own families. None of the daughters live close by. One daughter and her family live in Italy.

Albert passed away a few years ago. Both he and Alice had been in nursing homes. Bruce, JoAnne, and Alice moved to Kitchener, where the temple is, a few years ago. Alice had undergone a number of serious illnesses, including cancer. At this time Bruce and JoAnne became temple workers. They enjoyed this work and had many good friends among the workers.

But uppermost in their minds, was the desire to serve a mission. With Alice in the nursing home, she was their prime responsibility now, Bruce and JoAnne decided to serve a "stay at home" mission.

Our family and the Buckingham family have stayed very close through the years. We took camping trips together, and family vacation outings. Bruce called to tell me they had submitted their papers for a "stay at home' mission. This was not very long ago.

Paul passed away a few years ago, but I know he was as happy as I was to know that Bruce and JoAnne could finally serve the mission they had planned for so long.

Alice was doing quite a bit better. Her cancer was in remission. Then, to Bruce and JoAnne's surprise, Alice mentioned to them several times that she was "ready to go." Several nights later she slipped away in her sleep.

They began an investigation to find out what had happened with their mission papers. The Stake President put in a call to Church headquarters. The papers had never been received. No one knew anything about the papers.

Bruce called to tell me about the "great mystery." But he also called it a "miracle." They could now submit their papers for a foreign mission which was what they had hoped to do through the years. At this same time, a request came into Church Headquarters from a bishop in Dawson Creek, several hundred miles from Edmonton in Alberta, Canada. This bishop was in desperate need of a couple to help with what seemed like insurmountable needs in his ward.

The bishop already had a house for them to live in. He had it fixed it up, even putting in new appliances. We looked at this as another miracle. We had dinner together before they reported to the MTC in Provo, Utah. They were happy and delighted to finally be on their way to serve the mission they had looked forward for such a long time.

They were even looking forward to the challenges awaiting them at Dawson Creek.

Submitted by Josephine Foulger

Christmas Giving

How silently, how silently
The wondrous gift is giv'n
So God imparts to human hearts
The blessings of his heav'n
No ear may hear his coming;
but in this world of sin,
Where meek souls will receive him,
still the dear Christ enters in.

Looking For Nancy on Christmas Eve

Nancy Garnenez was our Navajo child. She came to us in August of 1976, from a place called Wide Ruins, Arizona. When our Prophet, Spencer W. Kimball, began what was called The Indian Placement Program, my husband, Jesse, and I decided to become foster parents. One of the reasons was that Jess had served his mission in 1956-57 among the Navajo people. He had great love, respect, and admiration for them. The other reason was that we had lost our baby the year before. There was such a void in our lives because of this. We hoped that having another child in the home would turn our grief in another direction.

Nancy was ten years old. She often complained of aches and pains that were not usual for a child. During her check-up with our family doctor, he discovered that she was a battered child. Old, badly healed fractures showed up on x-rays. Her father was an alcoholic. He no longer lived with the family. We did not know if he was the cause of her battering. No one had told us. Dr. MacKay did what he could for her, and counseled us about her care.

She had been in the fourth grade the year before, but we were advised to put her a grade lower. She was small for her age and this made it easier. We started her in the third grade at L. J. Muir School with Matthew, our second son.

She struggled in school. Navajo people are right brained. They are gifted artistically. They are good builders. They can make anything with their hands. They are born with a bent towards religion. They love nature in every form. They reverence life. Math, science, geography, history, (except for their own oral histories) are difficult. Thinking abstractly is not normal for them. They become frustrated in the American school system, which was designed by left brained men of European descent, such as Horace Mann, and John Dewey. (The exception is Elizabeth Peabody who founded the first kindergartens in Concord, Massachusetts. She fought all her life against the type of schools Horace Mann structured.)

Nancy brought laughter and her own joyous personality to our home. She liked to tease. Our white Maltese dog, Mopsy, who was fussy about who could come near him, took to Nancy immediately. She never tired of playing with Mopsy.

There were some hard adjustments for Nancy. She was very close to her grandmother. In traditional Navajo tribes, the oldest mother in a family is reverenced as the matriarch. She makes final decisions about whatever the family does. She is the one constant in a child's life. Nancy cried for her. For some reason she had a fear that her grandmother would die before she saw her again. She was homesick. We knew what it was like to long for a missing family member.

I learned much from my Navajo daughter. I learned the value of being quiet. I began to relearn about the differences in culture. (I had been taught this value in teacher training classes, but I had trouble practicing it.) For instance, Navajo children are taught that it is disrespectful to look an elder person in the eye. When you address them, they will always look over your right shoulder. In my everyday work as a teacher, many times a day I was saying to my students, "May I see your eyes, please." "Look at me when I talk to you." It took time for me to internalize this with Nancy.

We read bedtime stories together, and built reading readiness into our Home Evenings. We read the Book of Mormon. We went to the opening of the Jordan River Temple. At Christmas time we tried to emphasize the Nativity and always acted it out. One year Nancy was "the Angel 'Moriah.'" (She mixed up Gabriel and Moroni.) I had made each of my children a Christmas stocking, and I made one for Nancy.

We dealt with illness and tooth problems. Dr. Candland Olsen offered to donate his work to take care of her many dental problems. This made such a difference in her appearance. Our family was grateful to him.

There began to be problems between Nancy and our daughter Melanie, who was three years younger. It was probably sibling rivalry. But Nancy began teasing Melanie, and it did not bother her when she made Melanie cry. We dealt with it every way we knew. But when eighth grade was finished, we talked with the placement counselors, who had been aware of our problems. Nancy was moved to the home of Gerald and Margaret Jordan in Bountiful. She was able to graduate from Bountiful High School and from Seminary. We were there for the graduation. Her family came, including her old grandmother, who welcomed Jess and me in Navajo. She thanked us for what we had done for Nancy. Her mother, Mabelena, had not come, which surprised me. Through the years she had sent many letters of thankfulness, and lovely pieces of handmade art for Christmas gifts.

Every year just before Christmas, I would get out the boxes having to do with Christmas. When I took out the stockings to hang on the mantle, there was always Nancy's stocking. I had not thought to give it to her when she left our home. Replacing it in the box always disturbed me. Last year, I did not put it back in the box. I hung her stocking alongside the others. It began to concern me that, after so many years, she was no longer a part of our family.

We heard that she had married, and had a son named Nicholas, whom we had not seen.

When Jess and I retired from teaching, we put in our papers for a mission, which we had long planned to do. We asked to serve on the Navajo reservation. We were ecstatic when our request was granted. President Boothe of the Arizona, Phoenix Mission, was now the person in charge of our lives for 18 months. He told us we could stay home and have Christmas with our family. But we were prepared to leave for our mission. Our family would make it through without us.

I also hoped to share that Christmas with Nancy's family. In my heart I felt that this would be a gift to the Savior. I was prepared to leave the material part of Christmas, but not the emotional part. I cried a lot. I was homesick and humbled; which reminded me of how Nancy must have felt when she was away from her family for holidays.

We arrived at Tuba City on December 23rd. We immediately got our trailer house situated. Our place of residence was behind the chapel. We got up early on Christmas Eve to begin the search for Nancy and her family. It was a great leap of faith, for we had lost all contact with her.

We only knew that she was a practical nurse working at a care center for the elderly. Prayer decided for us that we should go to Wide Ruins, which was one hundred and fifty miles from Tuba City. We meant to rely on people at the Wide Ruins Trading Post to help us locate the Gaddy/Garnenez hogan. We had no address. There were no telephones. We had been to the family compound in 1979. All we remembered was that it was at the end of a long red dirt road. We also had memories of hills covered with juniper and cedar, and then a plateau between Wide Ruins Wash and Puerco Wash.

Finally, we found the turn-off road that led to the Wide Ruins settlement. Jess had taken me on a second honeymoon there. The Trading Post was built on the top of old Anasazi ruins. We had slept upstairs in the pioneer style home behind the Post. I will always remember being awakened by the Spirit as the sun came up; whether it was the Holy Spirit, or ancient Anasazi spirits I did not know, but there was the definite feeling that Jess and I were not the only ones in the room.

Going down the road that would lead to the Wide Ruins Trading Post, we passed a Mennonite Mission, the Kinteel Chapter House, (Kinteel means wide house) and came to a ruin. It was the remains of the Trading Post. All that was left of the old building were some sandstone block walls. It had been destroyed by fire. Gone were the Wide Ruins of the Anasazi, which refers to the square pit houses as opposed to the round hogan. Here a more recent Navajo history had been developed; excellent weaving, and the discovery of new dyes for weaving.

It had been a residence for Betaan Yazzie, (Little No Shirt) a famous Navajo artist, as well as a Post Office, and general store for the many scattered outlying hogans, which are houses for shepherds watching over their sheep. It is a place of rich forage for the sheep. Among the junipers and cedars, many species of desert grasses flourish in the area of the Wide Ruins Wash. One could almost transfer the landscape to Israel, and the shepherd's fields around Bethlehem.

We got out of the truck and stood in shock. Even the old pioneer house was gone. My hopes for finding Nancy and her son Nicholas were dashed. We went back up the road towards the school and the Kinteel Chapter House where a lot of vehicles were gathering.

Jess approached a group of Navajo men. They told him about the fire, one man with an American Legion insignia on his shirt, told us that the Gaddy sheep ranch was at the end of the Tanner Springs road. My hopes were revived. We started off.

After turning right and driving up Highway 191, we retraced our steps and soon found the sign: Tanner Springs Road. I thanked the Lord for another prayer answered. We were on a red dirt road that was well maintained for the school buses.

We thought we recognized the place down a side road, and followed it. It ended in a pasture. We tried half a dozen of these little side roads. They were all dead ends. One place was almost a clone of the Gaddy place, with its hogan and tar paper shed in the back. No one was home. But it was not the right place. The Book of Remembrance I had made for Nancy had a picture of the front of the house. It had a gable and this one did not.

I prayed again and the thought came that we should travel onward down the red dirt road toward the west. It was 3:30 in the afternoon.

We had to find the place before the sun went down, otherwise we would not find it. We drove on for a long time without seeing any settlements. But we kept going, following the Spirit's direction.

Suddenly, there it was. A house with a gable and smoke coming from the chimney. It was more dilapidated than we remembered, but brown siding had been put over the tar paper shed. The door opened almost before the truck stopped. A small woman wearing a bright Christmas sweatshirt, and snow boots came quickly toward us.

I got out of the truck and went to meet her. "Nancy," I said. My heart was beating faster. I was so excited to have found our girl at last.

"No," she said. "I am Mabelena, her mother." She seemed to know us, and even had been expecting us. But how could she? There was no way.

She took me in her arms and hugged me. Her hair was curly and cut short, and her face was covered with freckles. I saw that she had a curvature of the spine, and her chest was caved in. She looked beautiful to me.

We were invited into the house, and surrounded by members of the family who had gathered for Christmas Eve. A young roly-poly boy with a pleasant smile came up to us.

"This is Nicholas, Nancy's son." Mabelena said.

I nearly sobbed. "Nicholas," I said, "I'm your other grandma."

Nancy's brother, Denny, looking like a big bear, introduced his lovely wife, Delphine. They were bilingual. They spoke English well, switching back and forth easily between the two languages. They introduced one of their daughters, and told us about another one who was in the mission field.

They knew surprising things about their family genealogy. "But," said Denny, "It only goes back to 1882. After that we'd have to use Joseph Smith's Urim and Thummim to find information about the Glyphes." We all laughed.

Gene, another of Nancy's brothers who had been to our home in Bountiful, came in. He recognized us immediately. Elisa, Nancy's younger sister, came in. She had been on the placement program with Alan and Margaret Jorgensen. She was grown up and had a sweet two-year-old girl named Talia. Elisa remembered kids from Bountiful who were common friends with our children.

It was a wonderful reunion with a humble family with whom we had strong emotional ties.

I had made a stocking for Nicholas and filled it. When I presented it to him he received it politely and put it under the tree. I had brought Nancy's stocking from home. I had made a Book of Remembrance for her. The family all admired it, and then put it under the tree for her.

She was working at her job in Winslow, but was coming home that evening. They said she had a small red truck. That was interesting because our truck is also red. Jess and I kept listening for the sound of her truck on the dirt road.

Mabelena thought we should go ahead and eat without her. She had hot squaw bread, turkey, with potatoes and gravy, and peaches for dessert. They are a delicacy to the Navajo people, even canned peaches. Peaches are grown in small orchards here and there across the reservation. The original seeds were given to the Navajos when Mormons settled in areas just outside the reservation. The trees grew, and have been carefully tended for all those years.

We explained our mission assignment. They were excited for us, and glad that we would be a little closer than Bountiful, Utah. The light in the house grew dim. Dusk was settling on the land. There were no lights on the Christmas tree, there was no television set to blare out the news of the world. The family has no electricity, or running water.

Soon it would be dark and Nancy had not come. We had one hundred and fifty miles to drive back to Tuba City. Jess and I decided that we must leave. Mabelena took me by the arm and walked with me to the truck. She called me "ach' e' e'" and asked me to repeat it. She said that it means "daughter." I was touched beyond words.

As we left the compound and turned west, the moon rolled over the horizon, especially luminous because there were no city lights to detract from its glow. It was an almost new moon, so bright we could see the shadowed side. A star rose above it, the Star of Bethlehem shining over the shepherd's fields of the Navajo reservation.

Nancy's Christmas stocking was where it belonged at last. I was at peace in my soul for the first time in several years. The meeting with her came later. We see her often now.

Submitted by Barbara Manfull

Christmas Is About Giving

One day when we had a guest at our home for Thanksgiving Dinner, there was a discussion about the holidays, how wonderful it is to have special reasons for bringing families together, and how the spirit of giving is so much more intense then.

I love the holidays a lot, especially those surrounding the Christmas season. I've always tried to make Christmas a special time for our children. We could never afford to give our children all the material richness some families can provide. But I try to make Christmas a fun and pleasant memory for them.

When we were first married, we knew that we would probably never be rich. That did not matter to my husband and me because we were used to poverty. But we were concerned about not being able give our children as much as other people did; not for our own pride, but we did not want the children to be ashamed of how little we had.

We talked about this one evening before we knelt together for prayer. As we were praying the Spirit spoke to us both, 'Love is enough.' A burden lifted from our minds.

As a parent, you wish you could give your children everything they want even when you know it's impossible to do. We did truly love our children, and we tried to keep in our thoughts, "Love is enough." But the ways of the world sometimes caused me to wonder whether one or two gifts per child was enough on a festive occasion like Christmas. Thoughts like this would cause me to be discouraged.

That discouragement was finally put to rest this one Thanksgiving day as our guest greedily told how she couldn't wait to return to her home (on the mainland) and open all the gifts her family would give her. I put my head down, ashamed that I couldn't say the same for the number of gifts my children would receive that year.

But before I could feel sorry for myself and our circumstances, one of my daughters spoke up quickly saying, "Our special family tradition is that each Christmas we get to choose the name of a family member out of a paper bag. We become a secret Santa to that person." (A game we use as parents to save on the cost of gifts.)

We gave each child a minimal amount of money; they must choose a gift that fit the name they chose, as well as do a good deed for that person, or a give them a hand-made craft.

As she began to explain the fun of being Santa for someone in your own family, the other children chimed in, telling of how they could never keep a secret, and laughing at the fact that before Christmas Day came around, everyone would sort of know who their secret Santa was. They would ask each other questions about the person whose name they had drawn. This tradition, which began as a way to save money, had helped to bring our family closer, and I didn't realize it until that very moment.

I will never forget that feeling! I was overcome with gratitude and humility that my children did not think about the money we didn't spend on them during the holidays, but only thought how special our family tradition was. Never again was I ashamed to tell people about the meager way we celebrate Christmas. I realized it isn't how much money you spend, or the number of gifts you get that is important. The fun and joy that comes with choosing and giving a gift to someone you love, fulfills the real meaning of Christmas. My children have definitely taught me that lesson.

Now, we have added a new tradition. We randomly choose names of people we consider acquaintances, people we don't know well. We plan to do a special something for them during the holidays without them knowing it is us. The children love it a lot. They love to surprise the families. What I've learned is, sometimes it may seem a small thing to take some time, and a measure of creative thinking, to come up with something to do for someone else; but the gift you've given them comes from the heart. They will know this: what you give from the heart, in the end, is more precious than gold or diamonds you can buy. Isn't that what it's all about? Yes! Christmas is about love, and giving.

Submitted by Mapuana Jarrett

The Real Joy of Christmas

In the Ozark mountains, where I was born, there was a careful conspiracy among adults to keep the knowledge of a secular Christmas, with decorated trees, Santa Claus, and gift-giving, away from children. I was eleven years old before I realized this. By that time, a three-year drought had turned our farm into a dust heap reclaimed by the bank, and we had moved to Idaho.

The relativity of happiness soon distilled upon my senses. In the hill country, where everyone was equally deprived, I was content with a few possessions. I was unaware of the larger world outside my own where people were judged by material possessions. In Idaho, I became acutely conscious of my poverty of "things."

At Christmas time, in that place, far from familiar surroundings, family, and friends, I was told stories in school about a jolly old man with white whiskers who lived at the North Pole. He had elves who worked night and day in a huge work shop, making toys for good girls and boys.

On Christmas Eve, it was written, the little man wore a red suit trimmed with fur and flew through the sky in a sleigh filled with toys. The sleigh was pulled by eight reindeer who had no wings, but they could fly. He flew all over the world, stopping on rooftops, sliding down chimneys, putting thousands of gifts under Christmas trees. This was an especially delightful thought for I had never owned a toy, nor had my brothers.

I was the oldest child, the only one who attended school. Excitedly, I told my two brothers about Santa Claus, the elves, the reindeer, the sleigh filled with toys. My mother heard me one day. Her face got red; she grabbed me by the arm, and took me outside.

"I've a good notion to whip you for fillin' those boys' heads full of such nonsense. Where did you hear those stories?"

I tried to tell her that there were books at school with pictures of the elves, the reindeer, and Santa Claus. I told her what the stories said would happen on Christmas Eve. She shook me 'til my eyes bugged out and my brain felt quivery.

I was told to forget what I had heard. She warned me not to say "another word" to my brothers. "They'll believe anything you tell 'em. It's all lies. None of those things are goin' to happen."

I didn't say any more to my brothers, but I continued to believe in Santa Claus, until Christmas morning. Then I learned why Mama had said what she did. She was right. Santa Claus came to the homes of other Idaho school children. But he did not come to where we lived: a tiny tent in an apple orchard. He was a strange, capricious being that hill people had not talked about for good reason. They did not know of his existence. And he did not know of ours.

More than fifty years later I was reminded of those early childhood memories when my husband, George, and I arrived in Bulawayo,

Zimbabwe, Africa, two months before Christmas. The culture was totally alien to us. We shortly discovered that most of the ten million people who lived there were bereft of "things."

A few miles outside Bulawayo, the second largest city in Zimbabwe, is 'the bush;' a primordial place where lions run through tall grass stalking prey, (usually small antelope, whose sole reason for living seemed to be the provision of meat on the hoof for lions.)

Herds of giraffe moved with a rocking-horse gait across the plains, eating choice leaves from the tops of acacia trees. Elephants walked through the bush munching small trees, discarding only the trunks. Dung beetles were eternally busy, rolling balls of dung fifty times their size, to some unknown location, for reasons apparent only to the beetle.

African nights are nearly too beautiful to bear; the sky so dark, the moon so pale, the stars so thick and bright. As you watch, stars die in a brilliant streak, trailing fire across the sky. One here, and one there, mesmerizing your eyes.

All senses tuned, you become aware of distant sounds; the bawl of a wildebeest, a lion's roar. Something is being hunted. Something is being killed in the moonlight—a reminder that only a few miles away, all is not bright and beautiful.

Although our house was within the city limits, most of our neighbors kept chickens. Roosters who could not tell time woke us each morning well before dawn. Already, in the street outside, we could hear the sound of scurrying feet. The feet were carrying people to market, to work, to school.

The average Zimbabwean will never own a motor vehicle, nor a bicycle. Each morning, thousands of people get up before daylight, and begin walking.

We heard greetings, singing, laughter—the voices of men, women, and children, mixed with the squawking of go-away birds, who were the background sound for everything that went on in Africa. We knew without seeing that many of the women would have babies tied to their backs.

For several years there had been little rainfall. Rivers and stream-beds throughout the country were bone-dry. Animals in the bush were dying. Women in rural areas walked miles for a bucket of water. Africans are superstitious. Some Africans believed that God was punishing them for the war they had fought, and won, against white natives ten years ago. Before that, they said, the rains always came.

There was no grass around our house, only dark-red dirt. Johannes, our domestic helper, swept the dirt clean every morning with a broom he fashioned from broom straw, which grew at the back of our leased property. In spite of the drought, bougainvillea vines covered the walls that enclosed our house; blooming profusely in tangled masses of pink, red, and gold. Flowering trees, including a poinsettia, two flamboyants, and a jacaranda, also burst with color.

Large blue-headed lizards, which I first thought were blue birds, inhabited the trees. They socialized in the morning sun on the stone terrace outside our kitchen door, which was of Dutch design, split at the center.

I enjoyed standing at the half-open door, quietly spying on the life of the blue lizards. They are shy and do not try to come inside; their cousins, the geckos, and the small gray lizards do.

December is Zimbabwe's hottest month. In the department stores, (no air conditioning) perspiration ran down the faces of black Kris Kringles wearing red velvet suits trimmed with fur. Skies were brilliant blue and cloudless. Windows must be open for air movement. There were bars on the windows to protect us from thieves, but no screens. Houses are built with a two inch space between the tops of the walls and the roof. This makes it possible for hot air to drift up and out. It also provides an easy thoroughfare for lizards and insects.

A family of mongoose lived among the bushes along the farthest back wall. Their business was to kill rodents, and snakes. Not long after our arrival, a mongoose chased a small cobra and caught it under our car. I stood frozen at the half-open door. Johannes stood a few feet away from the car, his short-handled hoe at the ready.

Red dust puffs flew from under both sides of the car, attesting to the hidden struggle going on there. The mongoose emerged victorious with a lifeless cobra dangling from its mouth. I walked on trembling legs into the dining room and sat down. I had not considered snakes before agreeing to serve a mission in Zimbabwe. In her entire book about Kenya, Isak Dinesen made no mention of snakes.

The people who lived in the house before us had found a deadly black mamba in one of the closets. The place where it had got inside was now nailed over with tin. But while we were there, I told George and Johannes that the closet door must never be opened.

Recently I had gone to tea at an Englishwoman's house close to the bush. She told me that cobras were common in Zimbabwe. One day, when her kitchen door was open, an old, very large cobra slid through the door, skittered across the waxed wood floor of the living room, and disappeared under the organ.

A great discussion then ensued among her house boys about how best to dislodge the cobra from the organ. First, they carefully moved the organ outside to a large open area. They then squatted around it to decide on a plan. Since it was an old cobra, it was undoubtedly smart. They must figure how to be smarter. They talked much among themselves. Evidently the cobra grew bored with the talk and stuck its head out. In a split-second, a young man used his machete as a guillotine.

When I came home, I instructed Johannes to never leave the outside doors open.

We shared house space with flat black spiders the size of a child's hand, who have long hairy legs and move faster than lightning; mosquitoes, flies, cockroaches, praying mantis; and lizards, who eat all of the above.

Since Africa has a high mortality rate from malaria, we decided the lizards should be tolerated for disease prevention. (In any case, there was no way to keep them out.) However, deciding a thing rationally with your mind is one thing, seeing them run from under your pillow without hysteria is quite another. Two different principles are involved.

We became friends with Sabbath Maturure, a native African. He was President of a small branch of the Church just outside the city of Bulawayo.

Sabbath was aptly named; he was a gentle, good man. We gradually came to realize his immense spirit, and knew that he was one of God's chosen people. He was born with osteopenesis imperfecta, a genetic disease that causes brittle bones, with curvature of the spine both front and back. His arms were fused at the shoulders. He was confined to a wheelchair which he was dependent on other people to push around. He had limited strength and movement in his arms. He had never walked. His mother carried him on a pillow for the first year of his life.

Before we left Zimbabwe, we were able to join with the Methodists in purchasing a battery powered wheel chair for Sabbath. For the first time he was independent: liberated from his useless legs. We grew used to seeing him miles from home, always with a broad smile on his face;

using the power chair to attend District meetings, or in taking care of business, and personal duties. He was grateful with his whole heart for this unexpected gift.

According to tribal custom, the night when Sabbath became one-year old, he was taken by his father, and the elders of the village, to a high hill. There, after a special ceremony, he was lifted toward the star-studded heavens on a pillow, by his father. He was given a name and a blessing. Because his parents were Christian, his life was dedicated to the service of God, and his fellowmen. His head was then shaved. Before that, razors or scissors had not touched his hair.

When Sabbath was six years old he was given to the Methodists, who operated a large school with dormitories for students, close to the rural area where the Maturure family lived. His parents wanted him to be properly cared for. They wanted him to have an education, and learn a trade.

When we met him, Sabbath was thirty-eight years old. He had converted from atheism to Christianity. For the first twenty years of his life, he found it impossible to believe in a God who allowed all the suffering that he had experienced and witnessed since birth.

An older missionary couple taught him the gospel of Jesus Christ. He was converted in quite a miraculous way, and became a member of The Church of Jesus Christ of Latter-day Saints.

He was kitchen manager, and supervisor of students at the Jairos Jiri Center, a place where young disabled people came from many parts of Zimbabwe to be taught a trade. Some of those young people were members of the Jairos Jiri Branch.

They had varying disabilities. Some were deaf and mute. Others were blind. Some had been crippled by polio. We met a young woman born without arms. We watched in awe as she pinned a pattern, cut material, ran a portable sewing machine on the floor—all with her toes.

Few of the students had shoes. Most of them wore rubber thongs. Their clothing was an odd mix of cast-off apparel. Huge bales of clothing arrived periodically at the Center from various Western countries. The best things were sold to buy food and pay expenses. The students wore what was left.

Sabbath's wife was Susan, a pretty woman, who had been a victim of polio when she was three. She wore a heavy iron brace on her left leg. The polio had caused that leg to shrivel, it was four inches shorter than the right leg. Dragging the heavy brace, she walked two miles to work every day. She and Sabbath had three daughters, each one lovely, and perfectly formed.

Their family was fluid. Extended family members came and went. No one who needed a place to stay was ever turned away. People were called brother and sister, however thin the blood line. Their little house had one bedroom. We often wondered where everyone slept.

They were also raising Sabbath's baby niece, the child of his sister, Margaret, who was born with the same genetic bone defect as her brother. She was a teacher at the Methodist school. She died giving birth to the child. The father disappeared. No one knew where he had gone. He was not heard from after Margaret's funeral. Perhaps he went into the bush and was eaten by lions, sparing the life of one small antelope.

Sabbath's branch was part of our charge. We had a seminary class there.

As Christmas drew near, we began to think about how the Jairos Jiri Center would celebrate. We went to speak with Sabbath.

How many of the forty members would go home for the holidays? How many would stay? The answers were varied. Some would go home. Some had no money. Some had no place to go.

"Will there be a party?" I asked. "A tree?" "Presents?"

Sabbath's black eyes twinkled. He laughed: a dry mirthless chuckle. In the months ahead, that chuckle would become familiar. I can still hear it in my ears. Africans, who are thrust at birth into a life fraught with peril, hardship, disease, and death, develop a witty stoicism in order to live with what they daily see and suffer.

Like actors in a Greek tragedy, they sing, dance, rejoice at weddings, christenings, other happy events; giving themselves wholly to the event at hand.

They are enthralled by music. Using the primitive, traditional instruments: tambourine, drum, wooden flute, hand-held finger harp, they become absorbed, every fiber, every sinew; head to bare feet alive and vibrating to the music their voices emulate. They are lost to the world's trials for the length of time they allow the music to become a part of their being.

When someone dies, women will sit around the outside wall of the person's house, legs stretched straight out in front of their bodies. They will throw dirt upon themselves, and wail wildly for days. If the person was a close relative, they will shave their heads, showing utmost respect for the departed. In Africa, people die unexpectedly from snake bite, tetanus, malaria, pneumonia, auto-immune deficiency, (which has not been named to them.)

Born to expect the worst, when lesser things happen, they smile and make jokes. Events that would send North Americans into maniacal fits, will be met by a shrug of the shoulders, a smile, and the words: "Ah, well, God is great."

"No," Sabbath said. There would be no tree. No party. There was no money. There would be some meat for the tomato, onion, and chamolia relish they dip their sadza in. (Sadza is a thick cornmeal mush eaten twice a day.) Maybe there would be a glass of sweet punch.

"There will be flowers, and we will sing Christmas hymns. I have many times wondered," Sabbath said, with a pensive look, "how the Savior will like us to celebrate His birthday. Perhaps tinsel covered trees, and Kris Kringle with his bag of gifts may not be pleasing. Have you considered this?" Sabbath shifted himself in the wheelchair, and looked intently at us.

I smiled. He and my husband were kindred spirits. George leaned forward, and put his hand on the arm of Sabbath's chair.

"Yes," he said, "I have pondered this question. I think a bit of meat in the relish, a glass of fruit punch, and the singing of hymns will please the Savior as a celebration of his birthday. May we join you?"

Sabbath covered George's white hand with his large black one. Tears glistened in both their eyes.

We, along with three other missionary couples assigned to Bulawayo, met with the Jairos Jiri Branch on Christmas Eve. We took five baked chickens, and many packages of cookies. I also took a large assortment of balloons that my daughter had sent from Utah. The students had never seen balloons before. They liked blowing them up.

At first they really did blow them up. The thin rubber skin was stretched tighter and tighter, until the entire thing blew up in their faces amid much laughter. A number of such incidents happened before they were able to gauge the proper time for stopping with air input.

Great enjoyment came to those of us who helped the blind young people discover balloons. First, we put a balloon without air in their hands. We then blew up a balloon, and had them feel the round smoothness of it with their fingers. Next, we put their fingers at the opening and allowed the air to escape. They could then feel that the blown-up balloon without air was like the first one they had felt. We put the opening in their mouths and asked them to blow. It was an exercise in merriment, with wet balloons flying about the room, until they finally caught on.

My journal page for that evening reads: "In the center of the room, Susan covered an old table with a freshly-ironed white cloth. She set the Savior's picture there. Around the picture, and over the cloth, she scattered petals from scarlet hibiscus blossoms, which grow along the back of the building.

"After dinner, when we sang the hymns, (a capella) there was a feeling of perfect peace in that beat-up room, with the battered benches, and broken chairs. Tears kept coming to my eyes. My throat would close, I could not swallow, and I could not sing. I noticed that the other missionaries were having the same problem. Thankfully, we had Sabbath's rich baritone, and Susan's sweet soprano to keep us on course.

"In Africa, I have rediscovered an important truth that I learned as a child in the Ozark hills: happiness is relative, and "things" cannot buy it. Santa Claus truly is a capricious being who has nothing to do with the real joy of Christmas."

The Rest of the Story

Five years later, while my husband and I were on a mission in Thailand, we received a letter from Blessings, Sabbath's oldest daughter, telling us of his death from pneumonia, a complication of the malaria which he had nearly died from a few years before.

Very recently we received a letter from him, relating the most joyous day of his life. He had traveled across the country by car, and was in the Harare chapel when President Hinckley spoke to the saints there. Sabbath had the privilege of meeting the Prophet. He bore a heart-felt testimony in his letter; of his great love for the Savior, for the Church, for the Prophet, and his total joy when President Hinckley took his hand.

Sabbath was the kind of brother I never had. We became great friends. He was an artist. His final gift to us was a batik painting that was miraculously delivered just before we left Thailand. It had been sent months before. The cloth had been tightly rolled, covered with brown wrapping paper, and tied with string. It must have lain hidden in a small crack in the hold of a ship before it was finally found and posted to us.

Touched by the Spirit

An African, born and raised in the bush country, has little concept of how the world of commerce and trade works. You want a painting to reach a person all the way around the world? You roll it tightly, tie it with brown paper and string. You print a tiny address on it, in black ink and send it away. Surely it will arrive at its appointed destination.

Angels were watching over that small piece of cloth, or we would not have received it. It is now perfectly framed and hangs where I see it every day. I will miss Sabbath forever. But his lovely painting reminds me that he once was.

Submitted by Joy Robinson

(Author's note: This story was written as a memorial tribute to our brother and friend, Sabbath Maturure, and for his family)

About The Authors

Kathy Alexander - Kathy was born and grew up in Bountiful, Utah. She graduated from University with a B.S. in Nursing. She is also certified as an assistant teacher. She has six children. A daughter has just completed a mission in Mexico. A son is serving a mission in Mexico City. A daughter has graduated from BYU. She is married and teaching in Springville, Utah. Kathy's husband is President of the Torreon Mexico Mission. They have their three youngest children with them. They have all learned Spanish; love the people, and their mission.

Kyle Bills - Kyle was born in Corvallis, Oregon. He graduated high school in Seattle, Washington. He served his mission in Torreon, Mexico. He loved his mission, and the people. He was the Mission President's AP for the last part of his mission. He returned to his family, who had moved to Providence, R.I. while he was away. Two months later he moved to Provo, Utah, to enroll at BYU. He met Stephanie Alexander, the daughter of his Mission President. Five months later they went to Torreon, to be married in the Monterey Temple. He attends school at BYU, and works as a Spanish language Instructor at the MTC, a job that he loves.

Dorene and Ben Booth - Dorene is a talented musician. She began formal training on the piano at age five. She studied at the McCune School of Music. She then went on to study the pipe organ for four years with Dr. Alexander Schreiner. She worked professionally as an organist at the Bountiful Community Church, and the Episcopal Church of the Resurrection, which gave her respect for people of other faiths. She is married to Ben Booth. They have four married children. They have served two full-time missions together. They are both much engaged in genealogy research and temple work. Many spiritual miracles have happened to them in conjunction with this work.

Sherry L. Bratsman - Sherry and her husband spent their lives in Idaho, until recently, When they moved to the Big Island of Hawaii. They have traveled extensively, visiting Russia and other republics in the former USSR, in 1991 and again in 1994.

Linda D. Dodds - Linda grew up in Idaho, and Utah. She graduated from Murray High School. She married and moved to West Virginia. She then moved with her family to Page, Arizona, where they have lived for twenty-six years. She owned and operated a florist and gift shop until 2003, when she sold it to devote more time to leading, and directing the C.U.D.D.L.E. Foundation. She is married to James Dodds. They have three married children, and four grandchildren.

Isaac Fenn - Mr. Fenn was born in 1930 in Pomerene, Cochise County, Arizona. He served as a missionary in the East Central States, later he served a mission with his wife Pat in the Alaska Anchorage Mission. He served in the Military during the Korean Conflict. They live on the island of Keaau, Hawaii. He is currently a temple ordinance worker in the Kona Hawaii Temple.

Josephine Foulger - In 1976 Josephine became the historian for the Tabernacle Choir. In 1978 she also became recording secretary, keeping the minutes of all Choir events. Paul and Josephine had six children. She served for many years in the Ward and Stake Primary. She has always been active in Community affairs. She served as a PTA officer all the years her children were in school. She is a past president of the DUP's North Salt Lake Council. Josephine was a secretary for the directors of Church Hosting for the First Presidency and other General Authorities for thirteen years.

Stacy D. Garn - Mr. Garn was born in Fielding, Utah in 1906. He graduated from Bear River High. He served 30 months on a mission to the Western States. He was assigned to the New Mexico area. He was District President of the Mission for 19 months. He was set apart as a Mount Ogden Stake High Counselor by Apostle John A. Widtsoe. He served as High Counselor in several Stakes, and has held numerous other Church positions. He retired after 39 years from the Metropolitan Life Insurance Company. In 1975 he was set apart as First Counselor in the Mesa Arizona Temple by Spencer W. Kimball, where he served for 5 years. He performed 1,892 marriages during that time.

Jeffrey Hall - Jeff was born and raised in Pickerington, Ohio, by his beautiful mother and four older siblings. He served a two-year mission for the Lord in Puebla, Mexico, under President Juan Machula. Jeff received a degree in business Management from Utah Valley State College. He is employed by new York Life as a Financial Consultant.

Ray Hendershot - Ray grew up in the Boise Valley, in Idaho. His family attended the Marsing Ward of the Caldwell, Idaho Stake. He graduated from Nampa High School. He attended Utah State University. He and his family now live in the Pahoa Ward, in the Hilo Stake. Ray said they came to Hawaii via Alaska. They went to Hawaii to get warm and decided to stay. He is a building contractor on the Keaau Island. In his story about the school bus accident, Ray said that Stephen, the young man who was killed in the bus accident was one of his Boy Scouts. He also said, "My wife and I are very aware of, and thankful for, the angels who watch over us in our daily lives."

Mapuana Jarrett - Mapuana and her husband Waleka live in Keaau, Hawaii with their 6 children. Both parents are working towards College degrees. Their nineteen-year-old son is looking forward to his mission. They are active members of their Pahoa Ward.

Russell Jobst - Russell served two tours of duty in Viet Nam as a pilot. He later became a pilot for United Airlines. He is married to Joan Oviatt. They live on a farm in Hawaii. He serves as Assistant Ward clerk in their ward.

Jan Jonstun - Jan was born in Portland, Oregon. She has a twin sister and an older brother. She lived on a 100-acre ranch, with cattle, horses, chickens, ducks, and a peacock. Salmon spawned up a creek on their property. She loved to ride horses until she was in an auto accident that broke her back and the femur bone of one leg. She was in a body cast the last seven months of her senior year in high school. She entered University with the highest math score of any student up to that time. She has been a single adult, married, divorced mother of three, remarried, and is now a widow, mother of six, and a grandmother of twenty-one children.

Marlene Kettley - Marlene Conway Kettley was born and educated in Illinois. An avid genealogist and historian, she has published several family histories; and The History of Big Rock, Illinois. She is currently working with Arnold K. Garr, and Craig K. Manscill, of BYU, on a history of the early Saints in Illinois. The working title is 'Mormons in Illinois Before Nauvoo; to be published in 2005. The history will be in four volumes.

W. Herbert Klopher - Mr. Klopher was born in East Germany. Much of his early years are in the stories he has kindly allowed us to use. He is a master musician. He studied the organ with Dr. Frank Asper and Dr. Alexander Schreiner. He was President of the Eagle Gate Stake for nine years. He is a member of the General Church Music Committee. He is married to the former Carolyn Hamilton, who is also an accomplished musician. They live on the Avenues in Salt Lake City. They are the parents of four children, one deceased.

Werner Klein - As a young boy during WWII, he escaped from a Russian Concentration camp. He spent months alone, sleepless, and starving, trying to find his way home to Landsberg. Several years after serving an LDS mission, he escaped to the West; two months before the permanent erection of the Berlin Wall. He met his wife, Linda Trinny in Karlsruhe. They were married in the Swiss Temple. They have three daughters. Mr. Klein worked at the University of Heidelberg as their "Artist in Residence' before immigrating to the United States in 1971. He has served in two Stake Presidencies, and filled two Stake missions. He was a tour guide for German speaking tourists on Temple Square for eleven years. He is a wildlife artist. He has had showings of his paintings in Germany and in the United States.

Muriel Lee - Muriel is a registered physical therapist. She and her husband, Wayne Lee, are the parents of four children under the age of six. Their newest child is three days old as of this writing. Muriel teaches in the Relief Society. For a number of years she served as Relief Society President of the Genesis Branch, whose President is Darius Gray. Much of her history is told in the testimony she wrote.

Susan Land - Susan lives in Salt Lake City. She is an active member of the Canyon Road Towers Ward. Much of her personal history is included in her testimony. Susan is an altruistic woman. She regularly takes women who have physical impairments to the more accessible, 'User Friendly' temples.

Dell and Marie Madsen - Mathew Dell was born on a farm north of Willard, Box Elder County, Utah. He graduated from Weber College and the University of Utah with a degree in chemistry. In 1941, he took a job in St. Louis, Missouri, with the Mallinckdrodt Chemical Works. Dell served his entire working life with Mallinckdrodt, as a chemist, technical editor, patent liaison, and ultimately as a registered patent agent. He has served in varied positions in the Church, both in St. Louis, and in Salt Lake City where he and Marie reside. He was awarded the Silver Beaver by the St. Louis Area Council Boy Scouts of America.

Erma Marie Gillies - Marie was born in Milford, Beaver County. Her father died when she was five. Her mother became the live-in manager of the small telephone office in Milford. She later married Sam Cline, an attorney. Marie graduated from the University of Utah with a degree in home economics. Marie is an excellent cook, and an artist, with expertise in all forms of fine handwork.

Barbara Manfull - Barbara was born and grew up in Bountiful, Utah. She graduated from the U of U, with a Bachelor and Masters D. in Education. She taught fourth grade at Meadowbrook School 31 years, until her retirement. She hated to retire because she loved the children. She and her husband have four children. They are serving in the Arizona Phoenix Mission. This is same area where Jess served as a young man. They love the people in their mission; and the young missionaries, who seem like their own children.

Marylyn W. McBride - Marilyn was born and grew up in Grace, Idaho. She attended the U of Arizona. She married Vince Williams. He worked as a

Research Scientist for the National Center of Atmospheric Research. This required them to move often. Marilyn graduated from Cosmetology school and worked in this business from 1968 to 1994. She and her husband had three children. One child is deceased. Her husband died of cancer. She served as a missionary in the Mississippi Jackson Mission. She met and married Don McBride in 2002. They were married and sealed in the Bountiful Temple. "That is why I now live happily ever after in our Utah home."

Violet Seaver Mills - Violet was born in Arizona, 30 miles northeast of old Mexico. During World War 11 she worked with the Red Cross. She was the Junior Sunday School Coordinator for may years. She has worked in the Primary more than 30 years. She has served 3 home missions, and one full-time mission. Violet is 79 years old. She lives with her husband, Jack, in Hawaii, on the Keaau Island.

Jack Pearce Mills Jr. - Jack was born Feb. 22nd 1922 in New Mexico. He grew up near Tombstone, Arizona. He is a combat veteran of World War 11. He was awarded the Purple Heart, and the Bronze Star medals. He worked 5 years with the Atomic Energy Commission, and 5 years with the NASA program. He has served 3 times as Elders Quorum President. He served 7 home missions, and one full-time mission. He has served more than 20 years as a Temple Ordinance/ Veil worker, which is his present assignment.

John Morgan - John graduated from the University of Utah with a D. in Political Science and Business. He served two years with the 44th Army Division in Europe. He has been Chairman of the Board, President and CEO of Morgan Gas and Oil Company since 1982. He was Co-Founder with Daisy Morgan, and Sylvia Wunderli of the World Senior Games, now known as the Huntsman World Senior Games; which attracts more than 6,000 people each year from all 50 States, and foreign Countries, to participate in 22 different sports in St. George, Utah. He serves on many business, civic, and community Boards. He married Daisy Richter in 1950. They had four children. A son and a daughter are deceased. Daisy passed away in 2001. He married Wilma Clayton in 2002. They reside in Salt Lake City, and St. George, Utah.

Morris Mower - Morris was born and reared in Fairview, Utah. He received his BA at BYU, his masters at the University of Utah. His doctorate in education is from the University of Northern Colorado.

Annetta Mower - Annetta was born in New York, but reared in Salt Lake City. She graduated from the BYU school of Nursing, and then obtained her Masters Degree at the University of Utah. They are the parents of four children. Morris served a full-time mission in Western Canada. He and Annetta have served two

Church Service missions; in the inner city, and at Welfare Square. They have served four full-time missions in Bulgaria, Mexico, Vermont, and Ohio. They have four children.

Rod Olsen - Rod was raised in Golden, Colorado. He served a mission to Santiago, Chile. He graduated from BYU. He married Jeri Petersen. They have four children. He owns Old Home Realty Co., and Faucet Fixers. He is a High Counselor in the Ensign Stake.

Jerry M. Okabe - Jerry is vice-president of Audience Marketing for Primedia Business Magazines and Media, based in Overland Park, Kansas. He has twenty-five years experience in business-to-business publishing. He serves on several business media boards. He is a frequent speaker at Industry conference's, and journalism classes. He has received three National Awards for service. He and his wife, Shizuka, are parents of one son and two daughters. He has served in many Church callings, including a mission to Japan. He is first counselor in the Woodbridge Connecticut, Ward Bishopric.

Joan Oviatt - Joan received a Master of Arts D. from BYU. She won the BYU Sesquicentennial Playwriting Contest with her play, The Field Is White. She has won awards for several of her plays. She has appeared in more than sixty stage plays and films. She is a writer of note with more than six books published. She lives on a farm in Hawaii with her husband, Russell Jobst.

Angel Baby Pahoa - Angel is Samoan. She graduated from high school on the island of Keaau, Hawaii, where she lives with her family. She is an active member of the Church. She teaches in the Primary.

Linda Reeder - Much of Linda's biography is in her testimony stories. She has been blind since birth. She is amazingly independent. Since graduating from College, she has always held a job. She rides a special Flex-Tram bus, to and from work. She pays $68:00 a month for this service. Friends usually take her to the airport, and pick her up when she returns. Her travels usually have to do with various camps which she attends. Counselors meet her at the airport when she arrives. When she orders her ticket she tells them she is blind and will need assistance. (Editor's note: Linda was a member of the Singles ward where my husband was the Bishop. She carried three huge, heavy black Braille books to all the meetings. One was a songbook. Her life has become a bit easier since the advancement in computer technology for the blind.)

Bonnie Barker Rice - Bonnie was born and grew up in Salt Lake City. She attended the U of U, and BYU. She has two degrees; one in family development, with a Masters D. in Social Work. She is a licensed Clinical Social Worker. She is married to Kenneth Rice. They are the parents of four daughters. They are presently serving as Inner City Service Missionaries.

Brett Robinson - Brett graduated from Bingham High School. He obtained his Bachelor D in English at the U of U in 2002. He also carried a minor in Spanish. He served an Internship at the United States Supreme Court. He enjoyed this work immensely. Because of his language skills he was able to meet many interesting people. He works at MGIS Insurance Company. He will attend law school at the University of Utah in the fall.

Brooke Robinson - Brooke Robinson loves to read, especially her scriptures, which she reads every day. She likes to roller blade and play baseball. Her favorite people are her family. One of her favorite things is playing with her siblings. She attends Bella Vista elementary school.

Byron Robinson - Byron is the son of Loren J. Robinson, and Rosetta Baker Robinson. He was born and reared in Oakley, Idaho. He served as a missionary in the Central States Mission. He then served in the United States Navy with the Seventh Fleet, in Australia, New Guinea, and China for four years. He married Dorothy Price in 1946. They have two sons. In the church he has served twice as a Bishop, a Counselor to three bishops, and stake president of the Wilford Stake for nine years. He is a sealer in the Salt Lake Temple.

Devin Robinson - Devin graduated from Bingham High School in 2002. He is an inventor. He won the State Award in Applied Technology for inventing a radio controlled car. He attended UVSC before going on his mission to Santiago, Chile.

Dorothy Price Robinson - Dorothy graduated from South High School in 1935. She graduated from the Secretarial School at LDS Business College. Her first job was as an apprentice legal secretary with different firms of lawyers; who paid her $1.25 a week. This paid her carfare and allowed her to buy a five-cent sandwich for lunch. She then went to work for the University of Utah and retired from there. She married Byron Robinson in 1946. She has been active in the Church all her life, serving as a Relief Society President twice, and has filled nearly every women's position through the years.

Doug Robinson - Doug grew up in an Air Force family. He graduated from Utah State University with a degree in Journalism. He is married to Lori, they have three children. He has worked for the Deseret News since his graduation. Doug writes Sports, and Metro columns, and in-depth profiles. In 2003, Doug was honored with several prestigious awards by his professional peers; First Place—General Interest Column Writing, National Society of Newspaper columnists; First Place—Sports Features, AP Sports Editors (and other awards too numerous to mention). His favorite saying: "Writing is easy; all I do is sit at the typewriter and wait for big drops of blood to form on my forehead."

Jennifer Day Robinson - Jennifer grew up in Highland, Utah and graduated from the High School there. She attended BYU, graduating with a degree in Education. She is married to Warren Robinson. They have six children. She has always been active in the Church, serving in various positions in the women's auxiliaries. She is the mother of six children.

Justin Robinson - Justin grew up in Summerville, South Carolina. He served in the Arcadia Spanish Speaking Mission. He has a BS from BYU. He is married to Sarah Pittson. They are expecting a boy in June. He is a counselor in the Young Men's Presidency in the North Charleston Ward. He is a Claims Adjuster for All State Insurance.

Kent Robinson - Kent grew up in Bountiful, Utah. He served in the North Carolina, Virginia States Mission. He graduated from BYU. He married Tanya Denkowitz. They have four children. He is self-employed as an agent for All State Insurance. He has served the Church in many positions. He was a Bishop, a Counselor in the South Carolina Columbia Mission, and has served nearly nine years as a counselor in the Summerville Stake Presidency.

Tanya D. Robinson - Tanya is the mother of four children. She presently serves as Relief Society President for the Summerville, South Carolina Ward. She sits on the Board of the Tidelands Bank, works part-time for the School District in the 'Office of Public Information.' She is Co-president of her son's middle school PTSA. She has been named an honorary life member of South Carolina Congress of Parents and Teachers. She is a recipient of "The Golden Rule Award for Service to the Community" in the local Charleston area. She is a Life member of Junior League.

Vicki Jo Robinson - Vicki is the mother of ten children. She loves to write. She has published several books for LDS families. One of her articles was purchased by the Ensign. A noted scriptorian, she has been the Gospel Doctrine teacher in three wards. Prior to marriage she taught Middle School, and investigated child abuse for the State Of Utah. She is married to Bryan Robinson. They live in Bluffdale, Utah.

Warren C. Robinson - Warren grew up in Bountiful, Utah. He has an inventive mind. He is usually working on some kind of a new idea. He served in the Mexico Vera Cruz Mission, graduated from BYU, and got his MBA from Nova University. He is the manager of a title company.

Nola Sears - Nola was born in Star Valley, WY., in the town of Freedom. She grew up on a farm and learned how to work at an early age. She graduated from Star Valley High School. The children rode a bus 20 miles to school and back. She attended College at Utah State University. She met her husband, William Sears, while they were at school. Eleven days after their marriage he was called to serve a mission in Montana. Nola was sent to the same area. She had Sister Companions. The last six months of their mission, she and her husband were allowed to be companions. They have two children. William died of a brain tumor in 1997. Nola has served five years as a Service Missionary at the Conference Center, and seven years as a temple ordinance worker.

Marijke Shuttle - Marijke was born in Den Haag (the Netherlands), there with her parents, and her brother. Part of the war years they were evacuated to Delft. She and her Family lived through the Hungerwinter of 1944–45. She married in 1953. She and her husband emigrated to Brazil. Later they emigrated to Palo Alta, California. Their four children were born in the Bay Area. In 1978 she was divorced from her husband. He was excommunicated. She married Charles Shuttle in 1986. They were sealed in the Oakland Temple. They live in Salt Lake City in a lovely Victorian home they have restored.

Glen M. Seely - Glen was born in Malta, Idaho. He graduated from Box Elder High School. He graduated from Weber College with an Associate D in Science. He served a mission to Great Britain. Graduated from the University of Utah. He is a retired Major in the USAF. He is in the Reserve USAF. He is a Real Estate Broker. He serves as a counselor in the Canyon Road Bishopric. He is married to the former Nita Harrison.

Gyongyi (Momi) Szirom - Momi is a Registered Nurse and Massage Therapist. She lives in the Puna District of the Big Island of Hawaii. She loves communing with Nature, and the Spirit. She works her acre of land, growing flowers and edible food. She says the island holds a lot of mana (mah-nah, God's blessings) so everything grows well. She loves her peaceful home.

Ethelyn Taylor - Ethelyn's accomplishments in education and Church service are hallmarks of her years since graduation from Snow College. She served more than 20 years on the College of Business Faculty at BYU. She received her BA at BYU, and her Masters at Stanford, with graduate work at Northwestern, Denver U., USC, and UCLA. As the wife of Henry D. Taylor, she had the opportunity for special service in the Church. She served missions in Switzerland, and California. She sang with the Tabernacle Choir, and the Oratorio Society which performed "The Messiah" in Tel Aviv, and Jerusalem.

Guillermo A. Tolentino - Brother Guillermo was converted to The Church six years ago. Born in the Phillipines, he now resides with his family on the Big Island of Hawaii. He is seventy-eight years old. He enjoys doing temple work at the Kona Hawaii Temple. His son, Guillermo, Jr., served a mission in Oakland, California. He is now attending college.

Tiffany Wilde - Tiffany was born in Las Vegas, Nevada. She has five older brothers and one younger sister. She was delighted to become a big sister when a baby sister was born in 1989. She enjoyed high school. She took part in student council, and was a member of a dance group. She served a full-time mission from 2001 to 2003. For eleven months she served on Temple Square, and was then transferred to Miles City, Montana. After five months she returned to Temple Square as a Zone Leader. On July 19, 2003 she married Robert James Grine III, who had patiently waited for her. They are awaiting the birth of their first child, a baby girl.

Rodney Yamamoto - Some of his life history is in his testimony. He did not send a separate biography. He and his wife Jan teach the "Marriage and Family Relationships" class in their ward. They are active members of the Church.

Janet Yamamoto - Jan is a Relief Society Counselor in her ward. A daughter just returned from a full-time mission. She and her husband do volunteer work for the homeless shelter. Jan also volunteers her time at the abused women's shelter. They live on the island of Keaau, Hawaii, and attend the Pahoa Ward.